10-10-10

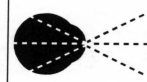

This Large Print Book carries the
Seal of Approval of N.A.V.H.

10-10-10

10 MINUTES, 10 MONTHS, 10 YEARS
A LIFE-TRANSFORMING IDEA

SUZY WELCH

THORNDIKE PRESS
A part of Gale, Cengage Learning

GALE
CENGAGE Learning™

Detroit • New York • San Francisco • New Haven, Conn • Waterville, Maine • London

GALE
CENGAGE Learning™

LIBRARY OF CONGRESS CATALOGING-IN-PUBLICATION DATA

Welch, Suzy.
    10-10-10 : 10 minutes, 10 months, 10 years : a
life-transforming idea / by Suzy Welch. — Large print ed.
        p. cm.
    ISBN-13: 978-1-4104-1721-3 (hardcover : alk. paper)
    ISBN-10: 1-4104-1721-2 (hardcover : alk. paper)
    1. Decision making. 2. Self-realization. 3. Problem solving. 4.
Success. 5. Life skills. I. Title. II. Title: Ten-ten-ten.
BF448W455 2009
153.8'3—dc22   2009015667

Published in 2009 by arrangement with Scribner, an imprint of Simon & Schuster, Inc.

*With love, respect, and gratitude,
I dedicate this book to the 10-10-10ers
who shared their stories of transformation*

CONTENTS

INTRODUCTION:
BEFORE SUNRISE

I was born in Portland, Oregon — *exotic* Portland, as I like to say, since it always seems to get a laugh. I guess people generally think of Portland as bland.

Portland is lovely.

Except for the snakes. When I was very young, one found its way into our backyard, and as I knelt to examine it, my mother ran outside from the kitchen and killed it with a shovel.

My mother was very beautiful — poised and stylish too. I don't want you to get a Wild-Wild-West kind of impression of her. It's just that desperate women do desperate things.

That I can assure you.

My father was an architect. Fifteen years after the snake incident, he taught me how to parallel-park in that way people do when they are engineers in their souls and understand physics in their brains, and are teaching people who are writers in their souls and understand poetry in their brains. We laugh about it now.

I spent every summer of my youth on Cape Cod, aboard a little boat, hauling in blues and bass by the cooler-full. For the record, and with God as my witness, I felt for the fish.

I went to college, became a journalist in Miami, watched the city burn twice, moved North, landed a job at the Associated Press, got married, went to business school, became a management consultant, and worked very hard to look like I knew something meaningful about industrial manufacturing.

I was later the editor of the *Harvard Business Review,* until I was fired.

At the age of forty-one, I got divorced. It was the right thing to do.

Three years later, I got married again. It was the rightest thing I've ever done.

I have four children. Actually, they're not really children anymore. But they're my children.

Not a one of them looks like me. Two are fair Nordic types; they look like Swedish farmhands. But even the two dark ones look like strangers by my side. It's OK — truly. It's a good reminder that they should have their own lives.

If I had a magic wand, though, I'd use it to teach my kids everything I know with a little tap on the forehead. Because like most parents, I wish they could skip all the hard parts.

They won't. And I guess that's OK too. As the Russian novelist Fyodor Dostoevsky once observed, "Suffering is the sole origin of consciousness." Learning how to live from experience is part of the human condition.

Still, there is just one thing I wish I could teach my kids without all the blood, sweat, and tears usually involved.

How to make good decisions.

Simply put, that is what this book is about — a new approach to making choices that will allow you to create a life of your own making, no matter where you were born, how you've spent your days, and what mistakes you've made along the way.

It's about a steady discipline that can help us replace chaos with consistency, confusion with clarity, and perhaps best of all, guilt with not-guilt, or to use another word for that condition, joy.

It's about an idea that changed my life and has transformed the lives of men and women around the world.

Now — please! I'm not suggesting that

11

I've got it all tied up in a bow. There are still plenty of times when I can't get out of my own way with my bright ideas and best-laid plans. And I know, too, that sometimes life is formed by chance or by events outside our control. Accidents and miracles happen. Of course they do.

But much more often, our lives are formed by decisions within our control, though it may not feel that way. In today's accelerated world, with its streaming information, confounding options, uncertain global economy, and ever-morphing culture, many of the decisions we face can seem unspeakably complicated, or as if there are just too many of them, in too little time. So we decide by not deciding or by letting our gut instinct guide us. We ask our friends for advice, consulting them like Ouija boards, or we look for signs, the way ancient people sought counsel in oracle bones. And we hope for the best.

Today, my life is renewed; my decisions deliberate, purposeful, and confident. But thirteen years ago, I was there, in that hoping place. Even with my credentials and accomplishments, my loving family, and dear friends, even with the affection and respect I was blessed to receive, I made many of my decisions as if I was watching them from a moving car. Sometimes things worked out. More often, they didn't. And my life showed it. It was fine one day or week or month, then crazy. It was tedious, then frustrating, then all wrong, then all right. It was happy and full, then lonely. It was moving forward, it was falling back.

I wasn't living my life. My life was living me.

Then came February 1996. I was in Hawaii, though not for a vacation. With a full-time job at the *Harvard Business Review,* four children under the age of six, and a rocky marriage, I didn't take a lot of vacations in those days. I was in Hawaii to deliver a speech to a convention of insurance executives who had offered to pay me a mortgage coupon's worth of dollars to enlighten them about the history of management.

My boss was thrilled about my trip. I was, as she put it, "getting the brand out there." But I knew that I couldn't leave my husband alone in charge of four kids. So I decided I could make it work for everyone if I brought my five- and six-year-olds along. Not to worry, I assured the trip's organizer. The clients might be "extremely demanding" — her words exactly — but my kids were extremely mature. They were practically

13

little adults! "The clients won't even notice they're there," I promised.

Back home, I gathered Roscoe and Sophia into my arms. "We're going on a wonderful adventure," I told them. "Mommy has to work a little with some clients. But you won't even notice they're there!"

With one clever plan, I had finally cracked the work-life balance code, all while putting money in the bank! Or so I had "decided." Hooray for me.

Hooray, it turned out, for the saintly flight attendant on our plane. Because she did not kill me when Sophia spent the entire twelve-hour flight demonstrating the use of those little white air-sickness bags. My poor lovely thing. She was green by the time we landed. Not to worry, though, I thought — a few hours at the beach will do her a world of good. It will do wonders for all of us. Family time! Sand castles, body surfing, happy memories!

And sun poisoning. No, I didn't forget sunscreen. I over-remembered it, slathering ladlefuls on Roscoe's luminous Nordic skin and then covering him with a shirt, hat, and towel for good measure. Prudent mother that I was, I had turned my little boy into a convection oven.

Not surprisingly, what with the ice packs

and soothing I needed to apply to stop the wailing, I ended up arriving late to the clients' festivities that evening. To compensate, however, I immediately leaped into mingle-and-chat mode, introducing myself to everyone.

My approach seemed to be working well enough — these were insurance executives after a day on the golf course — but I did notice a group of people at the party who didn't really seem inclined to mingle and chat back with me. It wasn't the attendees themselves, but their wives. Perhaps they were wondering where my husband was. Or maybe they thought, correctly, that I looked as frantic as a woman who had two moaning kids up in her room and a speech to give the next morning.

Hours later, the party ended and I rushed back to the kids, staying up with them most of the night, as all three of us battled jet lag — then each other. They wanted *The Little Mermaid,* I wanted the headline news. They wanted one more story about Nonnie and the snake. I wanted to close my eyes.

At 5 AM, to win the peace, I ordered ice cream for breakfast and, finally, sticky faces pressed close, we slept.

Not for long, though. At nine, I sent the kids off to a hotel-run hula dancing camp

15

on the beach and dutifully donned my power suit. Then I climbed the stairs to center stage, and pointer in hand, spent the next hour marching my bleary-eyed audience through Frederick Taylor's four principles of scientific management, Max Weber's seminal insights into command-and-control hierarchies, and Peter Drucker's groundbreaking views on outsourcing. I may not have been exactly scintillating, but I was earning my keep, one PowerPoint slide at a time.

Until, that is, the very last moments of my speech when, gazing toward the back of the auditorium, I noticed that two little people were trying to get into the room, their bodies pressed against the sliding glass doors, hands cupped around their eyes to peer in all the more intently.

It was Roscoe and Sophia, dressed in hula skirts. They'd made a jail break and come to hunt me down.

Up on stage, I wrapped things up with a quick thud — no Q & A as planned — then bolted toward the back of the room to head them off. I'll never forget how they frantically grabbed my legs when I reached them, or how the insurance executives who caught the scene regarded me, eyebrows raised high.

Yes, yes, I realize now that I should have packed my bags at that point and headed home. But in my make-everyone-happy, I-can-freaking-do-it-all mind, I still had twenty-four hours to go. I promptly decided I would spend the rest of the day scuba diving with the kids, tire them out, put them to bed, then show up at the client's luau ready to charm until sunrise if need be.

I didn't count on the saltwater making Roscoe shriek or the luau actually lasting until nearly sunrise, by which time I was decidedly not charming. I was confused and exhausted to the point of weepiness. At one point, I even put my head down on a table and shut my eyes. When I opened them again, I saw a client-wife looking down at me with a mordant grin. "You working mothers," she said, voice dripping with vinegar, "I don't know how you do it all."

"Just smoke and mirrors," I blithered.

"Your husband must be very patient," she responded archly.

"Oh, he most certainly is," I assured her.

With that big piñata of a lie hanging between us, the client-wife wandered off. Eventually, I wandered off too, to my room, bedraggled. I sent the babysitter away and collapsed into a chair on the balcony. A glorious, big golden sun — just like in the postcards — was lifting toward the creamy blue sky of morning above.

I didn't know it at the time, but a new day was indeed breaking.

"I have to end this craziness," I heard myself saying. I might have fallen asleep for a moment there, or I might have just zoned out. My consciousness was fading in and out like a cell phone call from a mountain pass. "I have to figure out another way," I muttered.

I don't know what happened next, or why, and I probably never will.

Perhaps I had simply reached the point where change had to happen; no alternative remained. Or maybe that trip was the last factor in the equation of experiences that added up to some nascent form of judgment, or vision, or understanding. Maybe I simply received a gift. All I know for sure is that, as the sun rose over the sea, an idea came into my mind.

It was a lifeline and my lifesaver from that moment forward.

It was the beginning of a journey of discovery and reinvention that I took myself, and that we are about to take together.

It was 10-10-10.

CHAPTER ONE:
IT WAS WHAT?

10-10-10 IN THE LIGHT OF DAY

To tell you the truth, I didn't know precisely what 10-10-10 was at the moment of its inception, except that I suddenly felt as if I had a new, different, and massively better operating principle in my (albeit tenuous) grasp. I had come upon, it seemed, an enhanced thinking process of sorts, a methodology for getting systematic about things. All I *really* had to do to reclaim my life, I realized that morning on my Hawaiian balcony, was to start making my decisions differently — proactively — by deliberately considering their consequences in the immediate present, near term, and distant future.

In ten minutes . . . ten months . . . and ten years.

If I did that, I figured with a fair amount of wonder, I might actually have my very own "life management tool."

And thirteen years later, that term continues to be how I define 10-10-10 in quick and easy shorthand. That said, I've certainly heard 10-10-10 described in other ways. One dedicated 10-10-10 practitioner I know calls it "a road map for clarity and courage," another, "my little guilt eraser." A grandmother from Houston once told me she refers to 10-10-10 as her "kick-start to get unfrozen." A Canadian minister who has preached about 10-10-10 describes it as "a great bridge enabling us to put things in perspective."

But none of those handles for 10-10-10 — mine included — really describe the nitty-gritty logistics of the process. So before we go any further, let's break them down.

THE HOW OF 10-10-10

Every 10-10-10 process starts with a question. That is, every 10-10-10 begins with posing your dilemma, crisis, or problem in the form of a query. Should I quit my job? Should I buy the house with the great backyard and leaky roof? Should I hold my son back a year in school? Should I stay in my relationship or end it?

Having a defined question is essential to 10-10-10, I've come to discover, because so many messy problems are intertwined with side issues and sub-issues, distractions and digressions, red herrings and bit players. Thus, the most effective 10-10-10s always tend to start with determining exactly what issue, underneath it all, you're trying to resolve.

The next stage of 10-10-10 is data collection. Not to worry; you can conduct this part of the process in your head, on your computer, with pen and paper, or in conversation with a friend or partner — whatever works. The only real "requirement" is that you be honest and exhaustive in answering the following prompts:

Given my question, what are the consequences of each of my options in ten minutes?

In ten months?

In ten years?

Now, to be clear, there is nothing *literal* about each ten in 10-10-10. The first 10 basically stands for "right now" — as in, one minute, one hour, or one week. The second 10 represents that point in the foreseeable future when the initial reaction to your decision has passed but its consequences continue to play out in ways you can reasonably predict. And the third 10 stands for a time in a future that is so far off that its particulars are entirely vague.

So, really, 10-10-10 could just as well be referring to nine days, fifteen months, and twenty years, or two hours, six months, and eight years. The name of the process is just a totem meant to directionally suggest time frames along the lines of: in the heat of the moment, somewhat later, and when all is said and done.

The last step of the 10-10-10 process is analysis. For this stage, you need to take all the information you've just compiled and compare it to your innermost values — your beliefs, goals, dreams, and needs. In short, this part of 10-10-10 impels you to ask: "Knowing what I now know about all of my options and their consequences, which decision will best help me create a life of my own making?"

And with the answer to that, you have your 10-10-10 solution.

IN THE BEGINNING

As I've said, a fully conceptualized version of 10-10-10, logistics and all, didn't exactly strike me like a thunderbolt that Hawaiian morning. Rather, my thinking was more like, "I have to stop running around tamping down fires and trying to make everyone happy. When the kids are in their twenties, they're going to love me or hate me for decisions far bigger than whether or not I took them on a four-day business trip in February 1996. I'm just living too much in the moment, for God's sake."

And with that, I formed the concept of "10-10." I was going to start making my decisions based on a balance of short-term and long-term considerations. What nonsense it had been, I told myself, to have schlepped the kids five thousand miles for a few piddling swims on the beach together. If I had left them home, their pouting would have lasted a day at most, had there even been any.

Almost instantly, however, I became aware of the incompleteness of my emergent idea. Over the next few months, I was actually going to be away from home twice more, for a wedding and then for another conference. Maybe my trip to Hawaii, taken cumulatively, had me absent from the children too much. Maybe, for true balance and perspective, my new decision-making process needed to consider a more middle-term horizon as well.

Thus 10-10-10 was officially born.

With nothing to lose, I started applying the process to all sorts of dilemmas both at home and work as soon as we returned to Boston. Should I stay at the office for an emergency when I promised the kids I'd be home at six? Should I spend the holidays with my parents or my in-laws? Should I confront a difficult writer about a late manuscript? Should I focus my time on an article submitted by a promising newcomer or a steady old-timer? Much to my surprise, I found that the process *invariably* led me to faster, cleaner, and sounder decisions. And as an unexpected bonus, it also gave me a way to explain myself to all the relevant "constituents" — my kids or parents or boss — with clarity and confidence. "Let me tell you how I came to that decision," I could finally say, and go from there.

Within months, 10-10-10 had served me so well that I couldn't resist sharing it with my sisters, Elin and Della, as well as a cadre of close friends and colleagues.

And so it was that the process first started to spread. One of my coworkers told his wife, who used it to untangle herself from a state of job-search paralysis. A friend "gave" 10-10-10 to her just-married daughter, who was struggling with whether to continue working or return to graduate school. Another acquaintance of mine described 10-10-10 to her husband, a doctor, and he brought it to work, where a group of nurses adopted it to confront — and resolve — a contentious dispute over patient visiting hours that had been simmering for months.

Eventually, 10-10-10 stories from outside my immediate circle began to trickle back to me. One day, for instance, I answered my phone to hear, "Are you the 10-10-10 lady?"

When I figured out that I was and said as much, my caller burst into friendly laughter and identified herself as Gwen, the sister of one of the nurses. "Sorry to surprise you," she said, "but I'm calling because I'm sitting here wishing you could see me. I'm smiling for the first time in months."

Gwen, it turned out, was a stay-at-home mother in Chicago. Like her sister, she had started with a career in nursing, but she had changed course after a few years to become a sales rep for a pharmaceutical company. The job was a perfect fit for Gwen's outgoing personality and professional drive. "You couldn't peel me away from my sales rounds," she told me. "It wasn't work to me. It was fun. Oh — and the money! It couldn't have been better."

Gwen enjoyed her career so thoroughly that she barely missed a beat through the pregnancies and births of her three children. Sure, there were challenging times when her job and motherhood collided, but she always felt supported by her husband, who was also a sales rep, in her choice to keep working. The couple hired a live-in nanny and communicated with her constantly by cell phone. They spent weekends reconnecting with each other and their kids.

One evening when Gwen returned from yet another long stretch on the road, however, her nanny put her fifteen-month-old son in her arms and he didn't recognize her, shoving her away with an angry squeal. Gwen was shaken to her core. Her husband, looking on, was too.

Overwhelmed by a growing sense of guilt, Gwen soon resigned. "I'll be back in a few months," she promised her boss, "just as soon as things get back to normal at home."

But weeks passed, then months, and bit by bit, Gwen found herself ever more entrenched in the "back to normal" she was trying to build, her days busy with driving the kids to lessons, friends' houses, and various and sundry appointments, her nights taken over by dinner, homework, baths, and story time. Her office off the family's garage, piled with the industry trade magazines she vowed to keep reading, began to fill up with skate sharpeners and costumes for the school play.

After a year at home, Gwen's heart started to fill too — not with sadness, but with a vague, persistent longing for the big career that could have been. Occasionally, she would reread an email from her old boss she couldn't bring herself to delete from her inbox. "We'll take you back whenever you want," it said. "Your old team needs you and misses you."

Gwen missed them too, but how much? Weeks passed with her mind seesawing in debate. Had she really chosen stay-at-home motherhood, she wondered, or had she fallen into it by not choosing otherwise?

In the middle of this quandary, Gwen's sister mentioned 10-10-10 to her, suggesting she might use it the next time she felt stuck.

That happened a few days later. "I was cleaning the refrigerator, my hands and face covered with cold water and detergent, everything melting all over the place, and Sammy was crying his head off. I just lost it," Gwen told me. "For once and for all, I needed to decide if I should keep being a full-time mom."

Gwen soothed Sammy and put him down for a nap, finished with the refrigerator, and poured herself a cup of coffee. Then, with an hour to spare before her daughter arrived home from school, she sat in her kitchen and started to 10-10-10.

Her very first emotion, as the process unfolded, was dread. "Short term, if I stayed home, I knew I was looking at a lot of diapers and spit-up, with my brain not really in high gear," she told me. "I was looking at a bit of boredom, and a lot of wondering about what might have been." As for the long-term, ten-year scenario, "I knew the kids would basically be on their way out the door by that time," Gwen said. "They would be gone, and so would my career."

But a different kind of revelation began to emerge as Gwen considered the ten-month scenario. "Suddenly, as I sat there thinking about it, I became conscious of how much I cared about the time in between the first and last 10s," she said. "When Sammy makes his first goal, Emma has her first flute recital, and Alex learns to shave, I'll be there. I realized I was giving up one dream, but I was getting a reality I couldn't walk away from in return."

Another mother might have landed at a different conclusion that day in the kitchen, but for Gwen, 10-10-10 crystallized her priorities. Her decision didn't mean she would jump for joy every time the baby cried; it didn't mean that she would delight in the hours spent waiting for ice hockey practice to end. It simply meant she had made a values-driven choice that she could — and wanted to — live by.

THE TOUGH STUFF

No wonder Gwen was smiling when she first tracked me down. Her ambivalence was gone — and in its place, the peace of mind that comes with intentionality. But for the sake of full disclosure, you need to know right here and now that every 10-10-10 process doesn't end so neatly. Sometimes the solution you arrive at will be an outright surprise, as the process can surface values, agendas, fears, and dreams you've never confronted before, or it can send you down paths you've long avoided in order to keep your world under control. Some 10-10-10 solutions can even be deeply challenging, as they "require" you to come clean with others about what you truly believe and how you want to live. The truth is, transformation doesn't always come easily.

About a year ago, I gave a speech about 10-10-10 on a college campus. Afterward, one student lingered, waiting to see me alone.

He was, it turned out, an aspiring entrepreneur from Romania named Razvan, who wanted to launch a mobile phone company back home. The problem, he quickly told me, was that his longtime girlfriend, a waitress waiting for him in Bucharest, wanted to launch it with him. "What happens when Mihaela makes a mistake with a contract or something? She's not very tough when it comes to money; her family was all Communist," he reported matter-of-factly. "Then I have to say, 'Mihaela, we're trying to make a profit here,' and she starts yelling, 'Profit, forget profit — what about ideals?' And we have a fight, like always. You know what I mean?"

I got the picture, at least enough to get started. I gestured for Razvan to step closer, so we could conduct a 10-10-10 together about whether he should work with Mihaela on his new business venture.

In ten minutes, a "yes" answer was enormously appealing, Razvan said eagerly. Mihaela would calm down and, at least for a while, throw her best energies into the project. A "no" answer would cause, in Razvan's words, "World War Three," as Mihaela's family and his own — they were close friends — were sure to get involved and lobby him to change his mind.

The ten-month picture was less mixed; it would be grim no matter which choice was made. If they worked together, Razvan said, he and Mihaela would likely be back to their quarreling. But apart, there would be misery too: "We've been together for many years and there is love between us," he reflected wistfully.

We turned to the ten-year picture, and right away Razvan grimaced as if he was seeing a photograph that disturbed him. If he asked Mihaela to join his venture, they would surely be married by then, an outcome guaranteeing, as he put it, "a life of daily battles."

"Because your hopes and dreams are fundamentally different?" I asked.

"Because all we really have is history," he replied. "And I know that's not enough. We will spend our lives hurting each other."

With that, Razvan's 10-10-10 decision was made.

Was he happy? Of course not. Indeed, as we parted, I could see tears welling in his eyes. But I could also tell he was relieved in some measure, and resolved too, about taking control of his life and his future. Happiness, he seemed to know, awaited him. Sometimes, that is all 10-10-10 can promise.

A TRICKLE TO A WAVE

By 2006, I had heard enough stories from people like Gwen and Razvan to get the

31

feeling that I was on to something with 10-10-10. And so I decided to write about the process in *O, The Oprah Magazine,* where I have a regular column about work-life balance.

My "on to something" feeling, however, did not prepare me for the response. Heartfelt emails and letters soon poured in. 10-10-10, I discovered, wasn't just useful within one or two or three degrees of separation. It worked for men and women, young and old, near and far, in decisions large and small and in-between, at home and at work, and in love, friendship, and parenting.

It even worked for a twenty-seven-year-old government employee named Antoine Jefferson, who wrote me to say that he was using 10-10-10 to guide him in his personal goal of reinventing the welfare system, one act of kindness at a time.

What the heck, I wondered, is this guy talking about?

And so I called Antoine, and later had the great pleasure of meeting him in his native city of Philadelphia, where hearing his story convinced me that 10-10-10 can work effectively in ways and places I had never imagined.

Raised by a single mother in a neighborhood of housing projects, Antoine stopped going to school in seventh grade, and was eventually moved into foster care, where he was bounced among five different families. His days were often lonely, filled mainly with television-watching alone; he missed his siblings painfully. But perhaps the most defining experience of Antoine's life was the realization, at age thirteen or fourteen, that he wasn't like anyone he knew. Not just because he was gay, but because he was so unrelentingly optimistic. Even with all its harshness, the world could be a better place, Antoine believed, if people just stopped hurting each other.

A few months before my article was published, Antoine was hired to work at one of the state's busiest welfare offices, greeting clients and directing them through the application process. The idea of helping people in need thrilled him at first. But his excitement soon turned to despair. All around him every day, he saw his coworkers address the people coming into the office rudely and dismissively. "Applying for welfare usually happens at your lowest moment in life. There is so much shame in it," he told me. "The system is supposed to be about lifting people up, not breaking them more."

One night after work, Antoine wrote an impassioned manifesto about the ways he thought office protocol should change. They were fighting words, he knew, and when he showed them to his sister Tiffany, she gently tried to warn him off. "Everyone is going to hate you, Antoine," she said.

For the next few hours, Antoine sorted through the 10-10-10 consequences of presenting his proposal at work.

In ten minutes, he reasoned, there would be hell to pay. He had expressed his views to his coworkers already, and they'd brushed him off. Their message, as he heard it, was "Stop rocking the boat."

In ten months, Antoine predicted, the contentiousness with his colleagues would surely remain, or even worsen, as he refused to back down from his role as the office cop. On the other hand, if Antoine stayed mum, he worried that a crushing sense of hypocrisy would likely be destroying him inside. Neither option appealed.

But Antoine's path of action became clear as soon as he considered the ten-year scenario. "I realized I was absolutely willing to take the heat — and I even *wanted* to take it — for the chance to improve the welfare system of this state," he said. "All I could think was, 'If not me, who?' Someone has to lead change, even on the lowest rungs of the ladder."

The next day, Antoine met with his boss to describe his concerns about the cynicism that pervaded the office and the mistreatment of its patrons. She received his manifesto very positively, he recalls. But after she brought it to a meeting with the whole staff, Antoine's coworkers, as expected, started to freeze him out.

Rather than manage the mess, Antoine's boss asked him if he would be willing to be transferred to another welfare office across town.

He agreed. "I wasn't sorry or angry for a second," he told me recently. "I feel as if I did the right thing."

Today, Antoine continues to 10-10-10 any and all dilemmas that he encounters both at home and work. In fact, he recently shared the process with his mother, who, he says, immediately used it to make what could prove to be a transformative decision of her own. At the age of fifty-four, she's entered a training program in hopes of starting a small business someday. "I believe this is the beginning of a whole new life for my mother," Antoine says. "For the first time, I see her trying to create her own future."

ABOUT THAT THIRD 10

How exciting that new journey sounds. 10-10-10 does have a way of galvanizing people into forward-thinking action and out of a fixation on the present. But it would be a mistake to think that the *only* purpose of 10-10-10 is to clang long-term alarm bells during the decision-making process.

Yes, heightening your awareness of ten years out is one purpose of 10-10-10, and a very good one. All too often, we make decisions just to avoid an immediate ouch — the sulking child, the disappointed family, the complicated logistics, the angry coworkers, and so on. The third 10 in 10-10-10 has a powerful way of mitigating that tendency. It helps us decide whether (or not) it's worth it to endure short-term flame-outs in the service of our larger, more deeply held goals in life.

No one, however, should make *every* decision based on its consequences in the long term. First, such prudence is pretty much guaranteed to make your day-to-day life a total bore. You cannot banish spontaneity! But the main reason not to set your sights exclusively on the third 10 is that it can be too damn risky.

Pete Turkel taught me that.

Pete was an editor on the swing shift at

the Associated Press back in the mid-1980s, when I was all of twenty-six years old and a reporter in the Boston bureau. At the time I met Pete, I was working the overnight shift myself, reporting for duty at midnight and released to freedom at 8 AM when, oddly enough, I found myself hungry for a burger and a beer. My skewed body clock was unpleasant enough, but at least I was still able to see friends and family at breakfast and dinner. Pete, who came in at 4 PM and left at midnight, missed *everything.* He was asleep when his kids left for school and his wife for work, and he was at work when they all came home, ate dinner, and went to bed.

One day, bitching and moaning about my own hours, I turned to Pete — twenty years my senior — and blurted out, "I don't know how *you* stand it. It's like you're living on another planet or something."

To this day, I admire Pete for not smacking me for my temerity. Instead he smiled in his familiar, good-hearted way. "You'll understand this when you're older, Suzy, and have real bills to pay and a family to raise," he said. "I'm paid a premium for working this shift. If I keep at this job, I'll be able to retire early, send my kids to college without loans, and buy a house with a dock on a lake. What I'm doing will be worth every minute of it when I walk out that door on my last day."

I was one year gone from the AP when Pete was killed in a car crash. (His wife was gravely injured and died later.) But it was never lost on me that Pete was postponing life — for all the "right" reasons — at the time of his death.

I still think about Pete. His life reminds me that while it's important to consider the long-term consequences of every 10-10-10 decision, they cannot be *consistently* more important than the short- and midterm. The far-off future often matters more than we give it credit for and should influence our thinking more than it usually does. But it should not trump all other time frame considerations, all the time.

TURNAROUND TIME

If there is one piece of push back I receive about 10-10-10, it concerns timing and it generally goes like this: "I'm just too busy to do that kind of thing."

With life-changing decisions, it's true that 10-10-10 can take hours or longer to conduct. Later on, we will meet an advertising executive who leaned on 10-10-10 to help her decide what to do about her career after her son was diagnosed with a genetic mental illness. Because it required the gathering of medical opinions, her 10-10-10 decision unfurled over the course of two weeks.

Far more often, however, 10-10-10 slows you down just enough to get your decision right. It doesn't squander your time as much as invests it wisely.

Take Natalie, a tech company manager I met last year. Along with her busy job, Natalie tries to stay deeply present in the lives of her two teenage sons, both high school athletes, and her husband of eighteen years. Most days, she keeps all of her balls in the air, but when a new one gets tossed into the mix, sometimes unexpected decisions need to be made — quickly.

Natalie's uncle, Charlie, had never been a big part of her life, but when he passed away at the age of eighty-three, Natalie felt more conflicted than she had expected about attending his funeral service. "I barely knew him. He was my mother's brother-in-law," she explained to me. "But I also knew that showing up would mean the world to my parents and the rest of my extended family. They would take it as a sign of respect."

With that realization, Natalie decided she needed to be at the ceremony. She made plans to leave work early, but just as she was about to head out the door, her fifteen-year-old son text-messaged her. His lift to soccer practice had fallen through; could she help? Before Natalie could even react, another text message came in, this one from her husband. He had to stay late at work. Could she cover for him and drive their younger son to the orthodontist?

"Well, there goes the funeral," Natalie groaned in frustration, picking up the phone to call her mother.

But then she stopped. Why not, she reasoned, 10-10-10 the problem? She had learned about the process from another working mother, and had been using it ever since to sort out the kind of mini work-life balance conflicts that come with the territory.

With that, she quickly defined her immediate question as, "Should I attend Uncle Charlie's funeral?"

In ten minutes, she knew a "no" would make her life flat-out easier. She wouldn't have to find another ride for Josh, or go through the elaborate dance of rescheduling Todd's appointment with the recalcitrant receptionist at the orthodontist's office. What a relief.

In ten months though, the consequence of a no-go decision made Natalie cringe. She only had one chance to bid her uncle goodbye. More than that, she probably wouldn't have another opportunity to see several of her elderly relatives who were quite dear to her.

And what about the consequences in ten years? As a parent, Natalie was a firm believer in the old saw, "Actions speak louder than words." If she wanted to teach her children the values of respect and responsibility, she had to demonstrate them herself.

The next number she dialed was her son's cell phone. "Josh, I can't help you," she told her older boy. "It's very important for me to attend my uncle's funeral — to show my family how much I love them. Please ask Coach to help you find a lift." She then called her son's orthodontist and canceled his appointment; she'd reschedule it, she figured, when she found the time.

Finally, on the road to her family's church, she called her husband to explain her choice. "I'm with you," he said when she was done. At first, Natalie thought he was simply saying, "I'm on your side." Instead, he meant it literally. He dropped an email to his boss and jumped in his own car — to be with Natalie at the service.

Later, when I asked Natalie how much time she spent on her 10-10-10 decision, she laughed in surprise. "Oh, I don't know," she said, "maybe two minutes."

But I wasn't surprised. I've seen 10-10-10 sort out even longer-brewing dilemmas just as quickly.

One summer evening a few years ago, I was chopping onions for dinner when my daughter Sophia wandered by the kitchen. The hula-dancing incident long behind her, she had grown into a young woman who loved to write, mimicked me to perfection, and could hit a wicked two-handed backhand. She had the varsity letters framed in her bedroom to prove it.

"Mom, I need to tell you something," she said quietly. "I'm quitting tennis."

My heart sank. Over the previous year, I'd certainly noticed Sophia cutting her practices short and, when I let myself listen, I'd certainly heard her complaining that she wasn't finding joy in the game anymore. But that had never kept me from hoping she was in a phase that would pass.

I stopped what I was doing and put on the steadiest voice I could muster.

"Absolutely, positively, one hundred percent *no,*" I said. "We've worked too hard and spent too many hours to get where we are to give it all up now."

I expected a fight, but Sophia surprised

me. Perfectly calm, she shrugged and simply replied, "OK, but let's 10-10-10 it. How about framing up the question as: *'Should Sophia stop playing a game that she's sick of?'* "

"I would prefer it without the editorializing," I said, "but fine."

Sophia started by stating her case. In all three time frames, she said, freedom from tennis would allow her to focus on interests she simply and truly enjoyed more. And she insisted that she wouldn't stop playing tennis entirely, she would keep at it, only recreationally.

"Colleges want varsity letters," I resisted, "and in about ten months, that's going to matter. Colleges want kids who stick with things, who don't give up when things get hard."

"Colleges should see the real Sophia," came the answer, "and I'm not playing tennis in college, Mom. Come on, I'm not good enough. It's not fun for me to keep getting beaten. It's not my sport. It's yours."

She was right, of course, but I wasn't ready to surrender.

"When you're a grown-up, ten, twenty years from now, you're going to wish you could play tennis with friends," I said. "And with me. We could play together."

"I could destroy you and your pathetic serve with one hand tied behind my back," Sophia said with the beginnings of a smile. She waited a moment before her final shot; I suppose she knew it was a winner. "Mom," she said, "this decision is about *my* life."

With that I had to smile too. The game was over, and Sophia had won it fair and square. 10-10-10 had been there as our trusted referee.

SEEING WHAT WE NEED TO

And 10-10-10 is always there. No matter what the scope of the dilemma it's applied to, no matter what the details. Since the morning that I found 10-10-10, or it found me, I have seen the idea evolve into its full form and spread from person to person, across boundaries of every kind.

Because it works.

In a time when the world moves at warp speed and decisions can feel inexorably complex, 10-10-10 can help you forge an intentional life, choice by choice. It can make you far less likely to find yourself outside looking in at your life, in shock, dismay, or the kind of regret that rusts in you forever. It helps you decide whether you want to be a career woman or a mother, or both, whether a relationship should go forward or end, or if a job is worth saving.

10-10-10 adds reason where it is lacking. It inserts deliberation where there is only instinct. It replaces opaqueness with transparency.

Or as Antoine told me once, 10-10-10 "hushes the noise so the mind can see what it needs to."

Which brings me back to my first description of 10-10-10 as a life-management tool.

The truth is, if you use 10-10-10 consistently, it becomes less of a tool or a process or a device or a methodology — and more of an infinite and sustaining heartbeat.

It becomes a way of life.

Chapter Two:
This Is Your Brain
on 10-10-10
THE SCIENCE BEHIND THE SYSTEM

One day when I was talking with Antoine Jefferson about his change campaign at the welfare department, it dawned on me to ask him how he had made decisions before he found 10-10-10. The question produced a long sigh. "Well, just gut, I suppose," he said, shaking his head as if the memory both amused and mystified him. "And let me tell you, when I made all my decisions by the seat of my pants, I was on my ass *a lot.*"

I heard similar admissions from virtually every person I interviewed for this book. "For thirty years, I let my stomach guide me," a schoolteacher in California told me. "I called it my 'uh-oh' feeling, and it worked about thirty percent of the time." A mother of three in New Jersey said that she had asked her husband and friends for advice and then picked the point of view she liked the most. "No one ever knew where I was coming from," she recalled. Another 10-10-

10er confessed, "I suppose I just waited for decisions to happen to me."

These kinds of comments got me wondering: If 10-10-10 was so successful in changing the way people approached decision making, how were decisions *usually* made? And how did 10-10-10 help people make them differently?

A BEAUTIFUL MIND

Now, I'm no scientist. The last time I was in a laboratory, I was dissecting a fetal pig that my classmate and I had dubbed Johnny Rotten. But for the past two years, I've been on a small mission to learn about how the brain works, guided by willing experts in psychology, neurology, behavioral economics, and evolutionary biology. Their insights, along with those limned from a pile of scientific texts, have unlocked some of my own about how and why 10-10-10 works so effectively.

The human mind, I've come to learn, is a wondrous product of evolution, designed to guide and protect us in the most common social situations. We excel, for example, at forming alliances, making deals, and discerning motives. We're good at picking leaders, working in teams, and sensing enemies posing as friends. Such skills came in very handy as human beings struggled to survive in the earliest days of civilization, and thanks to the process of natural selection, they carry on in our neurological "wiring" today.

While we can handle many types of social interactions with highly evolved aptitude, however, our minds are not nearly as adept at making decisions with multiple variables and time frames — and for good reason. As a species, human beings tend to place a decreasing value on both gains and losses as they stretch into the future. The psychological lingo for this dynamic is "hyperbolic discounting," which, in everyday parlance, essentially means that people tend to act as if the future doesn't exist or that it will be ideal.

There are countless studies that demonstrate this effect. A 1999 report published by the Johns Hopkins School of Medicine, for instance, found that as many as 80 percent of the people who undergo an excruciating coronary bypass do not make the relatively easy lifestyle changes required to prevent further surgery, continuing to eat fatty foods, smoke cigarettes, and avoid the treadmill.

But scientific research is hardly necessary to confirm that we routinely ignore the long-term impact of our actions. We've all said yes to an invitation to go somewhere or a request to help someone, knowing full well that we will be too busy to fulfill the commitment when the time comes. We've all skipped exercise, downed another glass of wine, or finished off the last of the brownies. Somewhere in our visceral psyches, at least to some extent, we've all bought into the age-old "Eat, drink, and be merry, for tomorrow we all may die" mind-set.

Few people, of course, operate *solely* in the present tense. Clearly, it's also within our nature to develop coping mechanisms to combat hyperbolic discounting and "force" long-term considerations into our decision-making process. Some people keep journals to hear themselves think; others compile scrupulous lists of pros and cons. I have some friends who never make a decision without praying about it, and others who live by the credo "Never decide alone." Before 10-10-10 entered my life, collective pondering was my favored approach too, when I had one. I'd try to run my messiest dilemmas by my sisters, both of whom were very good at asking down-the-road-type questions.

But let's be real. Few decisions occur in situations where we can turn to a journal or even a pair of level-headed sisters for the kind of 360-degree perspective we need. At the end of the day, many of our choices are so personal and so complicated that, by necessity and convention, we are alone with them.

And that's where 10-10-10 comes in. By bringing every option and its consequences to the surface and connecting actions to deeply held values, the process empowers us to override the counterproductive tendencies of our own minds. It helps us help ourselves.

GREAT EXPECTATIONS

To understand how 10-10-10 achieves that effect, we need to go back (very briefly!) to the eighteenth century. In 1738, a Dutch-Swiss mathematician named Daniel Bernoulli postulated that people facing decisions with multiple variables would survey the likelihood and severity of possible outcomes and assess the consequences of each, then choose the option that would maximize their gains and minimize their losses across all time frames. Or in essence, they would try to get the most personal "value," or upside, out of any decision.

Bernoulli's idea was so intriguing that two centuries later it was embraced and more fully developed by two renowned mathematicians from Princeton University, John von Neumann and Oskar Morgenstern, who termed it "Expected Utility Theory."

The problem with Expected Utility Theory, though, is that it has a rather inconsistent relationship with reality. People do not regularly survey the likelihood and severity of all of their choices. They do not habitually assess outcomes and consequences. They do not, in other words, act rationally all of the time.

The forces that undermine rationality in human behavior are many, most of them quite familiar to anyone who's, well, alive. There's time pressure, peer pressure, lack of information, and information overload. The list goes on. But the result of all these conditions is stress, the ultimate deterrent to rational thinking. When it kicks in, our blood pressure rises, our pulse quickens, and adrenaline rushes through our veins. Sometimes these reactions can be all for the good, sharpening our focus and intent, allowing us to act almost superhuman. My friend Skye, for instance, jumped out of the driver's seat after a terrible car crash and rescued her sister, who was strapped in the back. Not until later, when her sister was safe and sound, did Skye notice that she was hurt. She had a shattered pelvis.

But outside of such do-or-die emergencies, stress much more typically interferes with sound decision making. As stress hormones race throughout the body, they monopolize the prefrontal cortex, an area of the brain where complex reasoning occurs. And when stress ramps up into full-blown anxiety, our misfiring neurotransmitters can provoke what some psychologists call "closed-loop thinking," in which the mind starts to fixate on a single worry, like a song you can't get out of your head. The result can be feelings of confusion or paralysis — or both. I suspect that just before my 10-10-10 epiphany in Hawaii, my own poor brain, clamoring with the voices of people who had a stake in my life choices, was experiencing exactly such a meltdown.

I was rescued by the sunrise and an idea.

Most people, however, are rescued from stressful indecision by their brain's back-up generator: gut instinct.

SUBCONSCIOUSLY SPEAKING

Not long ago, while I was getting rehabilitation for a bum elbow, my physical therapist asked me what my ailing joint had been "telling" me lately. "You have to listen to your body," she said. "It's like your gut —

filled with wisdom."

I nodded; like most everyone, I would agree that gut instinct has its moments of blazing insight. It's a pattern recognizer, if you will. It's your subconscious saying, "Hello, you've been here before. This time, please factor in the lessons you learned."

But every time I hear someone talk about the "wisdom" of gut, especially for choices with true impact and no easy out, I balk. I know from experience — two experiences, in fact — just how inadequate gut can be as a meaningful and consistent guide.

The first experience occurred when I was twenty-one and, pounding the pavement in search of a journalism job, I ended up in Kansas City for an interview. It was 7 PM by the time I left the newspaper offices to walk back to my hotel, and an hour later when I finally admitted to myself that I was completely lost in the wrong part of town. Just then, a hefty, middle-aged man wearing a cowboy hat pulled up beside me in a white Cadillac. "I can tell you're not from here," he said. "Let me help you."

Like most young women, I had spent my life being told that getting into the car with a strange man without a Good Housekeeping Seal of Approval tattooed on his forehead was a form of suicide. But on that day,

I took one look at this particular fellow's goofy, gap-toothed smile and hopped in the front seat. The happy ending of this story is that I had a lovely ride back to the front door of my hotel, during which I learned all about my pleasant companion's perfect wife, children, and grandchildren.

As we said goodbye, I thanked him for his hospitality and then, almost as an apology, offered, "I can't believe I took a ride with you."

"You know what?" he replied. "Neither can I."

Fast-forward two years. Once again, I was lost, except this time in Miami, where I had ultimately landed a job. In fact, I was lost somewhere in the spooky maze of streets behind the Miami airport, having taken a wrong left or right turn (or both) on the way to an assignment. It was pouring rain and my car had died. This was long before cell phones, and I was desperate to get out of there and let the news desk know why I wasn't where I was supposed to be. I was literally crying with frustration when a man in a pickup truck pulled up in front of me and, braving the storm, sprinted to my window. "Need help?" he asked. "I'm on my way to the gas station about a mile up ahead, right off West Flagler. I'll give you a lift."

I took one look at him and thought, *"No freaking way."*

The funny thing is, the guy seemed nice enough. He too had a goofy, wide-open face. He was about my age and even sort of cute. But something made me tell him that help was already on the way. In reality, it was another hour before a police cruiser moseyed along, called for a tow, and took me home.

For some time afterward, I was actually embarrassed by my split-second discharge of that would-be helper near West Flagler Street. I'd only been a reporter for two years, I thought, but what a dark and hardened cynic I'd become.

Then one day, hanging around police headquarters as I was wont to do for my job on the crime beat, I spied a pile of mug shots sitting on the desk of my pal, Detective Joe Lodato. I'm sure you can guess whose picture was right on top.

"Oh, Joe?" I asked, voice quavering as I pointed at the photo. "What's this guy wanted for?"

"Him?" Joe said, grimacing in disgust. *"Everything."*

Now, from these two stories, you might

conclude that gut actually works quite effectively. My instinct, after all, led to two correct calls. But think about it. Neither taught me anything. In Kansas City, my gut said, "Go with the guy." In Miami, it said, "Don't go with the guy." And I have no idea why. To this day, I still wonder if I was just lucky.

Look, I'm not denigrating gut. As I've said, it's perfectly fine for small calls, and many times, it's all you have to go on. But as a way of making cogent decisions in your life that you can explain to others — and especially as the means to a deliberate, self-aware lifestyle — it's simply not trustworthy enough.

ONLY ACTING HUMAN

And there's actually a neurological reason for that. As I came to learn in my exploration of the brain's workings, gut is often no more than an inborn reaction that can have very little to do with the choice we are facing in the moment, and quite a lot to do with the choices that our evolutionary ancestors faced on the African Savannah.

Here's what I mean. Evolutionary psychologists today agree that a number of behavioral biases were hardwired into our brains to ensure survival. In primitive circumstances, for example, we were "programmed" to freeze in times of danger, as predators would rarely go after dead quarry. Today, we still carry that deep-rooted propensity toward paralysis, even if "danger" is coming in the form of a tight deadline or a big meeting. Similarly, during the earliest days of civilization, to break with your tribe and go it alone spelled extinction. As a result, people continue to have trouble bucking majority rule and consensus. Many of us have gone along with a terrible idea just because it felt awkward to contradict friends, colleagues, or even the status quo. In doing so, we were only acting human.

10-10-10 cannot erase the ingrained neurological biases that our brains developed to protect our species over the course of millions of years. But it can tame them; indeed, it can reframe them for the times in which we live.

Take how our minds process advice. When you have a problem, you may think you hear input from your wacky aunt, brainy boss, and too-young-to-know-anything son using an "educated" brain that sorts out who's giving you the most credible contribution. But studies in psychology would prove you wrong. There seems to be general consensus among scientists that several ingrained biases undermine our ability to sort out good advice from bad. We tend, for instance, to give the most credence to the last and first pieces of information we've heard and discount what we've learned in between, regardless of the information's veracity or relevance. Some cognitive psychologists also believe that we have a strong inborn tendency to believe the information we have heard the most times and give more weight to information from people we like and minimize information from people we don't.

10-10-10 interferes with such selective information "deafness." Your brain may want you to ignore something you heard two weeks ago or a comment delivered by a grumpy old neighbor. The discipline of the process won't let you. And 10-10-10 won't let you buy into information you've heard over and over again, either, because by definition, it "requires" you to test facts and assumptions.

LISTENING WITH OPEN EARS

For many years, Paula had struggled with her older son's rebellious behavior. A drinker, smoker, and all-around rabble-rouser, Kenny had two misdemeanor arrests by the time he was seventeen. But a chance meeting with an old friend in the military landed Kenny in a recruiting office, and he ended up enlisting himself. Within a year, Kenny was a changed man, Paula told me, responsible and mature. "He became an adult," she said.

With Kenny stationed in North Carolina, Paula could finally exhale. But not for long. One day, her younger son — a tenth grader nicknamed Hooper — received a report card filled with Cs and Ds. Paula was shocked. Hooper was her "easy" child — good enough at school, crazy about basketball, never a problem at home. She quickly met with school officials, and they seemed mystified as well. Hooper, they said, seemed to have "fallen off a cliff."

Paula and her husband, Jim, tried to get to the bottom of the problem, but Hooper would barely answer their questions. He did tell them that he hated his math teacher because his math teacher hated him. He assured his parents that not making the basketball team had nothing to do with his mood, and everything would be better if he just changed schools.

Paula ricocheted in every direction about what to do while Hooper continued to plead his case. His guidance counselor agreed that a change might be good. Jim, however, worried that taking Hooper out of school would only teach him how to run away from problems. On the other hand, neither he nor Paula wanted to keep Hooper in an environment that was making him miserable.

Somewhere in the middle of the mess, Paula had a short meeting with Hooper's math teacher, and she instantly understood why Hooper disliked him so much. He was stern-faced, impatient, and obviously not interested in engaging in the kinds of niceties that preceded most parent-teacher conferences. "Your son is depressed," he told Paula within a minute of meeting her. "He needs a doctor and he probably needs a prescription." Paula left the meeting so enraged by the teacher's audacity — he didn't even know Hooper! — that she found herself unable to repeat his comments to anyone, including her husband.

A dismal Christmas came and went, and when vacation was over, Hooper refused to return to school. Paula was looking for an opening in local parochial schools when a friend suggested she try conducting a 10-10-10 analysis. Feeling at her wits' end, she agreed.

Paula framed her dilemma as, "Should Hooper change schools?"

In ten minutes, she reasoned, removing Hooper from the source of his misery would be like taking a giant thorn out of her family's side.

The ten-month scenario was more confusing. Maybe changing schools would improve Hooper's behavior, and all would be well again. But what would she do if it wasn't?

For weeks, Paula had been fixated on advice from the principal and her husband. Suddenly, however, she found she could no longer tune out another voice — that of the math teacher. What would happen, she wondered, if she considered the prospect that Hooper was struggling with something more significant, something without an easy fix, like depression? How then would her thinking change?

All at once, Paula knew she could not make a decision about Hooper without gathering more information, no matter how upsetting it might be. She called her pediatrician for a referral, and within days Hooper had an appointment with a psychologist.

Hooper's diagnosis of depression ultimately filled Paula with relief — and gratitude. With its emphasis on testing assumptions and considering every possible option no matter what its source, 10-10-10 had compelled her to open her mind to hearing advice from a person she'd wanted to ignore. The process didn't let her.

Today, with Kenny stationed in Iraq, Paula is hardly without worries. But Hooper, now the manager of the school basketball team and a solid B-student, is not one of them. "Jim and I call Hooper our 'rebound boy,' " Paula told me recently. "I guess we have two of those."

KNEE DEEP IN THE BIG MUDDY

Along with helping us correct for selective information processing, 10-10-10 also interferes with two other common evolutionary biases.

Most of us can probably remember a time when we've felt compelled to hang on to a hopeless project or a failing relationship. In a nutshell, such behavior is what cognitive science calls escalating commitment, or the psychological drive to cling to "investments" even when they're clearly not working. There are a plethora of books and academic studies on this topic, but my favorite is the aptly named paper "Knee Deep in the Big Muddy" by Barry M. Staw, a professor of management at the University of California–Berkeley. It richly describes our tendency to sink into an ever-worsening situation in order to preserve our self-image, justify actions already taken, or both.

Now, you might be wondering, if escalating commitment is so pointless, why do we still fall victim to it so often? No one knows for sure, but social anthropologists have hypothesized that the world's early survivors were likely those who, even when faced with failures, refused to give up on activities such as farming, hunting, and reproducing. Natural selection rewarded such perseverance, and we can all be happy for that. But the neurological result is that we remain inclined not to bail out of our predicaments — particularly in high-stakes situations — no matter how disastrous they become.

By pressing us to ask, "What are the positive and negative consequences of staying in this mess over time?," 10-10-10 can break escalating commitment's gripping downward spiral.

"I CANNOT REACH THIS GUY"

Rachel, a thirty-six-year-old administrative assistant in Chicago who I met several years ago, is a perfect (if painful) example of how escalating commitment can get the better of the best of us.

Rachel is pure positive energy — smart, capable, and suffused with warmth. Her intuition about people, honed by years of traveling the world and working in successful companies, is ordinarily spot-on. But when she met Kyle, a handsome, redheaded contractor, her usual good sense soon started to seep away.

Rachel and Kyle's relationship started with a flirtatious conversation at the gym, and before the month was out, the two were seeing each other once or twice a week and spending hours each night on the phone talking about Kyle's work, his dream of getting involved in local politics, and the difficulties of his mother's ongoing battle with cancer. The conversations seemed so intimate that Rachel couldn't help herself. She was at the point in her life where fewer and fewer men were available. Was she finally, she wondered, hearing wedding bells?

There was just one catch; the relationship was completely platonic. Rachel convinced herself the reason was commendable. Kyle was too worried about his mother's illness to physically connect with a woman. And she didn't feel she could — or should — test that assumption.

Months passed. Rachel and Kyle continued to see each other often and talk nearly every night. Eventually, Rachel started making regular visits to Kyle's mother in the hospital, where she met and befriended many of Kyle's relatives. Yet not a single chaste kiss passed between the pair.

"Didn't you ever just think, 'Something has to be wrong?' " I asked Rachel when she recounted the experience to me.

"Oh, that thought might have crossed my mind," she replied with a sardonic grin. "Like every night, I would go to bed thinking, 'I cannot reach this guy.' "

A year and a half after Rachel first met Kyle, his mother passed away. At the funeral, Kyle's cousin pulled her aside. "Someone needs to tell you," he said. "Kyle has a girl he's serious with — we all know her. Her name's April. She's over there." In the corner, Kyle's sister stood huddled with a pretty young woman who looked barely twenty-one.

With a terse text message that night, Rachel finally ended things.

"You know, I think Kyle really did love talking to me," Rachel reflects now. "The lie was that he couldn't marry someone who wasn't Irish-Catholic. Maybe I sensed that. But at a certain point I just felt so deep into the relationship, I couldn't pull out."

10-10-10, says Rachel, would have prevented her "stupidest decision ever" to stick with Kyle, by forcing her to see that her commitment to the relationship didn't make sense in any time frame.

To prove that point, Rachel conducted a retrospective 10-10-10 with me, placing herself a year back in time, before Kyle's mother died. Her question, as she phrased it, was, "Should I get out now?"

In the ten-minute and ten-month time frame, Rachel admitted, the answer would have been no. "I would have been willing to invest another year of my life in Kyle," she explained. "I felt like we had something, and there were not a lot of alternatives on the horizon."

The ten-year scenario, however, was eye-opening. If she and Kyle were together, Rachel reasoned, she'd be married to a man who was charming, but so fixated on himself that there would always be a piece of him outside her reach. "It was only when I imagined the distant future that I saw the real consequences of my inaction," she told me.

10-10-10, in other words, would have put the brakes on Rachel's deepening commitment to Kyle. Without it, she can only be thankful that his cousin was there to do so instead.

Today, Rachel is herself again; she just returned, brimming with excitement, from a trip to Honduras, where she distributed microloans to women farmers, and she plans to go back again soon. As for Kyle — she considers him a memory with an important lesson. "I will never not use 10-10-10 again," she told me. "I see it as a way to protect yourself from your own emotions — as a way to preserve your self-respect. What a valuable gift."

FUTURE SHOCK

Research in the field of cognitive science has also identified a group of biases that tend to trap us inside negative emotional states. We tend to feel, to put it very simply, that when bad times arrive, they will never leave, nor will our feelings around them. It's like New York City in the aftermath of 9/11. Some residents fled for the suburbs or even farther away, vowing never to return to the city's "irrevocably" marred psychological landscape, while the many who stayed predicted that the city would never regain its hustle and bustle. Of course, no New Yorker will ever forget that tragic day, but few would tell you now that the city isn't back. It just took time.

In our personal lives, the same emotional dynamic occurs. Emily, a woman in Texas whom I met through a friend, lost her beloved husband of twenty years in a car accident. For years afterward, she continued to wear her wedding ring and even had her late husband's name tattooed on her arm. Her sense of loss was so profound that she was convinced she would never look at another man, let alone date anyone. Is it any surprise, though, that today Emily is happily remarried? Emotions have a way of repairing themselves, but in our darkest hours, science has shown, our minds tell us otherwise.

Again, it's valid to ask why such a bias exists, and again, there's no definitive answer. Some scientists have suggested that strong feelings gave the earliest humans the psychological energy to fight tenaciously, even in times of great strife. But the point for today's world is simply that the tendency to believe that ephemeral emotions will last forever undercuts good decision making. Carnegie Mellon University economics professor George Lowenstein calls this dynamic an "empathy gap" with our future selves. We may know we will be around — working at our jobs, raising our children, running errands, and so on — in five or ten years, but we just cannot imagine ourselves doing as much in anything but a permanent state of shock and grief.

10-10-10 counteracts the empathy gap not by insisting, "Come on, you'll be better someday," but by asking us to *create* who we will become when that someday arrives.

A DREAM OF A LIFE

I met Lynne Scott Jackson, a marketing expert with twenty years of experience in the corporate world, after she had found herself in a position to do just that.

Lynne's dilemma had erupted shortly after she had launched her own public relations firm focused on the African-American market. "My dream was to build something very special," she told me, "a successful venture run by a working mother who was the descendant of slaves."

But a week before Lynne was due to travel to Johannesburg to work on a consulting project for her first major client, her parents fell ill. Neither one's life was at risk, but there was a flurry of tearful phone calls, each one ending with Lynne's parents pleading for her to come to Virginia right away and stay with them while they recuperated.

Immediately, Lynne's instinct took over. "Don't leave," her gut told her. "Take care of your family. That's the right thing to do."

An avid 10-10-10 practitioner already,

Lynne used the process to push back.

In ten minutes, she knew one thing for sure: Canceling the trip would quiet her guilt. On the other hand, Lynne anticipated that canceling the trip would also let loose deeper feelings of panic and dread. Would her new client allow her to postpone everything? She doubted it, and even if they did, she feared making a bad first impression.

Lynne then moved on to an assessment of her life situation in ten months. Her parents would likely be settled back into their routine. But if she didn't go to South Africa, her company would probably still be struggling. It had taken her nearly a year to land the South African account, and could take months to find another.

Ten years out, however, the lay of the land shifted. Sadly, Lynne acknowledged, her father might be gone. But her mother, younger and in better health, would probably still be living. Health problems were sure to crop up now and again, and with increasing seriousness too. Would she keep flying to Virginia every time something went wrong? Even if such a step assuaged her guilt in the present, Lynne reasoned, it would undoubtedly deny her the opportunity to ever establish a successful enterprise.

And what of the ten-year scenario if she

didn't cancel the trip? Lynne pictured herself running a company with perhaps twenty or thirty employees, the fulfillment of her lifelong dream, and an achievement, she believed, worthy of her ancestors' sacrifices.

The next day, Lynne flew to Virginia, not to stay but to arrange the ongoing services of a visiting nurse for her parents. Her consideration of the three time frames had opened her eyes to a solution she hadn't been able to visualize in her "heated" emotional state. She also called her brother in California, long absent from caregiving responsibilities in the family because of his military service overseas, and asked for his help. He quickly agreed to come east the following week.

Then Lynne left for Johannesburg as planned.

"By imagining how I would feel in the future — and how I *wanted* to feel — the crisis ended up changing my relationship with my parents for the better," Lynne told me recently. "It's so much healthier now. It forced me to set up a sustainable system to care for my parents. It made me get on the phone and bring my brother into the equation. 10-10-10 helped me get over myself."

Lynne's business continues to grow today

and has led to a secondary career as a professor of communications at a college in New York City. "Without using 10-10-10 to tackle my dilemma," she says, "I might even be living in Virginia today, on call, with a life I didn't really want."

Instead Lynne is leading a life of her own making.

NATURE'S AUTOPILOT

When I first set out to explore the connection between brain science and 10-10-10, it wasn't long before I came to see exactly what Isaac Asimov meant when he observed that "the brain is the most complicated organization of matter that we know." Indeed, the main thing I know now, after spending two years grappling with behavioral economics, neuroscience, evolutionary psychology, and related fields, is that I am not alone in thinking that science, even with technology's great advances, will never fully understand the machinations of the mind. Asimov's "complicated organization" is as mysterious as it is wondrous.

Yet, science does know enough about the human brain to begin to explain how it makes decisions, both for better and for worse. And as I came to better understand that process myself, I was reminded of my old friend Fyodor Dostoevsky again, who once said, "It is not the brain that matters, but that which guides it — the character, the heart, the generosity, the new ideas."

10-10-10 can be one of those ideas. By having us methodically sort through our options in various time frames, the process challenges our deep-seated, neurological biases. It forces us to dissect and analyze what we're deciding and why, and it pushes us to empathize with who we might become. 10-10-10 disengages our decision making from nature's autopilot.

We will never, of course, be able to banish gut instinct from our lives. Some dilemmas are so complex and stressful that they resist our most disciplined and rigorous thinking.

But if you seek a new life of clarity and intention, then your brain sometimes needs an intervention on its own behalf to overcome the all-too-human proclivity to act without deliberation.

10-10-10 spurs us to deliberate, then act.

It gives us decisions we can trust.

Chapter Three:
Authentic at Last
THE VALUES EQUATION OF
10-10-10

So far in this book, I've mentioned "values" a mere five times. Mere because, when it comes to getting the most out of 10-10-10, that number hardly does the subject justice.

Without values, 10-10-10 is a device for surfacing decision alternatives, and far be it from me to knock it for that.

But it is with values as an integral part of the process that 10-10-10 truly becomes transformative, allowing us to live in sync with our authentic dreams, hopes, and beliefs. That's why whenever I hear people talking about their decisions — and especially when I work with people using 10-10-10 — I often end up proselytizing about the overwhelming, undeniable, Holy Cow importance of bringing values into the mix.

I can't help myself.

You see, back in my youth — OK, up until I was nearly thirty — I thought that most everyone held the same guiding moral beliefs and abided by the same fundamental operating principles: Do Unto Others, Love Thy Neighbor, that kind of thing. I also assumed that most people eventually came around to the same basic list of priorities in life: health, family, happiness, achievement, financial security, and some right-feeling balance among them all. Simply put, I thought values were so generic that I generally tuned out anyone who tried to tell me otherwise.

Then one day during my second year of business school, a classmate bounded up to me on the quad to invite me to a party at his dorm that night. For a long moment, I just stared at him.

"Don't we have an industrial marketing exam tomorrow?" I finally managed to ask in a tone that could only be described as "withering."

He rolled his eyes. "I'll take that as a no," he said.

"I mean — the semester isn't over yet," I piled on.

"It's May, Suzy," he groaned back. "Everyone has a job locked up by now, including you."

"But there are still two weeks until grades are due!" I cried.

My classmate shook his head sadly. "You

know what?" he said. "You just don't value fun."

And then he bounded away, leaving me floored.

It was a chilling revelation, and one that in time prompted me to look long and hard at why I was always working, working, working. The answer, it turned out, had a little something to do with my unusual Sicilian grandmother, but a lot more to do with something I now call the "Big Black Hole," a condition that results from a lack of values awareness. More common than you might think, the Big Black Hole manifests itself as a gaping emotional void at the center of our lives, begging to be filled with activities, commitments, children, studying — whatever busyness will mask the emptiness.

Thanks to 10-10-10, both my Big Black Hole and aversion to fun are now long gone.

And so too is my haziness around values.

Today, I can finally say that I understand my values, in all their ungeneric glory. More important, my hope is that by the end of this chapter, you too will have a sharper and more meaningful understanding of your own. Your 10-10-10 decisions will be far better — and truer — for it.

THE CATALYST WITHIN

As I've taken 10-10-10 on the road over the past few years, I've discovered that while plenty of people know their values cold, just as many are like me before my conversion experience on the quad. They may sense their values; they may intuit them. But they can't state them with any real nuance — let alone use them to make decisions.

Fortunately, the 10-10-10 process itself can be an effective catalyst for values identification, as it was for Jackie Majors, a woman from California who first wrote me in 2006 after my *O* magazine article about 10-10-10 was published.

Jackie's dilemma had been long in the making, but it came to a head when her six-year-old daughter, Leah, brought home a school project — a collection of biographies she'd written about her family. On the page about Leah's grandmother, who cared for her while Jackie worked sixty hours a week as a corporate vice president, Leah had scrawled four exuberant paragraphs. Similarly, she had covered the page about her father, a teacher, with effusive praise and a detailed description of his pitching and catching lessons every day after school.

On Jackie's page, the entry read: "My mom travels a lot. My mom plans birthday parties when she's in town."

Later that night, with the children in bed, Jackie found herself fighting back tears. Should she quit her job, she wondered, or was there another solution to the torment she was feeling? Her thoughts scrambled, Jackie suddenly remembered that she had my article about 10-10-10 in her briefcase; a colleague had given it to her earlier in the week, with the gentle admonishment, "Your life is too crazy. You need this."

Jackie pulled out the article and started to read. And as she did, the dam broke, and the tears began. "I saw myself in every sentence," Jackie recalls, "conflicted, running every which way, never totally happy. I just sobbed."

For an hour or more, pen to paper, Jackie struggled to sort out her options and their consequences. But she kept coming up against a wall. "Finally," she told me later, "it occurred to me that I couldn't figure out what I wanted to do or what it would mean until I knew what I wanted from life."

She found a new piece of paper, wrote VALUES at the top, and immediately, the words started flowing:

"I want to wake the girls up every morning and put them to bed every night."

"I want to get off the money train. It's not the

life I want to look back on twenty years from now."

"I still want to work. I'm wired that way. But my work can't control me."

"I love the house we're in."

"I don't want my worth to just come from my salary."

Jackie laughs now, remembering the experience. "Imagine, an executive like me, running a business, managing clients, developing staff, didn't have any idea of her real values. I sure wasn't living by them. I realized that night that I had sold my soul."

It took Jackie six months to plan her exit from the company, train a successor, and line up a new, more flexible job for herself. The week before she left, she prepared a stack of slides to explain her 10-10-10 decision to her direct reports. "I wanted them to know what I was doing wasn't arbitrary," she told me. "I was making the decision based on my values."

These days, Jackie works forty hours a week at a nonprofit organization close to home. She makes the girls breakfast and dinner, and attends all seven innings of their softball games.

None of this is to say that Jackie's life is now perfect. With her new job, Jackie took a reduction in pay, and her family has had to cut back on some of its familiar extras. And Jackie will tell you, too, that she sometimes misses the challenge and fast pace of the corporate world.

But would she go back?

Not a chance. At last, she owns her soul — and her life.

TIME MAY CHANGE ME

Jackie's values evolved with her circumstances, and that's certainly not unusual. We all know a certified Party Animal who, upon seeing his baby's first smile, became the kind of doting dad who wouldn't dream of going out on a Saturday night. And we've all seen our own values adjust with seminal experiences, like the death of a parent, a divorce, or a new job that opens our eyes to what we can achieve if we only try.

Along with identifying our values, one of the great advantages of 10-10-10 is that the process often reveals to us *how* and *why* our values have shifted, not to mention helps us explain them to those they affect.

Melanie, an editor I met at a party not long ago, was brought up in a home of musicians. Her parents both played violin with a city orchestra, and her brother, who grew up playing piano competitively, is now a conductor in Europe. Melanie's instrument was the flute, and although she stopped practicing daily after her son was born, she never stopped loving the elegance of the classical form. Her son Ian seemed to inherit her devotion, and by seven, he was playing Mozart and Brahms on the cello.

But when Ian turned eleven, he asked Melanie for a drum set. The request launched a yearlong battle, with Ian pleading and Melanie refusing to budge.

After our meeting, however, Melanie decided to 10-10-10 the question of whether she should buy Ian a drum set for his next birthday. Her first step was to take a quick pulse check of her values.

All her life, she had spurned modern music. But why, she asked herself, was she being so rigid? What harm would occur if she opened it up to accommodate for changing needs and circumstances?

With that question, Melanie's 10-10-10 came quickly.

In ten minutes, amending her value from "classical music" to "all music" — or even changing her value to "finding common ground with Ian through music" — would mean Ian would be able to experience music just as she did, passionately. And the same held true for ten months and ten years.

By contrast, if she held on to her old

value, she might turn Ian off to music — and to her — for the indefinite future.

On Ian's birthday, not only did Melanie surprise him with a drum set, but drum lessons as well. And to explain why, she walked him through her 10-10-10 decision. "That was the best part," she told me. "It restored a connection between us."

Just as important, Melanie found she had a new value — acknowledging, respecting, and enjoying her son's authentic interests.

A VALUES EXCAVATION

You don't have to wait for a 10-10-10 dilemma to discover your values or how they are changing, however. For a quick assessment, you can ask your friends and family for guidance. After all, they've seen you in action for years, and your behaviors over time have surely shown them who you are and what you care about.

I've also found that the widely available "Proust Questionnaire," created by the French memoirist Marcel Proust more than a century ago, includes an array of excellent, values-excavating prompts, from "What is your favorite virtue?" to "What is your motto?" to "If you were not yourself, who would you want to be?" But my favorites of all are, "What is your idea of happiness?"

and "What is your idea of misery?" If you answer honestly and expansively, those two simple queries can reveal quite a lot about your beliefs, hopes, and dreams.

And then there's my own values "questionnaire," which I developed about five years ago after finding that many 10-10-10 practitioners were having an easy-enough time coming up with decision alternatives and consequences, but getting stuck on the critical matter of their values.

My first questionnaire prompt concerns legacy: *"What would make you cry at your seventieth birthday?"*

This question, I've found, often gets right to the heart of a person's über-hopes; it reveals the size and shape of the footprint we want to leave behind. I have a friend, for example, who took less than a second to answer, "Knowing that my obituary wasn't going to appear on the front page of the *New York Times.* That would kill me on the spot!" He was laughing, but as we talked, I learned that his utmost goal in life was to achieve the wealth and renown of his stepfather. It also explained why he was so frustrated with his current lot in life, a high-paying but low-prestige job in public relations. He was experiencing a dreams-and-reality disconnect.

Not so for Shelley, whom I met a few years ago in St. Louis, where I was giving a speech about 10-10-10. Struggling with the question of whether to divorce an alcoholic husband, Shelley answered the birthday-party question with, "Not being surrounded by my whole family, all of us closer because we had weathered the storm." When I asked her what that reply suggested about her values, she began to reflect on her own rocky upbringing, and her sadness over the estrangement she felt from her adult siblings. By the time we were done talking, Shelley was naming "family stability" as one of her values, and "perseverance" as another.

The second questionnaire prompt I suggest concerns character: *"What do I want people to say about me when I'm not in the room?"*

To this query, I've heard everything from "That I run a great company because I'm smart and I'm fair," to "That I've raised great kids," to "That I'm honest and kind, but I'm no pushover." But the answer that has stayed with me for years came from Morgan, a former Las Vegas showgirl in her forties. "I couldn't possibly care less," she said with a huge smile.

Morgan was twenty-two when she fell in

love with a casino operator thirty years her senior. They had a daughter but soon broke up, and Morgan decided to start her life again in New York, where she landed work as a model and tour guide. Later, with modest savings, she and her daughter moved to Paris, then Prague, then Madrid, finding adventure and getting by with small jobs wherever they went. With her daughter finally grown and on her own, Morgan is now trying on another incarnation, writing screenplays in Los Angeles.

"I think I'm pretty fearless," Morgan told me when we got to talking in more depth. "I love being free and independent. It keeps me growing. Some people value conformity; they think being regular helps their kids. I think the exact opposite. Change makes people strong." She lived her life accordingly.

My final questionnaire prompt concerns lifestyle: *What do you love about the way your parents live, and what do you hate?*"

Remember Paula, the mother whose son Hooper was diagnosed with depression? When I asked her this question, she took a full, pensive minute before answering. "Well, there's a lot of silence in my parents' house," she finally replied. "I don't like that. Not a lot gets said. My dad's not one for talking about feelings." When I pushed her to identify something she loved, her face brightened. "My mother's a beautiful cook. She shows her love to everyone through food."

Through 10-10-10, Paula was able to translate both answers into values — and action. She wanted a home filled with openness, dialogue, and affection. Getting Hooper the medical help he needed was an essential first step in that direction.

DIGGING DEEPER

The three questions I've just outlined may tell you all you need and want to know about your values writ large, but if you'd like to keep probing, I've also developed value prompts that correspond specifically to decisions regarding love, work, parenting, friendship, and faith.

Love first.

Almost all romantic dilemmas, in my experience, come down to conflicts over the values of intimacy, commitment, and control. Sure, each relationship has unique dynamics. But when people get together, it's usually because they have a shared, realistic understanding of how their relationship will function and how much support and independence they need as individuals.

And when couples break up, it's usually because their expectations and beliefs about their relationship are no longer aligned, or they never were in the first place.

That's why, when it comes to love values, I suggest you ask: In my ideal relationship, how much time do we spend together? How much of myself do I keep to myself, and how much do I share myself with my partner? What kind of compromises am I willing to make? Am I truly comfortable with a partner who's different from me, or do I need to be with someone who shares my values? You might also consider: Do I need my partner to be in charge, or do I want that role? Or do I value most highly a balanced "deal" where both partners have equal agency?

Remember, there are no right or wrong answers to these questions. Their sole purpose is to help you assess your values with real depth and subtlety so that you can meaningfully apply them to a 10-10-10 decision.

As for work-related values, I encourage you to explore the matter of how central work is to your happiness and well-being. In this book already, we've heard varied answers. Jackie decided working was important to her, but not enough to supersede intimacy with her children, whereas Lynne determined she needed (and wanted) to put work first in her life in order to achieve her dreams.

For the purposes of making sound 10-10-10 decisions, it is also helpful to define what *kind* of work we want to pursue. Are we motivated by money, prestige, challenge, flexibility, or camaraderie? It's tempting, of course, to answer yes to all of the above, but it is a rare job that meets every criterion equally. To really know your values, you need to confront how they truly stack up.

Parenting may be complicated, but its underlying values tend to revolve around the answer to a single question: What do children need in order to be raised well? The answers range from tough love to unconditional love, from lots of activity to quiet focus, from wide exposure to the real world to fierce protection from it, from public school to private school, and perhaps most incendiary of all — whether children need stay-at-home parents or not. The challenge is to figure out where your beliefs land on the spectrum of possibilities.

The same holds true for friendship, where assessing our values is largely a matter of determining where our "voluntary" relationships fall in our list of priorities. I have an acquaintance in his late fifties, for instance, who would tell you he counts three people as friends. He'd rather spend his free time watching college football with his sons, playing catch with his grandchildren, and eating home-cooked pasta with his wife. Family trumps all.

By contrast, consider my old babysitter, Gladys. No one has ever attended more weddings or baby showers, spent more time on the phone listening to other people's troubles and worries, or more weekends helping other people move in and out of their apartments. She dedicates herself above all else in life to being a great friend, a sense of self that drives her choices large and small.

In a nutshell, that's how values work.

LIVING BY THE WORD

It is impossible — it would be wrong — to write about values without acknowledging the fact that millions of people strive to live by the overarching set of beliefs prescribed by their God. As one audience member told me after I spoke about 10-10-10 in Austin, "The values part of your idea is easy for me. I have the Bible."

But sometimes, devout people are a bit more stymied by 10-10-10. How can it possibly coalesce, they ask, with being religious?

My answer comes from experience.

If you're a Christian like I am, I say, you've certainly developed a few ways besides going to church that help keep you connected to God's word. You might volunteer with the homeless. Or garden to stay humble. Or pray during your headstands in yoga.

You can consider 10-10-10 another approach, in that it's a powerful means to make sure you are living in accordance with your values, no matter what their source.

That answer usually suffices, because most Christians, I've found, are already accustomed to blending their faith with the exigencies of the modern world. But if someone continues to press me about 10-10-10 and faith, I often refer to Colossians 3:17. In that verse, Jesus asks us to lead mindful and considered lives because doing so serves him. He doesn't tell us what to do in *specific* situations. How to handle the husband who seems bored, the boss who wants you to stay late, the child who's just been diagnosed with mental illness, the friend who stops calling. His teachings tell us how to live in general, which is deliberately, with truth and intention in every thought and action. If that's not in concordance with 10-10-10, I don't know what is.

In Proverbs of the Old Testament, God also asks us to live with patience. And that is how Ken Shigematsu first came to think about 10-10-10's role in a faith-based life. The leader of Vancouver's vibrant Tenth Avenue Church, Ken was preparing for a sermon in November 2006 when he read an article I had written. His topic that week was anger — or more precisely, how we can manage our natural propensity to feel fury, resentment, even rage. Ken wanted his congregation to understand that God does not ask us to repress or deny our anger, but to be patient with it, and with our actions, ultimately release it over to Him.

But how? In his sermon, Ken counseled his congregation that perspective is one of anger's most powerful antidotes, and offered 10-10-10 as a process to help in gaining it. When you feel hurt or pain and want to lash out, Ken suggested, ask yourself, will the source of my anger matter in ten days, in ten months, and ten years? Will it matter in eternity?

Along with Proverbs, Ken derives 10-10-10's theological support from Ignatius of Loyola, who was one of the principle founders of the Jesuit Order in the 1550s. When Ignatius was thirty-one years old, he wrote a book called *Spiritual Exercises,* comprised of meditations intended to deepen faith. One of those meditations concerns decision making, and in it, Ignatius suggests that when dilemmas arise, it's wise to step back and ask, "If I was standing before Jesus Christ giving an account of my life, what decision would He have wanted me to make?" Such a question, Ken points out, jibes with 10-10-10, in that it too prompts you to make decisions according to their carefully considered long-term consequences, often extending them to the eternal.

Ken continues to use 10-10-10 in counseling parishioners. "I think 10-10-10 acts as a great bridge enabling us to put things in perspective, whether they are challenges or even successes," he told me last year. "It's hard for people to think about eternity, but 10-10-10 helps with that."

FILLING THE BIG BLACK HOLE

Talking about 10-10-10 with people around the world has reinforced for me that each one of us has a profoundly unique set of values.

But I've also learned that not enough of us live by them. My friend Claudia, for instance, stayed married to an adulterous husband for twenty-two years because she couldn't bear to hurt her mother, who was a devout Catholic. She also struggled with her own values of conformity and reputation. "It's embarrassing to admit now, but I was really worried about what the ladies at our church would say about us getting a divorce," she told me.

Finally, after two years of counseling, Claudia's value of self-respect won out, and she decided to leave her husband.

As for the ladies at church, Claudia would tell you that they didn't really seem to care. They offered comforting words and then went about their own business. "I discovered that no one really holds it against you when you choose to live authentically," she told me recently. "I was trapped for too long. But I realized I had trapped myself."

Today, Claudia routinely uses 10-10-10 to make sure her decisions continue to adhere to her new values, which she names as "finding time to reflect every day and learning to trust again."

Most of all, she uses 10-10-10 to avoid the Big Black Hole that occurs when we have a sense of our values — even subconsciously — but can't find the wherewithal to live by them.

That was me, before my 10-10-10

epiphany in Hawaii. In those troubled days, I certainly knew my values, and contrary to what my classmate had said, I did like fun. I just didn't like it more than hard work or security, both values taught to me at the knee of my Sicilian grandmother. Married and divorced twice to the same man by the time she was thirty, Francesca Pilato raised her four children alone and sent all of them to college, debt free, from the profits of her own knitwear design business. Believe me when I say there weren't many other divorced immigrant women entrepreneurs in Rochester, New York, in the 1940s.

By her noble example, my Nonna's values made sense to me. And my own life experiences, too, amply proved that sacrifice and diligence paid off. In fact, one of the reasons I was so uptight about my classmate's party invitation all those years ago was that my employer had promised to pay for my entire second-year tuition if I graduated with a certain grade point average.

As time went on, though, I developed another value, deeper and stronger than all the rest. I wanted a good marriage.

And I was living a lie.

So I shoveled and shoveled and shoveled to fill the Big Black Hole at the center of my life. I threw myself ever more into my job. I had four kids in five years — and took two of them to Hawaii for no good reason. I hosted barbecue parties for the neighborhood. I taught Sunday school. I visited my parents once a week. I got a dog, and not just any dog, but a 180-pound mastiff. I kept a to-do list under my pillow and woke up at 5 AM to add things I'd forgotten.

When friends and family told me to slow down and ease up, I would reply with the joking refrain, "Desperate women do desperate things." But my behavior, beneath it all, was nothing to laugh about. My implosion in Hawaii was proof positive that I had been a values-disconnect train wreck waiting to happen.

10-10-10 forced — yes, forced — me to start making every decision according to my true beliefs.

Once I did, just about everything changed. My husband and I divorced. I also began to sort out conflicts between my job responsibilities and parenting with new success. As a result, my life began to be what I wanted, not just a picture of it. And my choices finally began to make sense to everyone, especially me.

I even started setting aside time for fun — my version of it. I attended my first U2 concert in a dozen years, and was so overcome by happiness during the band's rendition of "If You Wear That Velvet Dress" that I went flying off my chair, which I happened to be standing on. I replanted my garden and lassoed the kids into helping me sow and harvest. And every evening I made the time to take all 180 pounds of my dog for a long walk in the woods. Abby didn't stop to smell the roses, but she smelled the mushrooms, twigs, and rocks. She stopped to sniff other dogs, bark randomly at cars, and more than occasionally just to look at me, as if to say, "How's it going, girl? You hanging in there?" She is now in dog heaven, but I still thank Abby for her enduring lesson in proper pacing.

I value that now too.

In the coming chapters, you will meet many more 10-10-10 users, all making decisions based on their deeply individual values.

And in doing so, experiencing the joy of living authentically.

CHAPTER FOUR:
HAPPILY EVER AFTER

10-10-10 AND THE CODE OF
LOVE

Not long after my divorce, I developed a new Sunday-morning habit. Right after the kids and I got home from church, I would pour myself a cup of tea, lay out the Styles section of the *New York Times* on the kitchen counter, and read the wedding announcements — every one of them.

Usually the kids did their best to ignore me during this exercise, but one day, Eve, six at the time, couldn't stand it anymore.

"Why do you keep doing something that makes you so sad?" she demanded to know, looking up at me with her little hands on her hips.

"I'm not sad," I told her, surprised, because I truly wasn't, "I'm just curious."

I waved my hand across the sea of smiling photos. "Look at all these happy beginnings," I said. "Some of them will work, but some of them are sure to blow up."

Eve nodded solemnly, as if she knew all

too well what I was talking about.

"Maybe I'm looking for clues," I suggested.

She nodded again. It was, she seemed to silently agree, a reasonable investigation, given the changed circumstances of our lives.

Nearly a decade has passed since then. I've switched to iced coffee, Eve is taller than I am. And I'm not looking for the secret of Happily Ever After in the newspaper anymore. The greatest achievement of my life is that I'm finally living it.

And it's all due to a code-cracking theory of love, a woman called Lulu, a mountain-top enlightenment, a great man, an instantaneous 10-10-10, and a pack of grape bubble gum, purchased, incidentally, by that great man himself, my own Jack, in a fishing village on Cape Cod.

Look, love takes a lot of things to get it right. It can be mysterious. It can be crazy. It can feel impossible. It can cause deeper hurt and take us to higher peaks of joy than anything else.

In other words, I'm not going to sit here and tell you that 10-10-10 makes love easy.

But I will tell you that 10-10-10 can help forge healthy relationships. It can reinvigorate them; it can pull them back from a precipice and make them happier, better, and stronger in every way.

I've already made the case that relationships can only succeed when both partners share the same values — or at least respect each other's. But let me — Suzy Welch, love doctor! — further hypothesize that relationships are far more likely to endure when both partners have a way to openly discuss three key aspects of love: intimacy, commitment, and control.

10-10-10 transforms relationships because it plugs right into that dynamic. By surfacing values, 10-10-10 gives one partner alone, or both together, a chance to consider momentum, chemistry, inertia, independence, conformity, tradition, or whatever is keeping them together or driving them apart. It can intervene at any stage of the love cycle, giving one partner or both a framework for understanding what is enduring about the relationship and what may not be.

To the Precipice and Back

About three years ago, I received a call from Ajitha, a former business school student of mine. She wondered if I had a lunch hour to spare. Figuring it was career-related, I agreed and didn't give our meeting much thought after that. But when I found Ajitha across from me at a restaurant a week later, her normal composure and self-confidence seemed softened by a vulnerability I'd never seen in her before.

"Rohan and I were right at that point of no return," she told me unexpectedly. "But you need to know — with your idea, with 10-10-10 — we returned."

A brilliant engineer, Ajitha had emigrated to the United States at twenty-two. She spent her first few years here studying in that field, but by the time I met her in the classroom, she'd been signed on by a prestigious technology company and was earning her MBA at night.

Ajitha had always struck me as the serious, driven type. But as our conversation unfolded, I came to find out that her prim demeanor hid another side — she loved to party.

"I like to *socialize*" is how Ajitha explained it to me that day at lunch. "I love the freedom and the camaraderie. What is life without friends?"

For the first five years of their marriage, Ajitha's penchant for after-work revelry was never a particular problem for Rohan, another engineer. He adored Ajitha's good heart, respected her mind, and appreciated her spunk. Sometimes he joined her when she went out; most times not.

But then the couple's daughter Laya was born. At first, Ajitha responded by cutting back on her nights out, from five to two or three. Her mother, who lived nearby, was also able to step in and help with Laya's care. But for Rohan, that solution wasn't enough. He started to beg Ajitha to stay in for the family's sake.

Ajitha didn't see the point; Laya was perfectly happy with her grandmother, she told Rohan, and if she stopped going out with her friends, the balance of her life would start to feel off-kilter. "Why are you trying to control me?" she demanded to know. "Why can't I have my own time?"

After a year, Ajitha and Rohan's sniping had intensified into a quiet war. They spoke less and less. They split chores they used to do together, like bathing Laya and grocery shopping. In moments alone, they both started thinking about a divorce.

For Laya's sake, they soldiered on.

But every relationship has its breaking point, and Ajitha and Rohan's finally came when Ajitha announced she was going on a three-day ski vacation with her MBA friends. Rohan's response was immediate and anguished. "You just can't, Ajitha," he cried. "Three days is too much. How can a ski trip be more important to you than our marriage and our baby?"

In the heat of the moment, Ajitha brushed Rohan off, but the truth was, his question was too disturbing for her to ignore. That night, after putting Laya to bed, Ajitha climbed the stairs to her attic office and closed the door. Then she sat at her desk with three pieces of paper in front of her and one question on her mind. Would she go away or stay at home? In her heart, though, Ajitha knew she was grappling with bigger issues: her marriage, identity, and future were at stake.

She labeled the first sheet of paper, "Ten Minutes."

The notation came quickly. "Ajitha = Sad," she wrote. If she didn't go on the trip, she reasoned, she'd feel awful about missing the fun with her friends. But if she did go, she'd probably be feeling too conflicted to socialize with her usual abandon anyway.

Next, Ajitha imagined how Rohan would react as she walked out the door for the trip. "Rohan = Sad + Resolved. Done with us," she wrote.

And if she didn't walk out the door?

"Rohan = Relieved, Confused, Hopeful," Ajitha predicted.

Ajitha labeled her second piece of paper "Ten Months," but this time, the "Ajitha =" equation came slowly. She stared at the blank space for five minutes, then ten, watching pictures unfold in her mind. One was of her and Rohan holding hands across the dinner table the way they used to, another of them bathing Laya together, chatting about her toes and hair and noises, just like the old days. Surely, if she chose to stay home from this trip and kept making similar choices about how she spent her time, in ten months, she and Rohan would have started to rebuild the foundation that was now crumbling.

Ajitha filled the space next to her name with the words "Connecting again. Better."

"I knew Rohan didn't want me to stop having fun," Ajitha told me. "He just wanted me home a little bit more. If I could bend once or twice, if I could even meet him halfway, he would be overjoyed, and our life would be back."

And if she went on the trip? Ajitha felt she couldn't be 100 percent certain, but in ten months, the second half of her equation would most likely be "Alone."

Ajitha labeled her third sheet "Ten Years," and jotted down "Ajitha = Satisfied."

The equation surprised me. "Why not

'Happy' or something more enthusiastic?" I asked.

"Well, I was trying to be realistic," Ajitha replied. "I figured that in ten years, looking back, I would still wish that I had been able to go out more. But I was also certain that I would say, 'It was worth it. My marriage was worth it.' I gave something up and we both got something bigger back."

"You made the well-being of your marriage into a more important value than your happiness alone?" I asked.

"Yes," she answered simply, "and I'm indebted to 10-10-10 for that."

Ajitha and Rohan recently celebrated their tenth anniversary with a vacation alone — skiing. Ajitha tells me they're thinking about having another child, and together have run the decision through a 10-10-10 analysis. "But we just don't know yet," she says. "We're still trying to think about the long-term impact on our careers. We just need some more time to talk it through."

A CODE-CRACKING THEORY

What delighted me most in my conversation with Ajitha was her repeated use of the word "we." It made me realize how effective 10-10-10 had been in aligning the couple, and in giving them a disciplined and dispassionate way to talk about melding their values.

10-10-10 had made their relationship bigger than the both of them.

And that's how love looks in the most successful relationships, doesn't it? It looks as if both partners love each other as individuals — but they love their love even more. They exalt it. They celebrate it. They talk about it as if it is the third force in the room, created by their merged commitment. They revere it and routinely and willingly make sacrifices for it.

I wish I could claim this code-cracking "third force" theory as an original thought. But in fact it comes from *The Good Marriage,* a book by family psychologist Dr. Judith S. Wallerstein and *New York Times* science writer Sandra Blakeslee. During the nineties, Wallerstein and Blakeslee studied fifty successful marriages and observed that, in virtually every case, the partners treated their union like a precious, separate entity deserving respect and nurture. In good marriages, the authors concluded, both partners treasure their collective identity more than their individuality.

Ultimately, that's the destination to which 10-10-10 brought Ajitha.

The departure of a child, not the arrival of one, led to Jillian's crisis with her husband, Mike, a successful business executive who had once been the love of her life but had come to feel more like a stranger living under the same roof. For years, the couple had silently agreed to ignore the walls between them, but when their youngest son left for college, their detente collapsed.

"Suddenly," Jillian recalls, "I realized I had a very clean house and almost nothing else."

According to Jillian, Mike had never been hostile, just emotionally absent. He was physically absent too, and Jillian often wondered if he intentionally prolonged his business trips to avoid the muted awkwardness at home.

"When Mike married me, I was this carefree artist. Our whole thing was we were perfect for each other because we created a balance," Jillian remembered. "We'd spend long weekends sailing or camping, we'd always make dinner together. He'd come to my art shows. But as Mike changed, so did I. He became a big, roaring success at his company. I became a housewife. Sometimes I think I must have just bored him."

But when Jillian told Mike she wanted to

reenergize her spirit by painting again, he scoffed at the idea. "Forget it, Jillian," he said. "Those days are over."

Crushed and confused, Jillian begged Mike to attend couple's therapy with her. He agreed to go — once.

The first session piqued Mike's interest, though, largely because he sensed the therapist didn't have an agenda. Instead, she introduced 10-10-10 as a nonjudgmental way to simply discover if common ground still existed in the couple's marriage.

As a first step, the therapist asked Jillian and Mike to define their values. "The usual things" was Mike's quick response. "Financial independence. My kids making it in this world. Respect from the people who work for me."

"What about our marriage? Where's that on your list, Mike?" Jillian asked, incredulous. "That's my main value. Our marriage and our family."

"There is no marriage, Jill, you know that," Mike answered flatly.

Over the next few weeks, the couple worked with their therapist to imagine their worlds both apart and together. The sessions alternated between silence and acrimony and divorce seemed inevitable, especially after Mike admitted to something

Jillian had long feared, that he had been unfaithful to her on the road.

But a breakthrough came when their therapist made a compelling point.

"You both loved your early relationship," she said to them. "You talk about it as if it were a close friend who died. What would it take to resurrect a new version of your old marriage?"

Immediately, Jillian and Mike began to use 10-10-10 to brainstorm how they could recapture the satisfying marriage they had had in their first decade. And just as quickly, they realized that reinvention would require a world of change. Jillian would need to start accompanying Mike on his business trips. Mike would need to embrace Jillian's return to painting. And the couple would need to overcome a raft of emotional obstacles to reintroduce themselves in bed.

They would, essentially, have to elevate their marriage to a priority above all others.

For Mike, the main impetus to give the plan a try was the couple's children. He believed he owed them at least one real attempt to save the family. And he sensed that he still loved Jillian on some level, or at least the woman she used to be. For Jillian, the motivation was more romantic. She adored Mike, still felt strongly attracted to him, and yearned to rekindle the fulfilling partnership of their beginnings.

About six months had passed since that decision when I checked in with Jillian recently. I could tell by her voice right away that things were going well. She and Mike were feeling so positive about their future that "not a day goes by when we don't 10-10-10 something we're doing," she told me. "We're always saying, 'OK, how will this choice affect our marriage in the near, mid-, and long term?' It's just like a GPS device; it keeps us on track."

I love that image of 10-10-10 as a tool to prevent a couple from getting lost. Because, even in the happiest of relationships, it's all too easy for us to take a wrong turn, or for life to take a wrong turn on us.

A DAUGHTER AND A WIFE

When Nancy and Carl met in 1987, she was thirty-six, a once divorced and once widowed medical records coordinator with a teenage son from her first marriage. Staunchly self-sufficient, Nancy believed the only thing that could go wrong with her life would be another man entering the picture. Carl, the same age, was recovering from a divorce, and described himself to anyone who would listen as a confirmed bachelor.

But after a chance introduction to Nancy at a dart tournament in a local pub, he swiftly changed his mind.

Two weeks later, on their first date, Carl asked Nancy to marry him.

"Do you have a bank debt you need to relieve, or some kid you can't support?" she joked back.

"No, I'm just a lucky man who's finally met his lady" was Carl's steady reply.

The first twelve years of Nancy and Carl's married life together were nothing short of blissful. Sometimes, Nancy would awaken in the middle of the night to find Carl staring at her in wonder. She would smile back in wonder too.

"I was sure I had the happiest marriage in the world," Nancy told me.

Then Nancy's mother, Virginia, who lived on the first floor of their two-family house, was diagnosed with Parkinson's disease with dementia. Both Nancy and Carl were eager to provide care, but as Virginia lost her ability to feed and bathe herself, the responsibility began to wear heavily on the couple, physically and emotionally.

After five long years, Nancy reluctantly agreed to put her mother in a nursing home. But to assuage her guilt, she also decided to visit her every day after work.

Not surprisingly, the routine left Nancy more exhausted than ever. Her job at the hospital had expanded, and most days she couldn't make it to the nursing home until 7 or 8 PM. By the time she finally pulled into her driveway at night, all she wanted to do was collapse. Carl was patient, but even he had his limits, and the relationship grew strained in ways neither partner had ever imagined.

"I can't believe another marriage of mine is going to die," Nancy cried to herself in despair.

Then one night, as Nancy was driving home from visiting her mother in frustrated tears, she remembered reading about 10-10-10. All at once wondering what would happen if she tried to look past her feelings of obligation and opened her mind to other options, she decided to propose the process to Carl.

A few hours later, the two of them used 10-10-10 to decide if Nancy should continue to visit her mother every day. They skipped paper and pen for the exercise, instead sitting side by side on the living room couch, holding hands.

Their first ten came quickly — and presented a mixed picture. "I'll feel worse and I'll feel better," Nancy lamented to Carl.

"I'm just so afraid of the guilt. But at the same time . . . I can barely breathe. I need a break. I'm exhausted. I miss you, Carl."

"I miss you too, baby," Carl told her.

"As for Mom, well, you know — in ten minutes, she will be very angry," Nancy hastened to add. "She'll hate me."

"Virginia is not Virginia anymore," Carl reminded her softly. "Nancy, you've been the perfect daughter for fifty-seven years."

"In ten months, I'm sure other family members will visit a bit more," Nancy suggested hopefully. "God knows they've offered. And if they visit Mom, I don't have to as much. Maybe we could begin to get our life back."

"And in ten months, your mother will have adjusted to other visitors, if she even notices," Carl put in.

But something was still bothering Nancy. "Let's talk about ten years," she said to Carl. "When Mom is gone. I'll want to feel good about myself as a daughter. I don't want to think, 'Well, I was fine until it really mattered.' "

Carl let Nancy think in silence for a long moment. Then she surprised him.

In ten years, Nancy thought out loud, she wanted to look back and think not only "I did right by Mom," but, "I did right by my husband." At the center of her life, she wanted a lasting marriage, a marriage that was greater than the sum of its parts.

"I love you, Carl," Nancy said with sudden firmness. "You *are* my life. I don't know why I only think of myself as a daughter when I'm also a wife."

The next day, Nancy didn't visit her mother. Nor did she visit her for another three days. And when at last she did, her mother greeted her as if nothing had changed. Nancy read her mother the newspaper and, for an hour or so, the two chatted about the weather, a few neighbors that Virginia seemed to remember, and the comings and goings of Nancy's son and his new wife. At her departure, Nancy softly offered, "I love you, Mom."

"I love you too," her mother replied in kind.

Not long ago, I caught up with Nancy as she, Carl, and other family members were preparing their annual Christmas baskets of chocolate-covered marshmallows and pretzels. From the lively chatter in the background, I could sense that the couple's life had indeed been restored.

"We had put our marriage on a back burner, but it isn't anymore," Nancy told me when I asked her if I was guessing right.

And then, as if to finish the thought, she let out an affectionate laugh. "Sweetheart, please," I could hear her say. "Get your fingers out of the chocolate."

THE MATING DANCE

Now, I don't want to leave the impression that 10-10-10 is only relevant in established marriages. Just as often, I've seen it play a constructive role in new relationships, as they're being created and shaped. After all, the beginning of every relationship is always such a complicated mush of dynamics. First there's the seduction, or the "Hey, take a look at my best self" part, where both potential partners spend prodigious energy flaunting their assets, the way peacocks spread their tails. Then there's the investigation period, during which we try to suss out what's real about the other's "best self" and what's not. The early stages of love also include an element of imagination, where both people picture what the relationship could become, and just as important, envision how friends and family might react to it. And finally, there's the negotiation, in which the relationship's patterns, depth of intimacy, strength of commitment, and balance of control are debated, tested, and ultimately set.

It's not called a mating dance for nothing. And I don't want to be a schoolmarm about this either. The early circling, weaving, flirting, flaunting, and checking-it-out stuff that most couples go through can be incredibly fun and exhilarating. But for all the thrill, the mating dance has its drawbacks. Too often it's mainly about posturing and maneuvering — with little sound thinking or values assessment mixed in. Nothing can completely overpower the rush and the whirl, but in the getting-to-know-you process, 10-10-10 can help keep both parties centered.

STARTING OVER — IN CYBERSPACE

The daughter of two poets who bounced from job to job across the Midwest, Heidi finally knew her first real home at thirteen, when her father landed a teaching position at a liberal arts college. The tranquillity didn't last. Two years later, her mother died from breast cancer, and her father, grief-stricken, quit his job and took Heidi on the road again.

When she was eighteen, Heidi met an oil deliveryman named Jerome. Following a brief courtship, the pair married and moved into a basement apartment on the outskirts of St. Louis.

Their first years were happy enough, but eventually Jerome's behavior started to become erratic. Some days he seemed to be in a daze, others he would shout at Heidi with the slightest provocation. For a while, Heidi suspected that Jerome felt trapped by marriage. But after two years of waiting in vain for Jerome's "moods" to pass, the couple sought a doctor. The diagnosis was adrenoleukodystrophy, an inherited neuro-logical disease that usually strikes its victims in childhood, but in rare instances also af-flicts adults. Jerome died seven difficult years later.

After a few months passed, Heidi decided to start over by moving to a small town across the state where she had landed a teaching job at a public middle school. She realized right away that she loved the work, but at the end of each day, she still felt loneliness and isolation creep in. Where was there for her to go to socialize? How would she ever meet anyone? As a well-known figure in a sleepy town with few single men, Heidi reasoned, she couldn't really date anyone from the community.

Late one night, she found herself surfing an Internet matchmaking site. Like most first-timers, the prospect both intrigued and repelled Heidi. "I can't do it," she told herself.

Or could she?

Heidi had spent her whole life moving around, feeling alone, and struggling against adversity. Now, a widow at age twenty-seven, she yearned for a real partner, someone with whom she could share the intimacy and commitment of building a life together.

An early adopter of 10-10-10, Heidi opted to use the process to decide if she should look for love online.

In ten minutes, Heidi told herself, online dating would be awkward, embarrassing, and probably fruitless. She would likely get rejected — and feel even lonelier than before.

In ten months, she would have either abandoned online dating because it wasn't working, or she would have learned to avoid awkward encounters. Maybe she would even have a sense of humor about the whole thing.

And in ten years, Heidi reasoned, she could be alone because she hadn't tried, or she could have gotten lucky and be with a man she loved. With few other options, online dating was simply too promising to pass up. She had to give it a try.

Six months later, browsing a message

board for people who had lost their spouses, Heidi met a widower with the screen name "Been There Done That." Robert was forty-five, wry and gentle, with a teenage son and a passion for poetry. He and Heidi started emailing, then calling, then visiting. With each encounter, Heidi made sure to remember the values she'd uncovered using 10-10-10. She wanted to communicate honestly as she and Robert "investigated" each other. Having waited so long for love, she didn't want to undermine it by swooning or game-playing.

Today, Heidi and Robert are married and raising their young daughter in Robert's native Canada. Her 10-10-10 decision, she told me once, took her all of five minutes to conduct. But by reminding her to stay true to her values as she ventured into cyberspace to find love, it led to the life of her dreams right on earth.

PROCEED WITH CAUTION

It would be misleading to suggest that 10-10-10 always propels a burgeoning relationship into marriage. Sometimes, in fact, the process can reveal a relationship's fault lines, and in doing so, send a message to both partners to proceed with caution.

Blair and Andre made an unlikely pair

from the beginning. When they met in college, Blair was an art history major whose priority was to find a job — any job — in the New York area so she could be near her aging parents. Andre lived and breathed science, and had already drawn a detailed map of his future: a PhD in oncology, which would likely lead to a prestigious medical research position.

Despite their different sensibilities, Blair and Andre dated exclusively for the two years leading up to graduation. After school ended, both found jobs in Manhattan, Blair as a receptionist at a law firm specializing in civil rights, and Andre as a junior researcher in a hospital laboratory. The relationship remained a slightly more grown-up version of its college self until, one day, Andre's boss offered him a fellowship at a Tokyo hospital.

"Pack your bags," Andre emailed Blair, "we're moving to Japan!"

Blair was stunned. Was this, she wondered, an oblique marriage proposal? And, if so, did she want to accept it? If it wasn't a marriage proposal, what was Andre thinking? Suddenly Blair realized just how much the ephemeral, undefined nature of her relationship with Andre troubled her. She longed for a way to discuss that with him.

But first, she realized, she needed to

determine what she wanted from Andre — and life.

Blair had come to love her work at the law firm. Her boss was a former corporate attorney who was capping off a thirty-year career by taking on pro bono cases. Accompanying him to the courthouse, Blair had realized that she was deeply invested in the idea of social justice. She wanted to attend law school to pursue civil rights work, and her boss promised her he would support her application process in every way.

Another lawyer at the office, a working mother, had introduced Blair to 10-10-10, and that day, after she received Andre's email, Blair decided to use it to help her answer the question: Should I move to Japan with Andre?

To get started, Blair drew a chart with boxes for ten minutes, ten months, and ten years, and within each square she put the sub-labels of work, love, and family. She then prioritized work, love, and family as values. In the past, the order had been family-love-work. Now she realized that she had changed her ranking to work-family-love.

After that, the process swiftly led Blair to an unambiguous conclusion. She wanted to stay in New York to keep her career moving forward and to continue caring for her parents with the attentiveness they deserved. Not that she wanted to break up with Andre — she loved him and was bursting with pride about his fellowship in Tokyo. But if the relationship were to advance, he would need to join her in making its terms explicit.

"My decision was not an ultimatum; that's what I loved about the 10-10-10 process most," Blair told me. "I was happy he was going. I was happy I was staying. And finally, we were able to have the first real conversation we'd ever had about our future."

Would that future include marriage?

Blair told me she wasn't sure. "No matter what happens, I feel that at least with 10-10-10, we have a common language to talk about it."

Rather than ignoring her unease and assuming that they'd figure things out later, Blair had used 10-10-10 to determine what life choice would best fit her values. Indeed, she'd resisted the tendency to gloss over a sense of misalignment, simply hoping that something — the passage of time, a job, a diamond ring, a baby — would make the uncertainty go away.

It almost never happens that way.

A Woman Called Lulu

My own first marriage was born out of that kind of glossing — and its companion, momentum. My husband and I had met in high school and shared years of common history but not a single common interest except the Roxy Music song "Avalon." (Sadly, I am not exaggerating.) Neither of us was yet twenty-five as we walked down the aisle, but no one gave us a word of caution — at least that we could hear. As my mother told me later, "You both seemed so sure of what you were doing."

To this day, I don't really know what we were so sure of. But I do know for a fact that when you get married for the wrong reasons, they will eventually catch up with you.

For whatever reason a marriage or relationship ends, however, 10-10-10 can intervene, instilling insight, deliberateness, and solace during one of life's most painful transitions.

One spring weekend in 2000, my husband and I took a hike up Mount Lafayette with three other couples and our kids. The air was warming, the trees were in bud, and the plan was to climb for a few hours, then have lunch at a clearing on the trail where our friend Ron, who was delayed because of a work obligation, would join us.

At 3 PM, two hours past the expected rendezvous time, Ron still hadn't shown up, and his wife, Leslie, was frantic. "I don't want Ron climbing in the dark," she worried aloud.

Then, in the distance, someone spotted Ron running up the mountain, his heavy backpack bouncing up and down. Leslie saw him too, and suddenly she was flying toward him. "Ron!" she cried, her voice flooded with happiness. "You made it!"

"Lulu — I'm here!" we could all hear him call back.

I turned away so I didn't have to see their embrace.

A few hours later when we made camp, I found a rock ledge a couple hundred yards away and sat atop it, taking in the grandeur of the mountains as they glowed pink and red in the dimming light. They were millions of years old and would exist forever. I was forty; my life was rushing by. What would I make of my remaining time?

Another woman may have made a different decision that evening. But I felt I had no other choice. At my core, I believed that no one could live a meaningful life in a state of deceit. And I knew that my husband and I could never have what I so desperately wanted — that "third force" in the room, the sacred thing created when two people love their marriage more than themselves.

Up until then, my priority had been to guide and protect my children, to prepare them to lead their own healthy lives. That responsibility is what had always made divorce seem so impossible. But sitting atop that mountain, I suddenly realized that living a lie wasn't helping me be a good mother. What kind of role model was I? What could I teach my children about hope, tenderness, and connection if I had none myself?

My trip to Hawaii was only four years in the past, and 10-10-10 was still somewhat new to me as a process. But I turned to it at that moment for the most important decision of my life.

In ten minutes, I understood, a divorce would bring torrents of pain and confusion, as my kids reacted to the empty seat at the dinner table, the empty closet, and the empty space in our pew. I wondered too how I could break the news to my parents. For almost sixteen years, they'd seen me struggle in my marriage, and they'd pleaded with me not to give up. And how would I face my staff at work? I was supposed to be upbeat and confident. Could I pull it off anymore?

My thoughts turned to the ten-month scenario. Things might even be worse then, I knew. Reality would have set in for the kids. And surely, as with all divorces, a legal and financial boxing match awaited. I had never seen a truly amicable "division of assets."

Yet in ten years, I decided, I could finally be living a real life. I didn't have a clue what it would look like or where I would be. But it would be authentic; I would make sure of that. And, in my heart, I knew that my husband wanted that for himself too.

A few nights later, in a quiet conversation, we agreed to divorce.

My worst fears never did come to pass. My mother was very saddened, and friends chose between me and my ex-husband. I also stumbled terribly at work, trying to act as if my personal Waterloo hadn't happened.

But the kids never blinked. I took them through my 10-10-10 decision and they understood it as much as young children can. Once I even heard my daughter Sophia tell a playmate, "My mother couldn't take the pretending anymore. She had to make a decision."

Oh, yes, she did. And I'm grateful I had 10-10-10 as my guide through it all. My marriage would have ended eventually without it, but most probably in ways I would never have chosen.

A PACK OF GRAPE BUBBLE GUM

The day after Easter in 2002, 10-10-10 was there to guide my heart once again.

By that time, Jack and I were deeply in love. But the situation was complicated, to put it mildly. We lived in separate cities. I had just left my job in a cloud of scandal. And then there was the small matter of my four children, the very large dog, and the little cat. Where were we all going to live? How much time would everybody spend with everybody? What kind of family might we be?

These kinds of issues don't get settled in a conversation. They get settled with exposure and reflection. And so, that weekend, Jack and I drove with the kids to the fishing village of Wellfleet, where my parents' rambling old house stood empty. At first, things felt wonderful. Despite gloomy weather, we painted eggs, attended church services, and then sat down to a candlelit dinner that I'd spent hours preparing. Soon enough, though, I noticed the kids were getting a little — how can I put it? — frisky. They weren't used to my having a man in my life, and they weren't so sure they liked my attention being divided.

The next day, I awoke with the bright idea that a long walk was just what we all needed. We piled into the car and drove to the harbor, but the outing hardly provided the balm I was hoping for. The boys were tripping and punching each other, the girls arguing about TV shows.

On the way home, I could feel Jack's hackles rising. I knew he was thinking, "I love this woman, but obnoxious kids are not what I bargained for."

And beside him, I was thinking, "I love these kids, but losing this man is not going to happen."

At that moment, Jack spotted a convenience store by the highway and swung into the parking lot. "I need some gum," he informed us. What he really needed was a break from the shenanigans in the backseat.

"See ya!" I said brightly as he exited the car.

I waited until Jack was out of sight, and then I whipped around and faced my children. My expression, they told me later, was "deranged."

I grabbed the kid closest to me by the collar of his shirt. It was Marcus, and today he is a fine and upstanding teenager — his school adviser calls him a "gentleman among boys." But back in those days he was a goofy eight-year-old who could spend hours on end speaking in a duck voice. It was his unfortunate fate that day to be within my physical reach.

"Listen here, all of you," I seethed, tightening my grasp on Marcus's shirt. "You don't think I know what you're up to — acting like a little pack of animals back there, fidgeting and screaming and poking each other? You don't think I know you're trying to scare Jack away? Well, guess what? I'm not that stupid."

As all four kids looked at me in a state of shock, I glanced back at the store to make sure Jack was still inside. Time was short.

"Get one thing straight." I turned back to my captive audience and rushed on. "I've finally found the one man I love. I've found the one man I was born to be with. And if you think you are going to screw it up, you're wrong. Jack and I are a team from now on. We are together."

I drew a deep breath, then: "I am doing what is best for all of us," I told them. "I am telling you the new rule of our lives."

And then I shouted it.

At which moment, the car door opened.

"Anybody want some grape bubble gum?"

Jack asked cheerfully.

I released Marcus's shirt and turned to face Jack with a huge pasted-on grin. "No thanks!" I chirped. "Kids?"

From the backseat, there was dead silence.

Something you should know here. Two days later, when I told my sisters what had transpired in the car at the convenience store, they became completely undone. "You're wrong, Suzy!" they cried. "No man ever comes before your kids!"

"I wasn't putting Jack first," I corrected them. "I was announcing the terms of our new family."

At that point, I had been using 10-10-10 long enough to know and trust its power. That is why it was there waiting for me at the moment of truth, while Jack was buying grape gum. In fact, I made my 10-10-10 decision that day in almost no time at all. It required no paper and pen. I did it in my head in about, oh, three nanoseconds.

In ten minutes, ten months, and ten years, there were to be no wants and needs of mine or anyone's more important than the "third force" at the center of our lives — the greater sum of Jack and me together.

That choice was made.

"So, what's going on in here?" Jack asked, still perplexed by the new mood in the car.

"Oh, nothing!" I assured him.

"Nothing?" he pressed.

There was another long moment of silence. Then Marcus broke it. "Mom told us the new rules," he blurted out, neither mad nor defiant-sounding, just dazed. He was no longer, it should be noted, speaking in a duck voice.

"Mom says there's no more 'just her' now," he reported. "There's only you and her, together."

Jack burst into a happy laugh. Then he raised his eyebrows at me and I gave him a real smile. Not a word passed between us, but I could tell by the expression on his face that, on some level, he understood what had happened in his absence, and he was grateful to me for the gauntlet I'd thrown and, most of all, for my decision — deliberate, sustaining, and true.

There in the quiet, that shared and sacred thing between us drew a hopeful breath, and grew.

CHAPTER FIVE:
IN WORK, DIGNITY

ON THE JOB WITH 10-10-10

This chapter explores the power of 10-10-10 at work. But to save time, you can skip it if any of the following are true:

1. Your work doesn't really matter to you. OK, it matters, but not really.
2. Your work matters to you, but it's a cakewalk.
3. You've never had an out-of-body experience during a staff meeting, a performance review, a negotiation with a client, or any other work occasion, where you've found yourself wondering, "My God, what have I done?"
4. You have absolutely, positively no interest in the work decision that I kept secret for sixteen years.
5. Your inner goodness and lack of *schadenfreude* prevent you from wanting to hear about how I was

fired twice.

If none of the above applies, read on.

Read on if you love your work yet sometimes dread it, or if you wrestle with your job daily but still want to wake up early the next morning and get at it again. Read on if you would embrace a process that would make your work more fulfilling. It doesn't matter if your work is washing dishes or running a corporation. All work is good work if it fills you with satisfaction and purpose.

10-10-10 will meet you there.

If only it had existed the first time I got the ax, back in the summer of 1975.

"WORK IS A DUTY, *CAPISCE?*"

The scene of the crime was the Cumberland Farms convenience store in Wellfleet, Cape Cod — the very store, it just so happens, where, twenty-seven years later, I was to lay down the new rules of family life for my stunned children while Jack went inside to buy a pack of grape bubble gum.

But back when I was a cashier at that store, I had no such backbone. Most sixteen-year-olds don't, of course, but I was particularly spineless. I was fired because I couldn't stand up to my mother. Clever and willful, she was such a force to be reckoned with that no one ever tried. Me included.

My downfall took just a month to unfold. The store manager, Mr. Antonio Scibelli, a sweet-natured Italian immigrant with a huge handlebar mustache, wanted me to work nine to five, five days a week — like any normal employee. Unfortunately, whenever the weather was good, my mother insisted that I join the family on our boat, hauling in the bluefish.

"But Mom, what about my job?" I would mumble from the backseat as we drove past the store on the way to the harbor most mornings.

"Mr. Scibelli loves me," she would blithely reply. "He'll understand. Family comes first."

Mr. Scibelli did seem to have a small crush on my mother. On the days when I made it to work — mainly when it was rainy — she would make sure to present me at the store, proclaiming, "Look, Tony, Suzy's here!" and his face would break into a big, goofy grin.

One rainy day, however, I didn't show up — my mother had decided the basement needed cleaning — and Mr. Scibelli called my house in a rage. "The store, it's crazy-busy! You get in here!" he yelled in his thick accent. "What do you think I pay you for?"

Quivering, I asked my mother to drive me over, but she'd have none of it. I considered running to the store myself — it was only a half mile away — but I couldn't bear the thought of my mother's reaction. And so, defeated, I stayed in the basement sorting junk.

The next day, the weather was still cloudy and my mother agreed to drop me off at work on her way to town. But when I walked into the store, my pigtailed head bowed in shame, Mr. Scibelli stormed over. "What are *you* doing here?" he demanded to know.

"I'm here to work," I volunteered meekly.

"You don't know *how* to work," he exploded. "Work is a duty, *capisce?* Work is not just — 'I feel like it or I don't.' You're never gonna keep a job, you act that way."

"I know! I know!" I bleated in protest.

"Basta!" Mr. Scibelli shouted over me. "Get out. Go, go, go!"

I went, and I've been apologizing to Mr. Scibelli ever since — in my head. Even at sixteen, I believed work was a commitment to be honored. But I didn't live as if I did.

THE DAYS OF OUR LIVES

Sociologists have long held that work is a primary source of identity in our lives, giving us direction and purpose and serving as the organizing principle of our days. My own career as a business journalist has only confirmed that concept. In my years as a newspaper reporter and magazine editor, I spent time in union halls and on factory floors, at small entrepreneurial start-ups and in sprawling high-rise boardrooms. In literally every instance, I saw and heard that work isn't just what people *do* all day. It's who people are.

In recent years, my understanding of work — and how people experience it — has been radically expanded by an avalanche of newer data. Each week, my husband Jack and I receive hundreds of letters in response to our column, which appears in *Business-Week* magazine in the United States, and throughout about fifty countries internationally as part of the *New York Times* Syndicate. Even with our diverse audience, one common message comes through loud and clear. People care passionately about their work. It fills them with satisfaction; it maddens them to distraction. In sum, work gives people meaning. An elementary school softball coach once wrote us, "I've got friends who say, 'You're just a gym teacher, Bob, don't get so high and mighty.' And I tell them, 'Yeah, but I'm a *teacher.* I can change a life.' " A friend of mine counsels executives who find their companies in some form of crisis. She sees her work as essential to keeping the economy afloat. My older sister Elin runs a photography business focused on graduations and Christmas card portraits. Her work, she says, celebrates families; it fortifies them.

A Latin philosopher once said, *"In opus, maiestas"* — In work, dignity. Some things never change.

But in these intense times, dignity at work doesn't come without intense effort. Work moves blazingly fast; its demands are increasingly complex. It's constantly changing. It's never complete. You can give it your all, but it never seems to give you security in return.

For most of us, work stopped being a nine-to-five thing a decade ago. Technology is one reason; for better and worse, Black-Berrys, cell phones, and laptops make our availability ubiquitous. In the always-on exigency of the global economy, business never sleeps. And so more and more, we bring our whole selves to work, and our

136

work into our personal time.

Now, more than ever, we need a process to ensure that our work decisions don't happen to us, but that we make them happen *for* us.

A Virtual Consultant

At work, 10-10-10 can play two main roles.

First, it can help with complex managerial, strategic, and operating decisions — from hiring and promotion picks to budgeting allocations. And second, 10-10-10 can be used as a tool to manage, teach, or counsel the people we work with. In both cases, 10-10-10 provides a framework for constructive debate and a common language to explore conflicting values and agendas.

In my experience, 10-10-10 works so well at work because it goes right to the heart of work's fundamental challenge. No matter what kind of job you have, whether you're an entrepreneur deciding where to manufacture a new product, a sales representative planning customer visits, an engineer selecting members for a special project team, or an executive opening a new office halfway around the world, virtually every decision involves a clash between the countervailing demands of the present, midterm, and future. Every decision calls for trade-offs and requires an evaluation of potential consequences across different time frames. At such crucible moments, 10-10-10 can act as a virtual consultant in the room, prompting us to gather data, test assumptions, identify options, and explore their varied consequences.

I discovered 10-10-10's consulting utility for myself when I was the editor of the *Harvard Business Review.*

Our goal at *HBR* was to publish articles that would, according to our mission statement, "improve the practice of management." Usually, we had a wealth of insightful, cooperative contributors to work with, but every so often, a renowned Harvard professor with an obtuse or otherwise half-baked idea would insist we print his text virtually unedited. And if we said no, the professor could raise a ruckus with the dean of the business school, the magazine's official boss and owner.

One day, a few members of the staff and I found ourselves struggling with exactly such a scenario. The offending contributor was a big kahuna on campus — I'll call him Professor Hampton here — who had submitted an article that was a retread of previous material he'd published in *HBR* and written in the kind of academic jargon we'd been trying to eliminate from the publication for years.

One of my colleagues had spent the day trying to negotiate with Hampton and was near her wits' end. Nonetheless, at our meeting, she argued to forge ahead. "We're in this so deep, we can't turn back now," she said.

"Why run an article that's not ready?" another colleague pushed back.

"We're running it so Suzy won't get a call from the dean," someone nicely suggested. "Although that's sort of what she's paid for —"

"Can we 10-10-10 this?" I interrupted when it suddenly struck me that the Hampton decision was just another dilemma with multiple constituents and varied consequences over different time frames — and inasmuch a perfect candidate for the process I used all the time at home. I quickly described 10-10-10 to the people in the room.

"Let's try it," one editor responded, to general agreement around the table. "The question is pretty simple, isn't it? Should we publish Hampton or not?"

The ten-minute time frame sparked a speedy consensus. If we went forward with the article, it would stall our efforts to change our brand image from stodgy to accessible. But if we rejected it, there could be a certain, unwelcome level of noise from the higher-ups.

In ten months, the outcomes weren't much better. Publishing the article would set a precedent for other difficult faculty contributors, making it harder for us to reject their less-than-optimal content down the road. And if we canceled Hampton, our bosses might still be so peeved that we could be stuck accepting an even less engaging article.

In ten years, though, the picture took on a clearer hue. "Who's going to be here a decade from now?" I asked the editors in the room. All of them raised their hands, and one immediately jumped in with an altered perspective.

"OK, hold on. We do have to kill the article," he said, receiving a nod or two from around the table. "Otherwise, in five years or eight or ten, we could still be sitting here having these exact same discussions."

"Just the opposite — we need to cut our losses and publish Hampton," another editor countered. "The brand is bigger than one article. Why cause trouble?"

Everyone looked at me. It was well known that I wanted *HBR* to modernize; I loved and respected the magazine, but I also felt that it could be too staid. On the other hand, I valued being in Harvard's good graces. I knew that even with my title and purported authority, I was hamstrung without my boss's support and the resources it brought *HBR.*

"Look, I think we have to run Hampton this time," I finally said. "If we want to change *HBR* in the long run, canceling this piece will carry too high a price. If we drop bombs, we'll become the 'enemy,' and that's no way to get anything done."

I'm not sure everyone in the room agreed with my decision. But at least everyone, including me, understood why I'd made it. And that's part of a leader's job.

GROW OR LET GO

Since that time, I have used 10-10-10 in countless other work situations.

Several years ago, for instance, I used it to prevent what would have been a truly dumb decision to fire my assistant. Megan La-Mothe was a very bright Colgate graduate with a degree in math and philosophy. Unfortunately, she was also the Amelia Bedelia of assistants, making one blooper after another and redeeming herself only by the graces of her huge heart.

One day after Megan had been working for me a year or so, I was standing by her desk when the phone rang. It was my brilliant friend Nancy Bauer reporting that she had just received tenure at Tufts University. I let out a shout and literally jumped up and down for joy. As soon as I hung up, I told Megan why. "Let's send flowers!" I cried. "This is fantastic news."

About two hours later, my own phone rang. It was the principal of my daughter's elementary school, a rather ornery woman who just so happened to share a first name with my best friend. "I have two dozen yellow roses on my desk," she said dryly, "and I can't imagine why."

That's it, I cried to myself. I ran to Megan's office down the hall. Surely some invective slipped out of my mouth, but then, catching the better of myself, I scuttled back to my own office to pull my thoughts together.

In the short term, I knew Megan was going to continue to drive me insane. She was a whirling dervish of creativity and inexperience, heavy on the latter. But, I realized, hadn't I been like that once too? And hadn't patient managers tolerated and tried to educate me? Given her vast potential, integrity, and good intentions, Megan might very well be an improved version of herself in ten months. And in ten years, she would surely be mature enough to be flourishing in the right career.

So what did I do? Instead of firing Megan on the spot, I told her why I wanted to. Then I informed her that I would give her another three months of my energy, but if my investment didn't appear to be paying off by then, she'd need to move on.

Today, Megan is just about to graduate from a prestigious business school. She's still overflowing with goodness and creativity, but has become poised, thoughtful, and a complete stickler for details. Every time she tells people I am her mentor, I want to faint from pride. She taught me how to be a better boss.

THE ENTREPRENEUR'S ALLY

For people who are self-employed, 10-10-10 can be especially valuable — it's a way to bounce around ideas when you have few or no colleagues to bounce them off. That's no small matter when you consider the statistics. Companies with fewer than twenty employees number close to 21 million in the United States, and while precise figures are difficult to obtain, perhaps as many as 15 million businesses have fewer than five people employed. And even in these times of economic disruption, an estimated 2,500 individuals go into business for themselves every day. As unemployment rises, we can only expect that rate will increase.

Fortunately, the government provides some low-cost support services to small business owners, and entrepreneur groups exist all over the country. But 10-10-10 can also help individuals get their companies up and running, providing a quick and easily accessible process to examine tough choices and test the gut calls that so many entrepreneurs tend to rely on.

Joan began her career as a teacher, but after a surprisingly fulfilling stint as her elementary school's guidance counselor, she decided to go back to school herself to obtain a degree in social work. A few years later, bolstered by a loan from her older sister, she decided to make the leap into the world of the self-employed. She hung her shingle as a family therapist, and drew her earliest clients from among friends, former colleagues, and the families of her old students. Soon, however, Joan came to realize she needed a more steady flow of income if she was going to be able to pay for her own health insurance, cover the mortgage, and continue to maintain her other household expenses. She spent weeks trying to set up appointments with local doctors and insurance providers, hoping they would refer patients her way. Some did, but not nearly as many as she needed.

In a moment of exasperation, Joan called Mary Louise, the principal of her old school and a good friend. "I knew going out on my own wasn't going to be easy," she lamented, "but I may not even survive my first year."

"Vin started three businesses before one finally stuck," Mary Louise replied, referring to her husband, who had recently turned his first profit with an eBay store-front drop-ship site. "You just have to keep trying things. I mean, try everything, Joan. Try something with the Internet. That's the future."

Joan balked. In fact, she had been considering launching a small website for herself, but her instinct had been to spend just enough to list her name and contact information. "I didn't have a lot of money to spare," Joan told me of her early thinking, "and I just asked myself, 'Come on, who finds a shrink online?' "

But Mary Louise's comment prompted Joan to reexamine her assumptions through 10-10-10, which she already used frequently in her personal life. Her question, she decided, was financial. "How much money," she wanted to know, "should I put into marketing myself online?"

To conduct a thoughtful 10-10-10, Joan knew that her first order of business was to get some hard data.

That didn't take long. A brief online search revealed that therapists of all disciplines were promoting themselves on the web, not only by listing details about their training and approach but also with blog entries from patients, videos clips, photos, and podcasts. And when Joan looked at message boards and forums, she learned that potential clients were using such websites in the therapist selection process, and coming to expect them.

"I'm very risk-averse," Joan observed when we spoke not long ago. "But now that I'm a solo act, I have to get used to risk; I have to find ways to manage it. 10-10-10 showed me that it was riskier from a business point of view not to spend money." Ultimately, Joan invested $5,000 to design her website, even taking a course to learn how to manage it herself. The new endeavor proved so enjoyable to Joan — and fruitful for her business — that now, two years later, she is thinking about expanding her digital presence with a subscription-based email newsletter to reach all the new clients the site has brought in.

Those clients, incidentally, are enough to keep Joan's new business afloat for the time being, but she has no plans to cut back on her web presence. If being an entrepreneur has taught her anything so far, it's that you can never let down your guard.

You need to keep pushing yourself, with every tool available, to improve your business not just today, but in the months and years ahead.

NOT JUST GUT, GUT, GUT

Shortly after I started to research this book, a friend sent me an email. "I just Googled your idea," she wrote, "and I'm assuming you know about all the life coaches out there using 10-10-10."

In fact, I had no idea. Every 10-10-10 user I'd met up until that point was a person like me, deploying the process individually, or, in a few cases, with the help of a friend or partner.

But since that time, I have come to learn that 10-10-10 has become part of the toolkit for many people in the helping professions — teachers, nurses, therapists, and psychologists. Anne Jolles, a family counselor in Massachusetts, for instance, uses 10-10-10 to help parents who are having trouble letting go of their children as they grow up and seek independence. Meadow DeVor, an online life coach, uses 10-10-10 with clients who are struggling in their marriages and with work-life balance issues. And remember Heidi, the teacher who used 10-10-10 to muster the courage to try online dating? She also put 10-10-10 to use in her classroom, asking her senior students to select one big decision in their lives and conduct a retrospective 10-10-10 analysis, laying out what they might have done differently had they methodically thought about repercussions.

"You almost never *see* kids learn," Heidi told me of the experience. "But those papers were the best, most profound pieces of writing I got all year. Nearly every kid — and these were tough kids — had their eyes opened by the process. They saw the consequences of their actions, and in some cases, realized they'd made a mistake."

Kimberly Smith-Martinez, a psychologist in San Antonio who just entered private practice, frequently used 10-10-10 in her previous work as a counselor in the juvenile justice system. The teenagers in Kim's care were typically in the throes of crisis, and many were on the verge of dropping out of society altogether. To help them sort through the potential outcomes of their choices, Kim took the 10-10-10 process and made it graphic. Sitting with each young client, she drew a 3-by-2 grid. Above each column, she wrote: Ten days, ten months, and ten years. Along the side, she labeled one row "Pros" and the other "Cons," and then she and her client worked through the current conflict, cataloging its consequences.

The day I talked to Kim, she had just conducted the process with a pregnant teenager who was trying to decide whether to stay with her disapproving but stable family or move in with her loving but erratic boyfriend, a drug user. Using 10-10-10, the young woman ultimately chose to stay at home, reasoning that her family would provide an environment that would allow her to return to school after her baby was born. She would miss the company of her boyfriend, but in the end she decided that she valued the possibility of independence more.

"Realistically, I don't know what will happen to this young woman," Kim told me, noting that most of her clients had at least one family member who had died or was incarcerated. "My kids don't ever look forward. But 10-10-10 gives them a little glimpse of something they usually don't see — themselves in the future," she said. "It's not all gut, gut, gut."

TWELVE ANGRY MEN

When I was not much older than Kim's clients, I made a gut call at work that was to become my secret for sixteen years. It was only 10-10-10 that finally helped me understand and make peace with that painful chapter of my personal history.

The year was 1985. I was twenty-six, working at the Associated Press in Boston as an overnight shift supervisor.

What a joke. Not because a twenty-six-year-old can't be a boss. In family companies and entrepreneurial start-ups, it happens all the time. But it doesn't usually happen — and for good reason — in situations where the employees are cranky old union members embroiled in a longtime pissing match with management.

You can imagine how happy such employees were to see me. I had just four years of newspaper experience under my belt, and a Suzy Sunshine approach to the job that must have made them feel positively homicidal.

I wasn't particularly crazy about them either, with their snark and swagger. Since they couldn't take their resentment out on top management, some of them took it out on me. They informed me that they didn't trust anyone who couldn't name the Irish county of their mother's birth. They also wanted me to know that college was for rich sissies, and my college in particular was for rich sissy morons. At 4 AM every morning, they left for their "lunch" break, and a few of them regularly returned an hour later in a toxic cloud of booze. To my friends, I dubbed my employees, such as they were, the Twelve Angry Men. (There were, in fact, usually no more than five of them on any given night.)

Now, I didn't mind the minor hazing — being called "Miss Harvard," or being left alone in the dark now and again when they threw the switch in the fuse box. What I couldn't stand was the way a few of the guys would go into the bathroom about ten feet from my desk and pretend — at least, I told myself they were pretending — to "pleasure" themselves whilst shouting my name.

My supervision of the overnight shift was to last about a year. In that time, I never complained to my boss about what happened. I never told my parents, a friend, a colleague, or my then-husband. The first person I told was Jack. I was forty-two years old.

"Are those jerks still alive?" was his response. "Because I need to go kill them."

And then more seriously, he asked, "Why didn't you put a stop to it?"

I walked him through my thinking at the time, using 10-10-10 in retrospect.

First I reminded him of the context. In 1985, "sexual harassment" as a concept may have been floating around, but it had yet to gain any kind of traction. Most women were still gaining a foothold in the working world, and those who complained about inhospitable conditions were labeled whiners and fired or swiftly warehoused in divisions far from the real action. To get ahead, you had to prove you had the mettle of the next guy — or more. I'm not saying those conditions were right; I wouldn't want my daughters working in them. But they were the reality of the times, and like so many women of my generation, I had to choose my battles.

In ten minutes, if I reported the actions of the Twelve Angry Men, I had nothing to gain and much to lose. As union members, they couldn't be fired without a lengthy grievance and litigation process. That would leave me managing a bunch of men who hated me more than ever before. I could ask my boss to move me off the night shift, but unless I told him why, it would look like I was wimping out over the hours or couldn't hack it as a manager.

In ten months or so, if I kept my mouth shut, I knew I'd be back on the day shift, triumphant. In those days, you couldn't advance in newspaper journalism without working the overnight; it was a rite of passage. If I survived mine, I'd also have the satisfaction of knowing I hadn't let the bastards get me down.

If I complained, in ten years, I'd still be known in the industry as "the girl who couldn't take a joke," as the Twelve Angry Men were likely to deny what had really happened. If I didn't complain, I'd be the woman who had risen through the ranks playing by the men's rules.

My decision, then, wasn't entirely wrong, as the trajectory of my career went on to prove. But I paid a price for my silence too. For a year afterward, even while on the day shift, I constantly felt uncomfortable in the office. I didn't know exactly why; I didn't even consciously link it to the Twelve Angry Men. Finally, I quit to attend business school. But whenever the subject of being a boss came up in class, I could feel my confidence ebbing. What did I know? I hadn't really managed anyone; my employees had run roughshod over me.

How sad that seems to me now. With 10-10-10, I came to see that by tolerating the Twelve Angry Men I had learned much more about men, management, and myself than I would have if I'd tattled or bolted. Today I even use the experience when I lecture at Babson College's Center for Women's Leadership. Working conditions for women have come a long way in the last thirty years, and most of my students will never have to confront what I did. But they surely will find themselves in dilemmas where a choice will have deep and lasting impact on their sense of identity. Don't make a decision, I tell my students, unless you can explain it to yourself, and to others.

And no, I don't use my first firing as an example. I use my second.

"You Did This to Yourself"

It was October of 2001 when I flew to New York to meet Jack for the first time. He had just retired after twenty successful years as chairman and CEO of General Electric and was in the midst of a publicity tour for his bestselling autobiography. My assignment was to interview him for *HBR*.

Jack was known to be charismatic and opinionated. On the phone call to set the meeting up, he had made no secret of how much he disdained my scholarly journal. ("Never read the thing" were his exact words, I believe.) And so I arrived at his office for our allotted hour a nervous wreck, armed with a stack of meticulously prepared questions.

I'm not exactly sure how long it took us to fall in love that day. Nor can I explain why it happened. I asked Jack a question about leadership, and he answered with a few ideas I recognized from his autobiography. Then I asked about strategy, and the same thing happened. On my third question, he rolled his eyes, as if he was exasperated with me. "Turn that tape recorder off," he ordered. And when I dutifully complied, he asked, "Do you have a guy?" Flustered, I told him I was dating a doctor in Boston, which I was, tenuously. "Get rid of him, he's a bore," Jack announced, adding presciently, "He's not right for you anyway." Then Jack asked why my marriage had ended. His question was blunt, and, reflexively, it made my answer that way too. "My ex-husband would tell you I never loved him," I admitted, "but I spent sixteen years pretending I did and he pretended back.

Eventually, we decided to stop pretending." Jack met my eyes directly and nodded as if he understood exactly what I meant, and then, to my disbelief, our conversation traveled to the daunting nature of marriage and the impenetrable mystery of love.

A half hour later, our "interview" feeling frighteningly close to the edge of intimacy to both of us, the tape recorder came back on, and for our final hour together, we talked about mergers and acquisitions, technological changes in the stock market, the role of human resources, and the quality improvement program known as Six Sigma.

Saying goodbye at the door of his office, Jack said, "You're nothing like I expected," and I answered, "Neither are you."

Over the next few weeks, Jack and I talked frequently on the phone — ostensibly about the progress of the article, but about everything else too. Politics, movies, my kids, his kids, religion, baseball, and the mortifying fact that I did not play golf. We had, it felt like, a lot of catching up to do.

A month later, I traveled to New York to have my photo taken with Jack for the Editor's Letter page of *HBR*. I was so (inexplicably) overjoyed to see him again that I was literally shaking in the elevator, and when I walked into his office, he bounded over to me, beaming, arms outstretched. Then we shook hands awkwardly.

That afternoon, we went to lunch, confessed what we were feeling and decided together that, given the circumstances, nothing could happen between us.

But a few weeks later, it did.

So it was that we created the perfect cocktail for a scandal — well-known, married CEO, a much younger woman, associated with Harvard, no less. The media had a party. But if they were having fun, we weren't. Even though Jack and his wife had periodically discussed divorce and had recently been living on separate continents on and off, there was no sugarcoating the fact that our relationship had started before theirs had legally ended. And because of that, and the sensation it caused, we had very regretfully allowed Jack's wife's privacy to be invaded.

I was also distraught over the awful disruption I had created at *HBR*. While my interview with Jack never saw the light of day, some members of my staff were livid about what had happened and how poorly I had behaved — and they wanted me gone. As one of them angrily told me, "You did this to yourself when you put your personal life ahead of your responsibility to the magazine."

Of course, he was absolutely right. My decision to have a life with Jack had caused so much turmoil at *HBR* that I needed to leave.

So why didn't I? Looking back at those four months when I hung on to my job knowing that I shouldn't, my best explanation is that events were happening too fast for the kind of attentive deliberation I so desperately needed to deploy. Yes, I had 10-10-10 in my life. I also had TV trucks camped outside my house. Reporters were calling my parents and showing up on my ex-husband's front stoop. A photographer chased me as I carried Marcus into the doctor's office for a strep test. Advice was coming from every direction — Jack, lawyers, colleagues, family, friends, college classmates, even strangers on the street. A priest approached me in a supermarket and told me he was praying for me. Running on a treadmill at my local gym, trying to act normal in the midst of the mayhem, I watched a panel of "experts" on TV debate how I should handle my dilemma. And then there was my gut, one minute shouting, "Quit now!" and the next, "Stay and fight." Amid all the noise and confusion, 10-10-10 didn't fail me. I failed it.

In the end, my boss fired me with the words, "You. Will. Never. Work. Again."

She must have been talking with Mr. Scibelli.

OK, I can joke like that now. But the truth is, I had turned my family's life upside down and put Jack's family into the kind of spotlight they abhorred. I had hurt colleagues I once considered friends. I'd thrown a respected magazine into disarray. My firing was a disaster like none I'd ever known, and it was my own fault.

THE POWER OF 10-10-10 AT WORK

It didn't have to happen that way.

Much of the time — most of the time, really — work decisions can be taken apart, examined through a prism of values, biases, needs, and fears, analyzed piece by piece, and, with due consideration, reasonably resolved. They are, in that way, no different from the problems we face in our personal relationships. Every one of our choices has consequences, now and in the future. We need to confront those consequences with candor and courage, and only then decide what kind of lives we want to lead.

Starting at that little convenience store on Cape Cod, I've learned that work has the capacity to draw you into moments of deep confusion and conflict. But I've discovered too that work undertaken deliberately can and will fill you with meaning, purpose, and the better measure of joy. Today, much of my career continues to involve the exploration of work and the ways in which people embrace it, with their energy, creativity, hope, and passion.

Because in work, there is dignity.

10-10-10 helps you keep it there.

CHAPTER SIX:
YOU CAN GET THERE FROM HERE

CHARTING YOUR CAREER WITH 10-10-10

Competitive strategy. Global markets. Monetary policy. Those were the kinds of weighty business topics that Jack and I expected to hear about when we first started inviting people to send in questions to our weekly column.

And we did hear about them, to an extent.

But we heard about career dilemmas more — by an order of magnitude. Indeed, to this day, most of the mail we receive still concerns the daunting dynamics of finding the right job and getting ahead once you do.

Jack and I try to answer many of the career questions that come our way, but what often stymies us is the fact that each one we receive is as individualized and values-dependent as the person behind it. "I dream of a career in music, but I'm afraid I'll never be able to afford a house and a car and my kids' education," a typical email goes. "How do I choose?" Another correspondent worried to us that her desire for professional achievement was pitting her against her family's demands that she reduce her stress level. "Why can't anyone at home understand that I love my job?" she asked. "I want to travel. I want to work late. I'm not stressed. I'm fulfilled."

A Way Out — and Forward

When career dilemmas become emotional or confounding, as they so often do, the rigor and discipline of the 10-10-10 process impels you to sort through the mix of needs, dreams, hopes, and assumptions that are making it so hard to find a way out — and forward. It's your guide as you weigh options and explore unknowns, comparing them to your values and goals. And just as important, the transparency of the process helps you explain your decision to yourself and any "constituents" who might be affected by it.

Carol Ann, a longtime real estate agent and a single mother, approached me at a conference in Florida two years ago. She was tall, blond, and dressed in bright yellow, with an out-there, ballsy demeanor — the kind of woman once referred to as a "great broad." Her only son had just left for college and at long last, Carol Ann told me with a smile, she was ready to have some fun with her friends instead of running home every evening after work.

Carol Ann's company, however, had another plan. They wanted her to relocate from Tampa, where she had lived and worked for twenty years, to their Houston headquarters to lead corporate training. The title, prestige, and significant pay increase of the new opportunity thrilled her. The potential for loneliness did not.

At Carol Ann's request, we started to 10-10-10 together.

In the ten-minute time frame, and even for weeks afterward, Carol Ann knew she would be elated by her promotion. She'd delight in the sense of achievement and the relief of paying off her son's student loan. She'd even be excited about finding a town house in Houston's buyer's market. "I love a bargain," she told me with a hearty laugh.

The ten-month picture was more mixed. "My job will be great, but my social life will be dead. I don't know anyone in Texas," Carol Ann said. "In ten months, the quiet nights will be killing me."

And what about ten years? Carol Ann paused before answering. "I'll have a nice bank account and a good pension plan by then. After the financial struggles in my life,

I have to tell you, I'd love that." She sighed deeply, her ambivalence tugging her face into a pensive frown. "But I'll have lost all my old friends in the process."

"You'll lose some friends," I said, more as a test than anything. "That always happens when you move. But with your personality, I bet you'll make plenty of new ones."

"Probably," she agreed. "Hey, maybe I'll even meet a man." She laughed again.

Then Carol Ann surprised me.

"You know what? I don't want to be clipping coupons in the supermarket circular," she announced. "I want a nice, comfortable retirement. And I want this new job. It will be fun. There's no better saleswoman in the company. You can ask anyone."

Before I could congratulate Carol Ann on a decision, though, she reversed herself. "But — I just can't leave my friends," she said.

I asked Carol Ann if the problem wasn't leaving her friends, but *telling* them she planned to do so. Maybe she feared her announcement would seem to say, "Guess what, everybody — money matters more to me than you do."

"Do you think your friends are going to be mad at you forever?" I pressed her. "Some of them may understand the value you place on financial security."

A smile started to spread across Carol Ann's face. "I get where you're going," she said. "In a year, I won't even remember the day I told everybody." Carol Ann grabbed my hand. "I can't build my life around fear. I'm taking the damn promotion," she exclaimed. "I knew I wanted to."

10-10-10 was her partner in making sure.

Carol Ann's dilemma stemmed from a conflict between the joy of her old life and the promise of a new one. But there are three other issues that most commonly set off career quandaries, and if you were to categorize them, they would sound something like this: "I'm worried I'm in the wrong job," "I think my career has stalled," and "My work-life balance is driving me crazy."

My hope is that by looking at each one of these tinderboxes in turn, and suggesting ways you might think about them, your next career 10-10-10 will be more focused and informed, providing the sustainable solution that's right for you.

WHAT SHOULD I DO WITH MY LIFE?

When I speak on college campuses, I'm often asked how I decided to become a journalist.

"I'm not sure I ever *decided,*" I usually answer. "I just knew — I always knew — there was nothing else I could do with my life." As evidence, I confess that in fourth grade I started keeping a diary in a little hand-decorated book with a cover inscription stating: "I shall write in here every night to practice for my future." (Yes, "shall." How mortifying.) In tenth grade, I could name the newspapers published in every American city, and by my freshman year in college, I had a poster of the audacious Italian war correspondent Oriana Fallaci hanging over my bed. She was my role model and my idol; I longed to be her.

OK, so I missed that particular mark by a mile. But I still am, basically, what I wanted to be as a kid, practicing for my future in the pages of my diary.

And that actually ends up making me more of the exception than the rule. Most people, I've found in writing about career formation, ultimately discover the profession that feels right to them through a vastly more iterative process. They try on one line of work, then zig and zag through related areas and positions, until they finally land in a good place.

Unfortunately, that process can take a decade or more, leading to the somewhat ironic reality that you finally discover "what you want to be when you grow up" when you've finally grown up. For women, it can be an even longer path, as their careers often involve stops and starts and flexibility-friendly digressions due to having children.

That said, it is possible to expedite your career's progression and arrive at the coordinates you so desire sooner rather than later. But that outcome takes a certain intentionality along the way.

10-10-10 can be your guide. To facilitate the process, however, I recommend first considering four questions about your job. The answers should stir up the "data" you need to start making meaningful career decisions.

Does my job allow me to work with "my people" — those who share my sensibilities about life — or do I have to zone out, fake it, or put on a persona to get through the day? The key word in this question is "sensibilities" — the values, behaviors, and personality traits that make you feel as if you're among kindred spirits. If you share sensibilities with your colleagues, you tend to work at the same pace, confront each other about tough issues with the same level of intensity (or lack thereof), and tell the same sorts of jokes in meetings. I'm not saying that people with shared sensibilities are all alike, but they pretty much all like one another.

I will never forget the firecracker of a woman — her nickname was "Sunny" — whom I met through my family a few years ago. "When I graduated from college, all I knew was that I wanted a job where I could wear high heels and carry a briefcase," she told me. "For a country girl like me, that meant you'd made something of yourself." Without much more thought than that, Sunny nabbed a position as a paralegal.

Two years later, she was out of there. "It was torture," she recalled. "No one laughed at what I laughed at. No one thought it was OK to argue now and again if you had to get some issues off the table. No one even enjoyed the same kind of music I did."

"I'm not saying it was a bad place," she concluded. "I just realized it wasn't *my* kind of place."

Sunny's next job was in catering — at least there were no suits involved — but when the work started to bore her a year later, she quit. Next, to pay the bills, she took a position as a project manager at a museum installation firm. Almost immediately, Sunny realized she was on to something. She loved the creativity and camaraderie involved in the job, and for the first time, it felt completely natural to her to stay late, suggest ideas, and connect with clients. One promotion led to another, and today, Sunny has found success in the related field of aquarium administration. She wears a T-shirt, shorts, and flip-flops to work, and doesn't even own a briefcase. Most important, she says, "I love the people I work with. We agree about what matters. I mean, we just see the world the same way."

The fact is, no job or profession will ever be right for you if it requires you to work with people who don't share your values or appreciate you as you are. You spend most of your life at work — a point well worth factoring into any 10-10-10 career dilemma. You have to like your colleagues — and feel authentic around them — if you are ever going to have a career you like.

Does my job make me smarter by stretching my mind, building my skills, and taking me out of my comfort zone? Without a doubt, it's appealing to hold a job where you feel like the smartest person in the room. In time, though, such efficacy can be a real career-killer. To feel fulfilled, you have to be growing.

Here's the catch: people tend to gravitate toward and stay ensconced in certain professions simply because they are good at them.

English majors go into publishing. Math majors go to Wall Street. My own sister Elin, who excelled in science through high school and college, "naturally" followed the current to graduate school and became a medical researcher.

But aptitude doesn't always equal passion. Thirteen years ago, when she was forty, my sister finally admitted to herself and her friends (not to mention our parents) that she never wanted to look through a microscope again. She quit science and started to look for an authentic vocation. She found it in photography.

Changing careers was rough going at first. Elin apprenticed herself to experienced photographers to expand her knowledge and scrimped to attend summer workshops on lighting and technique. She designed flyers and sent them to her neighbors and painstakingly sought new ways to market her services to communities across Boston's North Shore.

She loved every minute of it.

I am delighted to report that Elin's business is thriving — and she is too. Moral is, if your career 10-10-10 involves a change of direction, don't just ask, "Do I have the right skills?" Ask: "Will I enjoy the challenge of gaining new ones?"

Does my job open doors for me? As contradictory as it might sound, you can be pretty sure you're holding the right job if it has the potential to lead to another job elsewhere. That's because careers, by definition, don't have dead-ends. They are comprised of opportunities that lead to other opportunities.

In teaching at Babson College, I'm sometimes approached by seniors who are using 10-10-10 to decide between two job offers. I remember one student, Kristin, who came to our meeting with a carefully prepared list of pros and cons for both of her options, and a look of total exasperation on her face. "I'm stuck," she explained. "One of the jobs would be great for me for the next year or two. It's a little start-up. The work is fun and the people are great. But the company may not even survive. The other company has a great reputation, great training programs, and lots of upward mobility. It makes much better sense for me in a ten-year time frame. It's such a toss-up that I don't know what to do."

I reminded Kristin that every 10-10-10 solution depends on the values of the person conducting the process, but that didn't seem to help. Both opportunities gave her what she wanted from life, she said —

intellectual challenge, teamwork, and enough money to stay afloat.

I pushed Kristin to think more deeply about her career values. "Well, I'm not big on titles or prestige," she finally said. "I'd rather have responsibility than authority." Kristin, it turned out, dreamed of a résumé filled with stints at small ventures where she could have true impact, and hopefully a piece of the ownership as well.

"Which job opportunity opens those doors for you?" I asked, but we both already knew the answer. Kristin soon accepted her offer from the start-up.

The days of one-company careers are fading fast. So as you consider your career choices with 10-10-10, make sure that each job you hold at least offers you the chance to launch to another.

Does my job give me meaning? Every holiday when my kids return home from school and we start to select their courses for the following semester, we invariably end up in the "What should I do with my life?" conversation. And every holiday, I have to remind my kids that no one ever built a great career doing something they hated.

Do what you love, I tell them, and the rest will follow.

"Sure, Mom, sure," they brush me off,

"but isn't biotech a hot industry right now?"

"It is," I try to tell them, "for people who happen to like biotech."

Look, the perfect job — and the perfect career — are only perfect if they make you happy. Something about the work — the thrill of making a big sale, the excitement of hitting a deadline with your colleagues, the reward of coaching a newcomer or helping a customer — just turns your crank. It feels important; it fills your soul.

I am reminded of the first real stepping-stone of my own career, my job as a reporter at the *Miami Herald.*

For an Oriana Fallaci wannabe, there was no better place to be a reporter than Miami in the 1980s. In 1981 and 1982, the city was engulfed in riots, as residents of the Overtown and Liberty City neighborhoods protested the jury acquittals of white policemen accused of racially motivated violence. The burning and looting were so severe that the National Guard was called in and curfews were declared. Then in 1983, Miami was besieged by thousands of refugees, most of whom were hardened criminals Fidel Castro had just released from Cuban prisons. Meanwhile, cocaine traffickers battled one another in street-corner shoot-'em-ups in broad daylight.

The city wasn't a full-on war zone, but it was close.

Oh, to be a girl reporter then! I remember wearing a bulletproof vest during one assignment, which in the greenness of my youth filled me with pride. As we were creeping into a cocaine-processing factory in Perrine with a SWAT team one night, a rookie cop handed me a revolver and said, "You may need this." Another morning I remember waking up to see government tanks rolling down my quiet residential street in Coconut Grove, and not thinking, "Help!" but "Hallelujah!" There was just so much to write about. Not all of it was exciting, of course. For many of Miami's longtime residents, the city's implosion caused fear and sadness, and for residents of the riot areas, the violence took a dreadful toll. But I desperately wanted to hear their stories too; I wanted to tell them in all their heart-wrenching detail. My job gave me that great gift and opportunity.

Nearly thirty years have passed, but Miami has never left me. The experience taught me what a career should feel like. And in time, it taught me too that you simply cannot, and should not, 10-10-10 any career dilemma without acknowledging the "joy factor" of your options.

KEEP YOUR NOSE ABOVE THE HORIZON

I have a friend who takes flying lessons, and whenever I express terror at his idea of fun, he shrugs me off with a laugh. "It's actually very easy to fly, Suzy," he says. "You just keep the nose of the plane above the horizon."

Careers are like that too. To stay aloft, you need to keep your sights just high enough.

And you have to pay attention — quickly — when your nose starts dipping. You miss a promotion. Your bonus is flat. Your boss stops inviting you to important meetings. In such cases, something is usually off.

Something is stalling.

If you use 10-10-10, the next thing you know, you'll be applying the process to a "Do I stay or do I go?" kind of dilemma.

As you do, however, it's all too easy to get caught up in the feelings of rejection, confusion, and anxiety of the moment. After all, almost nothing is as disconcerting as the sneaking suspicion that everyone is in on something that you're not. To overcome your emotions, once again a certain intentionality is required. You need to stop, step back, and make a pact with yourself that you have work to do before deciding anything.

Now, identifying the source of your stall

may sound easy enough, but I've found that many people assign the blame for their situation to the economy, a bad boss, a scheming coworker, or any number of other forces outside their control. Extenuating circumstances may indeed be involved, but before conducting any meaningful career-stall 10-10-10, you need to determine if your own behaviors can be implicated as well.

The hard truth is, our careers rarely stall when we're performing well. And I don't just mean performing at expectations, I mean above them. For better or worse, over-delivering is what our bosses want, need, and expect in these competitive times. So if you notice your "nose" dipping at work, you need to have an honest conversation with yourself or a colleague you trust about your results. How good are they, *really?*

Unfortunately, we rarely know the answer to that question until it's too late. And there's an incontrovertible reason why. Most managers don't have the guts or the time — or both — to tell their employees where they stand.

I plead guilty.

Dave was the first person I ever fired. He'd worked at our company for many years before I arrived, and after I was promoted to being his boss, never seemed to get comfortable with my authority. As for his performance, it started out as adequate, but over time disintegrated to poor. He was political, divisive, and unproductive. Finally I decided he needed to move on.

Looking back, how could I have expected Dave to take the news sitting down? He had no idea it was coming — because I had never told him how he was doing.

The fallout of Dave's firing was a mess. He screamed at me in the meeting, waged a campaign through his coworkers to be rehired, and later threatened to sue the company unless he received a substantial cash payment. (Eventually, we settled.)

If your career seems to be in a stall, try to pinpoint the date and content of your last *real* performance review. Don't assume you're doing OK because your boss hasn't told you otherwise. And remember, don't conduct a stay-or-go 10-10-10 until you get the candid feedback you need on your performance. Only then can you decide whether your stall is reversible, or if a bailout is your only hope.

Along with problematic performance, our careers tend to stall for two other reasons. We have the wrong leadership mind-set or we're suffering from an embedded reputation.

FROM HERO TO ZERO

You don't need me to tell you that not everyone can be a leader, but if there's one thing I've learned over time, it's that most companies want everyone to *demonstrate* leadership qualities. That's why, if we start showing signs that we're not a person who can take charge — at least, someday — we stand the chance of slowly but surely being moved aside and then out the door.

And what does a person who can take charge actually look like? There's no universal leadership profile. Some companies want their leaders to be technically proficient. Others want them to have global experience. Still others like their leaders to have certain educational credentials. But virtually all companies know that the most effective leaders share one trait — they understand that success is not about them. It's about the team. Being a good leader means being turned on by the reflected glory of the people who work for you. Being a good leader means you honestly think it's more fun to see your people grow than to get your own ego stroked.

About three years ago, Jack and I received a poignant email to our column from a man who signed his note, "From Hero to Zero." A "quant jock" at a financial firm, his career had soared for six years, and along the way, his salary growth had never let up.

But then something strange happened, our correspondent said. He grew tired of just crunching numbers. He wanted to be a leader. And so, he asked to manage a department within his firm.

"You must be kidding," his bosses replied.

"They said I didn't care about my colleagues' ideas, and I never wondered how I might help them do better," he wrote. "They told me my results were great and that I could have my job forever if I wanted it, but I wasn't moving up, ever."

"Hero to Zero" never wrote again to tell us the next chapter of his story, but I would wager he's still a quant jock somewhere — unless his mind-set has radically changed.

Again, not everyone can be a leader or even wants to be. But if you're in the midst of a career-stall 10-10-10, it's worthwhile to ask yourself how you're perceived. If your company doesn't think you can manage, it may be managing you out.

STUCK ON THE OLD YOU

And then there's the career stall that occurs because we've got a reputation, earned or not, that we can't shake. Maybe we royally screwed up an assignment a few years back,

179

or we were involved with a project or product that failed, or we were hired by a manager who later left the company under a cloud of controversy. In such cases, we're tainted by a prior activity or association.

But sometimes our embedded reputation has to do with something less concrete: limited expectations.

The daughter of a trucker and a restaurant manager, Jody was the first person in her family to attend college, and she still counts her graduation day from the state university as the proudest of her life. With a degree in accounting and a 3.5 GPA, she soon landed a job as a bookkeeper with a machine manufacturer in Ohio.

For five years, Jody flawlessly executed her responsibilities, and according to her manager, brought energy, insight, and creative solutions to the job. Her colleagues liked her too; she was considered a team player who valued honesty and hard work.

No wonder Jody was perplexed when she didn't receive the small promotion she applied for in her division. She sought out her boss and asked why. "I know I can do the job," she insisted.

"I know that too," her boss agreed. "But that position is for an MBA."

Undeterred, Jody went back to work with

increased determination — and earned her MBA on the side. Eighteen months later, degree in hand, she applied for a promotion again — and again was turned down. She was devastated.

"I don't understand," she confronted her manager. "I got the credential you wanted."

Her boss had no good answer — at least, not an answer she could admit. But I've seen cases like Jody's enough times to know that Jody was the "victim" of her embedded reputation. In her company's mind, she would always be a bookkeeper, MBA or not.

In time, Jody put her advanced degree to good use at another company, which was able to see her credentials, skills, and potential with fresh eyes.

And that's a happy ending to remember if you find yourself in a career dilemma where probing with 10-10-10 leads to the realization that you're stalled because you've changed, but your reputation has not.

THE WORK-LIFE MYTH

A final source of career angst — and perhaps the most emotional one — is work-life balance. Think about Lynne Scott Jackson, whose dreams of a new business were just coming to fruition when her elderly parents suddenly demanded her attention. Or recall

Jackie Majors, the high-flying corporate executive who was spurred to use 10-10-10 by her young daughter's remoteness. 10-10-10 opened both women to the consequences of their options across three time frames, and helped them discover solutions that met their deepest wants and needs.

Those wants and needs, incidentally, were quite different. Lynne wanted more work in her work-life balance equation. Jackie, less.

My point? That you cannot 10-10-10 a work-life dilemma without being very clear with yourself about the relative importance of your values. Because balance is a myth. When it comes to conflicts between your work and your personal time, you need to make trade-offs. That's why I prefer the term "work-life choices." If you value professional achievement and wealth, you are de facto *choosing* that the amount of time you devote to work will be more than the amount of time you devote to all other activities. If your top value is being there all the time for your kids while they grow up, you are de facto *choosing* not to be a CEO. Climbing the corporate ladder requires unimpeded availability and unfettered commitment. And so does being an ever-present mother.

You cannot have it all, all at the same time.

But if you think that point is obvious to everyone, or even widely accepted, you'd be surprised.

Time and again, I've encountered women who are struggling through a 10-10-10, thinking it has the magical ability to put their lives in perfect "balance," with a big job, great kids, a happy marriage, fun vacations, and toned thighs.

Invariably, I tell them something's gotta give. Eliminate two of those goals. Or be realistic — eliminate three. I offer my own case as evidence. In the years when building my career at *HBR* was a top priority, I missed school plays, ice skating performances, and plenty of nights of homework. Dinner was often hot dogs and apple slices. And my thighs were definitely not toned.

I was living by a set of values that I had chosen with my eyes open — and therefore I had to own the consequences.

Sure, I could have blamed my company for not being more family-friendly. But I knew business exists to make profits, not to make my life pleasant. I could have blamed society for not making men carry half the load of child-rearing. But why be angry at a system that is thousands of years old and predicated on the biological reality that women bear children?

I was a realist, I guess. I still am. That's why when it comes to career dilemmas around work-life "balance," I urge you not to just think hard about your values but to actually rank them. Only then will your 10-10-10 reflect the trade-offs you've chosen to live by.

We're Going to Disneyland

Not to sound harsh! I know all too well that those ten or fifteen years when you are trying to be all you can be at work and at home can feel like an unmitigated series of little agonies. I know you can have days and weeks on end where you feel as if your choices are making no one fully happy, especially you.

I know all too well also that working mothers spend each day in a constant inner dialogue, endlessly making King Solomon–like choices. 10-10-10 can help, but even with its assistance, many work-life choices still carry their fair share of *weltschmerz.* I just want to be honest about that. 10-10-10 is the best parenting tool I know of; I've seen its power and effectiveness more times than I can count. But it won't *banish* your work-life conflicts; it will help you understand them, manage through them, and make peace with them.

Barbara, a West Coast retail executive, married in her twenties, but she and her husband, a neurologist, never found the time or inclination to have children as both of their careers expanded. But just after Barbara's forty-fifth birthday, a case of "baby fever" struck, as she puts it. "Both John and I suddenly realized something huge was missing from our lives. We had each other, but we desperately wanted a family. It was like we woke up."

After an unsuccessful year of trying to get pregnant, the couple decided to adopt an infant from China. They had no mixed feelings — "A child is a child, and every child is a blessing," as Barbara told me — but the process delayed their dreams of creating a family for another year. Finally, the couple flew to Beijing to pick up their new daughter, Amy.

On the flight back to the United States, however, Barbara began to feel nauseous. And she stayed nauseous for another three weeks after the family arrived home. It was morning sickness — and seven months later, another daughter was born. The couple named her Jesse and moved a second crib into Amy's room.

The years that followed were one continuous juggling act, as John and Barbara adjusted to dual career parenthood and the jolt of two children arriving within one year. Yes, they adored the girls; yes, they were happy. But they were constantly exhausted. John changed hospitals to work closer to home and switched to the more predictable schedule of the emergency room. Barbara learned the fine art of managing babysitters. And, in order to spend more time with her daughters in the morning, she started going into the office every Saturday night to do paperwork.

Finally, when the girls were five and six, Barbara and John decided they needed to feel normal for a change; they needed a vacation at Disneyland.

Ever the good corporate employee, Barbara gave her bosses six months' notice about the dates of her week off. Meanwhile, at home, she and John started to spend evenings with the girls in front of the computer, planning every minute of the trip. There would be breakfast with Tinkerbell, lunch with Cinderella, with rides on Space Mountain and It's a Small World in between.

Then, a week before their departure, Barbara's boss, a woman about her own age, sent her a curt email. The CEO was coming for a visit; Barbara's vacation had to wait.

Fighting waves of shock and anger, Barbara walked to her boss's office a few doors away. "I just can't cancel my trip," she said, trying to sound composed. "I promised the girls."

Her boss considered her coolly. "Do you think I got where I am in this company without making sacrifices?" she asked. "Do you think just because you have young children you're exempt? Men have young children too, by the way."

The executive checked her BlackBerry and then returned her attention to Barbara. "My children are nineteen and twenty-four now," she said. "They're healthy, happy adults. And I worked fifty hours a week every year of their lives."

That evening at home, Barbara turned the problem over to 10-10-10. First she reviewed her values. Not only did she love her work, she was the major breadwinner for her family. But she had started motherhood so late in life, she told herself, that she couldn't take a moment of it for granted. More than anything, she wanted her girls to know her as an individual, not as a cyclone whipping through their lives. She wanted to know them too, not just when they were in trouble and she *had* to be there, but also in the unstructured moments.

In ten minutes, either decision left her with a crisis on her hands: a disappointed boss or a dejected pair of girls.

The ten-month picture was more nuanced. Barbara sensed her boss might back off from her hard-line stance. "She knew, underneath all that bluster, that I'd paid my dues along the way," Barbara told me. "I had some chits in the bank. I'd canceled many a vacation before. In fact, I probably had enough chits to go back to her and make a strong argument about my record of 'sacrifice.' She couldn't use one incident to define me."

On the other hand, Barbara reasoned, the ten-month impact of a no-go decision would still be reverberating at home, as the girls continued to live with the fact that Mommy's work always came before them and that her promises were not to be trusted.

In ten years, Barbara calculated, she and John would be sixty-two, three years from retirement, and the girls would be teenagers. At that time, she asked herself, wouldn't trust and intimacy with her daughters be worth more than finishing her career one rung higher?

The family left for Disneyland as planned. A week later, Barbara returned to work to find an email from her boss, reporting that the meeting with the CEO went very well, and suggesting ways she might immediately follow up with him on certain strategic initiatives.

"I admit, I felt a real pang when I saw her message. I thought, 'Oh no, I *did* screw up,' " Barbara told me. "But then I remembered how I had made my decision — with my eyes wide open. 10-10-10 was my little guilt eraser."

She made a note of her boss's request and got back to her life.

OLIVIA'S LAMENT

A few nights ago, I looked up from writing a column to see Sophia standing in front of my desk with a beautiful young woman. I must have looked confused, because Sophia burst into laughter. "Mom, come on — it's Olivia!" she cried.

Of course it was — all I needed to do was squint, and I could see the spunky little next-door neighbor I had once adored and hadn't seen for a few years. Now, it turned out, she was a college student in search of a major, and after an evening chatting with Sophia about her confusion, they'd decided to seek my advice.

"Oh, Mrs. Welch, it's making me crazy,"

Olivia started in. "I want a great career, something important and exciting — and not ditsy. I just don't know doing what."

I loved the "not ditsy" part, but that's not what struck me the most about Olivia's lament. It was the realization that she was experiencing her first career dilemma. I knew that if she was like the rest of us, many more would surely follow.

I told her so.

"Oh no," she immediately protested, "I want to be like you."

I was touched by her vote of confidence. But the truth is, I may have known what I wanted to be when I grew up long before I grew up, but when I finally did grow up, I still had moments of career confusion and even despair. I left Miami with my heart torn in two, one side pounding with grief over leaving the work I loved, and the other with excitement about the career I thought I might be able to build in Boston. As I stood in my driveway saying goodbye to my coworkers, my car packed with my every earthly belonging for the trip North, I remember taking a long, last inhale of the soft tropical air and wondering why I couldn't muster a little of Oriana's courage when I needed it most. I was still crying when I crossed the border into Georgia.

No matter what your career, I assured Olivia, you will have career dilemmas.

And you will resolve them. By understanding where they come from — and by understanding yourself.

CHAPTER SEVEN: TEACH YOUR CHILDREN WELL

10-10-10 AS YOUR PARTNER IN PARENTING

One day when Marcus was five, apropos of nothing, he announced, "When I grow up, Mommy, I'm not going to tell you where I live." There wasn't an iota of malice in his words; I still remember the guileless smile on his face as he spoke, delighted as he was with his personal emancipation proclamation. But I still felt stung. I'd spent every day of Marcus's life pouring love into his adorable little vessel, only to discover in the most offhanded way that the payback might not be lifelong devotion.

"Oh no," I remember thinking, "this mommy thing is getting harder by the minute."

Oh no, indeed.

After twenty years on the job, I would submit that parenting is the most complex endeavor in the world. It can reduce you to putty; it can enrage or humiliate you. It can break your heart. It can suffuse you with feelings of intimacy, pride, and joy so profound you don't know what you did to deserve such a blessing.

I'm not sure parenting can ever be easy, but by introducing greater clarity, consistency, and calm, 10-10-10 can make it easier, releasing you from guilt and doubt and building trust in both directions, child in parent and back the other way. All in, 10-10-10 markedly decreases the days when parenting feels haphazard and overwhelming, and increases the moments when you feel, "I'm being the parent I want to be, and heavens to Betsy, it seems to be working."

And — here's the best part — 10-10-10 can make family life a lot more fun. In fact, I hold 10-10-10 responsible for one of the best laughs I've ever had, which occurred when the adorable little vessel of Marcus had grown into a strapping young man of sixteen. We were walking home together from a swim practice one afternoon when he turned to me and, apropos of nothing, gave me a hug. "You know, Mom," he said, "when I get married, maybe you can move into my house and raise my kids. That would be good."

MOMMY IN THE MIDDLE

I started 10-10-10ing parental decisions soon after I returned from Hawaii, the hula skirt incident fresh in mind, and I haven't let up since. But one of my earliest applications of the process remains my favorite. One morning not long after I became a single mother, I promised the kids I would be home in time to make them dinner, and more important, to watch our favorite sitcom, *Malcolm in the Middle.* The kids loved that show because wily young Malcolm always ended up getting what he wanted in life, despite the interference of his screwy family. I loved it because Malcolm's mother had occasional bouts of so-called Level-Five Rage that her children managed to find endearing.

But at the office that evening as I was packing my briefcase, my boss caught up with me. "Bad news — the Carter piece just fell through," she said. "I need you to stay late."

I cringed. "How late?"

"A few more hours," she answered apologetically. "I'm sorry, but it's an emergency."

Now, my values as a mother were actually very clear to me at that point in my life. I firmly believed that my main responsibility was to teach my children the character trait of goodness — meaning compassion, honesty, and authenticity. I also believed that children benefited when their parents led happy, meaningful lives, which was why I needed to work full-time. My final value as a parent was shared respect. Some mothers might strive to be adored or obeyed. I wanted to build a family that could talk.

In ten minutes, staying at work would mean there would be talk all right. There would also likely be serious moaning and groaning, as in, "You promised, Mom!" and "Why does work always come first?" On the other hand, staying at work could only engender a positive response from my boss, as she noted my availability in her moment of need.

In ten months? Well, about that time, I knew I would be coming up for my performance appraisal, and I could be pretty certain my boss would still hold in her mind the memory of me hanging in there when it mattered. At home, my kids and I would be watching the continuing saga of *Malcolm,* my one MIA episode washed from their minds by my more typical conduct, which was a pretty solid record of being there and relatively rare bouts of Level-Five Rage.

In ten years, my decision was a moot point. Staying at work or leaving for home

— one little choice about one little evening wouldn't matter either way in the big picture.

My dilemma suddenly became a no-brainer. The foreseeable future of my professional life trumped my kids' pressing desires, and would perhaps even remind them that the world did not revolve around their uninterrupted satisfaction, not a bad lesson from my perspective. I walked back to the office and told my boss I was in for the duration. "Thanks a million, Suzy" was her grateful reply.

Then I called home to report the news. The eruption was as predicted, but it was over in about five minutes; it ended right after I asked the babysitter to put me on speaker phone and I walked the kids through my 10-10-10 thinking. There was a moment of silence, then a chorus of little "Hmms" and "OKs." Sophia even promised to fill me in on the missed episode the next morning.

GETTING STRATEGIC

Soon after that incident, I started mentioning 10-10-10 to my working-mother friends, and they were among its earliest adopters. One used it to decide whether to heed her son's plea to quit an extracurricular science

196

program, another to work through a conflict with her teenage daughter about summer plans. 10-10-10, I was told by these mothers and others like them, just made thorny parenting decisions simpler and more efficient.

Over time, I've come to realize that 10-10-10's immediate appeal as a parenting strategy is linked to its dependable capacity to backstop gut calls. Some parenting decisions give you time to ponder, but plenty don't. Can we take the car to the party? Can I sleep over at John's house tonight? Can I borrow twenty bucks to go to the mall with my friends? It's not like your kid ever asks you such questions with a week to spare, or in circumstances conducive to clearheaded thinking. These questions are typically posed on the fly, with an audience of friends in the room. Just as often, kids ask you to hurry up and make an important judgment call when you're distracted. My own children, for instance, have perfected the art of asking for permission when I'm on the phone, running late, or about to get in the car.

Fortunately, you can conduct a 10-10-10 analysis in the same amount of time it takes to hem and haw and finally give in. And you can deliver the reasoning behind your decision in the same amount of time as it takes to deliver your gut call with all its qualifiers and warnings attached. Remember Natalie, the mother who was trying to decide whether to attend her uncle's funeral? One son was pressuring her for a lift to soccer, the other needed a ride to the orthodontist, and every instinct was telling her to surrender to logistics. But in less than two minutes, she made a more sound decision. If she were to teach the values of responsibility and respect to her boys, she had to demonstrate them with her actions. She went to the service.

Just as with problems in love and at work, 10-10-10 also overrides our autopilot neurological biases and interrupts the closed-loop thinking that so often accompanies stressful parenting situations. That was the case with Paula, whose son was begging her to change schools. 10-10-10's methodology opened her mind to advice coming from an unlikely source — a taciturn math teacher. Ultimately, by impelling her to listen to someone she didn't like, 10-10-10 helped Paula get to the root of Hooper's real struggle.

THE G-WORD

But 10-10-10 transforms parenting decisions for another reason: it's an antidote to

the cultural zeitgeist around motherhood —
the white noise of opinions and directives
that has an inescapable way of infusing
doubt into our minds and guilt into our
lives.

There, I said it, the G-word — guilt.

If you're a parent and you don't have a
consistent operating principle like 10-10-
10, guilt can be your constant companion.

That's in no small part because American
society today is engaged in a contentious
debate about the right way to raise children,
with the main battle line drawn over whether
mothers should stay at home or work, or
some of both. The so-called Mommy Wars
have spawned a cottage industry of books
and articles, but they play out perhaps most
widely among dueling mommy blogs, one
of the most active communities on the web.
From what I have observed, some mommy
blogs are entirely neutral, serving as cyber
coffee shops for the friendly exchange of
parenting tips. But others are virulently
politicized, creating a kind of electronic
public square for mothers to lambaste each
other about their respective work-life
choices.

You don't have to go online, though, to
step into the fray. I'll never forget the
cocktail party I attended where a stay-at-

home mother I'll call Lillian grew so annoyed with a story I was telling about my job that she abruptly cut me off with the salvo, "You working mothers think you're so important, it kills me."

"I don't think that!" I automatically shot back.

Lillian groaned in disgust. "Yes, you do," she said. "You think stay-at-home mothers like me just don't have the balls to get out there and cut it in the working world like you do."

Again I objected, but Lillian waved me off dismissively. "You go into your offices with your working-mommy friends and you laugh at us and say, 'What do they *do* all day?' " she asserted. "You think we're trivial. Don't you?"

My response was yet again denial — this was a cocktail party after all — but Lillian had me. My working-mother friends and I had on occasion cluck-clucked stay-at-home mothers. Some of my colleagues couldn't imagine how full-time mothers could stand the tedium of child care and household drudgery. Weren't they bored to death? Didn't they understand that they'd wake up to an empty house in twenty years, only to discover their kids had meaningful, rewarding futures — but they did not?

"Stay-at-home mothers *confuse* working mothers," I finally offered.

"You confuse yourself," she replied, "by not listening to what your guilt is telling you."

The G-word hung in the air between us for a moment before I made one last lame attempt at detente. "My sisters stay at home with their kids," I said, "and they feel guilty about *not* working about as often as I feel guilty *for* working."

"I doubt it" was Lillian's dry retort.

It was my turn to groan. There was, it seemed, no middle ground between us. We parted ways, and while I don't know Lillian's take on the conversation, I can tell you that it left me feeling just like every kind of mother today: defensive and not a little ambivalent.

A BLACK BELT IN TRUST

10-10-10 is your companion, and a very effective one too, in the never-ending quest to eradicate those feelings.

A year or two after my *Malcolm in the Middle* 10-10-10, work was continuing to plug along, but a possible promotion for me was looming. Because of that, my boss had suggested I grab every opportunity to show my commitment to the organization. I did, usually without any major impact on the home front. But then — a big break. I was asked to moderate a weekend offsite for the company.

Except . . . the offsite was scheduled for the exact day and time that Roscoe — twelve years old at the time — was going for his junior black belt. The test was a very serious affair, which would be held at the Uechi-Ryū karate headquarters in New Hampshire in front of a panel of sensei judges. It certainly stood to be the most important event in Roscoe's life to date. I knew this because every time Roscoe mentioned it to me, his cheeks flushed crimson and his voice got all wispy, like he might faint.

In ten minutes, I knew there was no easy way out. Agreeing to moderate the offsite was a huge boost for me professionally, and a huge loss for Roscoe, who would be hurt and confused. Hadn't I been telling him for years how much I admired the hard work and discipline he devoted to karate? Why did he have to be the only kid whose mother wasn't there to watch?

In ten months, I figured, it would be roughly the same zero-sum game. Yes, I could work harder than ever at work to make up for my absence at the offsite. Or I could fawn on Roscoe unrelentingly, attending every karate lesson and reiterating my admiration for its principles. But I couldn't fool myself: the consequences of either choice would still be reverberating.

Ten years out, though, there was a mind-clearing vision. I knew that, in the distant future, my career writ large would have reached the level where it belonged, a level not decided by one appearance at one offsite, but by a marathon of twists and turns along the way. Roscoe, however, would only get his black belt once. In ten years, he would be away at college. Our time until then could be precious or fraught. And I could not deny that it stood too big a chance of being the latter if I abandoned him at his first big moment of truth. He might never trust me to be there for him again.

That weekend as I watched Roscoe move through his precise *katas* one by one, not for a moment did I doubt I was in the right place.

Technically speaking of course, attending Roscoe's black belt exam was 180-degree turnaround from my previous *Malcolm in the Middle* 10-10-10 decision. My values hadn't changed. My assessment of their impact did. And nothing got in the way of my acting according to that insight — not gut, not guilt, not anxiety, and not the cultural static about what mothers should and shouldn't do.

Raising Cain

A few years ago, I was very intrigued to read *The Nurture Assumption: Why Children Turn Out the Way They Do* by developmental psychologist Judith Rich Harris. The provocative thesis of the book would give pause to any parent in today's environment, as it asserts that children are primarily formed by their genes and the values of their peer groups. Parents, Harris concludes, deserve neither credit nor blame for the way their children behave.

If only everyone agreed! Think of the huge exhale we would hear. But instead, our popular culture sends a radically different message: "Perfect parents produce perfect children; wayward parents reap what they sow." And so it is that, along with the *sturm und drang* over whether mothers should work outside the home, parents are also bombarded with an encyclopedia of advice about all the things they can do to raise successful progeny. Sign your kids up for the soccer team in the fall and Little League in the spring. Make sure they start piano lessons by age three. Buy them the high-end laptop. Put them in SAT tutoring in tenth grade. And don't forget the Chinese lessons.

On TV, Dr. Phil and Dr. Laura (not to mention a scad of lesser lights) scold parents on a daily basis. Every bookstore has aisles devoted to the topic of rearing kids the right way. And consider the magazine features devoted to Britney Spears's mothering skills or the reality shows that shine a spotlight on dysfunctional parenting styles. I myself will admit to an occasional evening with the series *Wife Swap,* which, despite its prurient name, is nothing of the sort. Rather, it's a moralistic cautionary, in which two families exchange mothers for a week, only to see mayhem erupt as disparate values collide.

The pressure to turn out super-children can afflict even resistant mothers who claim to place a high value on character. I confess! For years, I walked around saying I didn't care about my kids' grades and other credentials as long as they were "good human beings." But you should have seen me when Roscoe was competing in the national high school wrestling championships. I was cheering so hard for him to win, Jack practically had to revive me with smelling salts after every match. And when Roscoe ultimately lost in the sixth round, I literally had to lie down.

Afterward, a psychiatrist friend of mine gently helped me understand my ghastly behavior. "Mothers these days compete with each other by keeping score with their children's successes," he said. "Given society's fixation on how to raise perfect children, it's nearly impossible not to."

He then urged me to call Roscoe and apologize for my sullen moping around when he decided to retire from wrestling in college. I definitely plan to get around to that very rational edict . . . someday.

A SEAT AT THE TABLE

As if the debate over child-rearing wasn't fraught enough, there's yet another complicating factor in the mix. The command-and-control model of parenting, where "father knows best" and everyone else shuts up, is long gone. Most kids today think they're adults by age fourteen or fifteen, and inasmuch, expect a seat at the decision-making table.

What's the source of this presumption? Surely it stems from the fact that modern kids know more about life at an earlier age than did children of generations past. How could they not? You can try to turn off the TV and outlaw the Internet in your house, but good luck banishing all forms of media unless you're living in a cult compound. I tried diligently to keep my home G-rated for years; I'm somewhat embarrassed to say I even banned *The Simpsons* for about a nanosecond because I feared it was too subversive. But I gave up the ghost in 1998 when Sophia, then nine years old, took one look at a photo of Monica Lewinsky in the newspaper and, with more insouciance than a mother might like, opined, "What's the big deal? It wasn't real sex."

I don't want to sound like a cranky old lady here, decrying the lost youth of "kids these days." I can see one perfectly legitimate reason why teenagers now believe they're grown-ups — so many of their role models are doing adult things. We live in an economy where Mary-Kate and Ashley Olsen, once sitcom starlets, were running a multimillion-dollar enterprise before they finished high school. Miley Cyrus, heroine of the adolescent set, and Lil' Bow Wow, the teen rapper, are staples of the music industry. If these young people have adult supervision, it's usually kept out of sight.

But in the real world, most adults do stay on the scene. And because that scene is more complex than ever before, 10-10-10 is that much more relevant, lowering the cacophony of commentary from experts, scolds, fellow parents, and your kids themselves by helping you make choices based upon your own deliberately selected parenting values. It provides a framework and a shared language to bring our children into the decision-making process without undermining their essential independence. In sum, 10-10-10 produces the kind of decisions that parents in this era need and kids want: grounded, consistent, and transparent.

Mean Girls

Rick, a single father from Minneapolis, found himself in a painful parental dilemma when a rude wake-up call — literally — alerted him to the fact that his fifteen-year-old daughter was spiraling away from him.

Tina played on the school soccer team and received decent grades, but her hobby, according to Rick, was "clique warfare." She would spend hours each night on the computer, gossiping on Instant Messenger and starting catfights with other girls. Rick hated the behavior but felt helpless to stop it. "I told myself that all teenage girls acted like Tina," he recalls. "I thought her meanness would stop."

It didn't, and a few weeks later, the mother of Briana, one of Tina's targets, called Rick and angrily demanded he do something. Rick was mortified, not just by the details of Tina's Facebook posts about Briana, which Briana's mother read to him, but by the fact that Tina seemed to be preying on Briana because she had a speech impediment.

"I was raising a daughter whose character was getting really ugly," Rick told me.

He turned to 10-10-10 to formulate a course of action, first surveying his options. He could punish Tina by taking away her computer access or he could send her to therapy to get at the root of her behavior, though he worried about the cost of the latter. Or he could concede to Tina's intermittent suggestions that she live with her mother, who, after a long struggle, was finally sober.

Next, Rick revisited his values. He regretted the emotional damage caused by his divorce and felt strongly that his children should be raised in the same household. Together, they had a family; apart, they had none. He also had a strong desire to teach his children his own midwestern values of humility and common sense.

Rick knew that he couldn't make his decision alone. Tina, like most teenagers, believed she had as much say in the particulars of her life as he did, if not more. He set aside an hour with Tina for a 10-10-10 conversation.

The talk lasted twice as long. When it got contentious — which it did more than a few times — Rick steered the discussion back to the 10-10-10 framework. If Tina, for instance, began to revisit old territory, Rick would redirect her by saying something like, "Let's look out at ten months." Finally, father and daughter settled on terms that they could both live with. Tina would remain with Rick and keep her computer access. They also decided it was worth it for Tina to enter therapy to work on her aggression toward Briana and other vulnerable girls. But before that even started, they agreed, Tina would write a note of apology to Briana and invite her over for dinner.

"Together we found the best solution for all three time frames," Rick reflected recently. "Because my focus was on getting Tina back on track so she would stop damaging people around her, I knew there had to be repercussions for her actions in the immediate term, as well as counseling for her underlying issues in the mid- and long term." He admitted that he was surprised and pleased by the insights Tina added to the conversation. For example, it was her idea to write Briana an apology, and she also suggested that perhaps her longtime association with another well-known "mean girl" should end. "There was no way Tina would have bought into any solution," Rick concluded, "if she hadn't been part of the process of reaching it."

BEYOND THE CALL OF DUTY

Rick's trauma with Tina was trying while it lasted and certainly gave Rick more than a few moments of bona fide, bone-chilling concern. But at its essence, it was the normal stuff of parenthood. Our kids step outside the lines; we nudge them back in. They step out again, we nudge a bit harder. Most days, raising our kids is simply a matter of making sure they live by the golden rule of Do Unto Others. They test; we correct.

Unfortunately, however, there are times when parenting goes far beyond the ordinary. Indeed, along the way, every parent faces a truly major crisis . . . or two or three. A teenage pregnancy. A drunk-driving arrest. Anorexia.

For Ana, a mother of three in the Detroit

suburbs, the crisis was drugs.

Ana's son Bobby started smoking marijuana at thirteen. By seventeen, he had dropped out of school and was living with other drug users in a party house in the city, a move that sent shock waves through the tight-knit family. Ana's daughter, Kara, who was eleven at the time, lost her focus in school, and her eight-year-old son, Brian, withdrew into video games. Eventually, both kids dragged their mattresses into the basement to get away from the noise of their parents' nightly fights over Bobby's situation. Ana wanted to do everything to save her son; her husband, Gary, a metal worker in an automobile factory, wanted to disown Bobby and throw away the key.

For five years, Bobby came and went in his family's house, staying only a few days at a time and invariably wreaking havoc. He stole money and sometimes punched Brian without provocation. The family continued its routine of school and work, but behind closed doors, nothing was normal. Bobby and Gary never spoke a word to each other, but their mutual hatred was palpable. Kara and Brian seemed to lead their lives in an invisible universe, coming and going on tiptoe. And yet, Ana repeatedly welcomed

Bobby home, relieved to have him off the streets.

The situation finally came to a head when Bobby was twenty-three and Gary told Ana that if Bobby ever moved back in again, he would move out.

Ana's first reaction was fear. How would she support herself? What would happen to the kids? But soon anger rushed in too. Why was her husband making her choose between himself and their child?

In her turmoil, Ana was haunted by one question: What if Bobby died? She considered the piles of books stacked on her bedroom dresser, each full of advice on handling family members with addiction. One counseled her to have Bobby arrested for trespassing if he returned home, another argued that a mother should never "go negative" on a troubled child.

Ana needed to hear her own voice. Alone in her room one night, she turned to 10-10-10, and with it she discovered she had a powerful emerging value. She had to rescue Kara and Brian from the silent despair she had so long tried not to see. Her only choice was to draw them back closer to her, to give them hope for the future, and instill a sense that they had a mother who cared not just about her eldest son, but about them as well. It had been ages since she had attended one of Kara's softball games or asked Brian about his homework. And she couldn't even remember the last time she had asked either child to return to their old bedroom from their basement retreat.

Now, facing the question of whether she should allow Bobby to come home again, she considered her options — and their consequences — in ten minutes, ten months, and ten years.

In the first time frame, Ana reasoned, she simply couldn't let Gary walk out. His absence would destroy Kara and Brian, and undermine any chance of rebuilding the family they all so desperately needed to move forward.

In ten months, if she devoted herself to Kara and Brian and kept Bobby at bay, perhaps she and Gary could begin to reestablish their trust, and together they could start to create an environment in which their family could reinvent itself.

The ten-year picture was more painful for Ana, but she could no longer ignore it. Time and again, she had tried to rescue Bobby to no avail. Ultimately, she knew, he would live or die not because of her actions, but because of his own. The greatest gift she could give him — and her family — was a closed door.

That night, Ana told Gary of her decision to heed his wishes. In return, she asked him to join her in realizing her own dream of bringing Kara and Brian back into the fold.

When I checked in with Ana not long ago, she told me Bobby had spent time in jail for drug possession and was currently working through a court-ordered rehabilitation program where she was able to visit him once a month. And yet, she sounded optimistic about her family's future, whether Bobby would be able to rejoin it or not. She mentioned Gary's plans to take Brian fishing over the summer break and Kara's improved grades.

But what excited her most was a change that had just occurred. Both children, she told me, had moved their mattresses back upstairs.

THE LONG HAUL OF LOVE

After I got off the phone with Ana, I had a real "There but for the grace of God go I" moment. Ana had clearly been a loving mother, yet her son had grown from a precocious toddler, to an errant teen, to a living nightmare. Yes, there were times — and plenty of them — when Ana felt gut-wrenching guilt over her decision to let her eldest son go. But she pushed through her doubt by revisiting the logic of her 10-10-10 thinking and dwelling in its good sense.

Although the details of every crisis differ, all parents with profoundly troubled or otherwise impaired children need a decision-making process to get them through months and even years of challenges, a process that will withstand the pressures of fear and instinct.

Connor was twelve when his mother, Maggie, began to notice that something about his behavior didn't seem right. While Connor was often funny and endearing — he loved science fiction with a passion and showered love on the family's old dog — he often panicked over getting to the bus on time and he could become positively frantic about the tiniest disturbances of order around the house, such as how his sock drawer was arranged.

For weeks, Maggie watched Connor slip deeper and deeper into a well of anxiety. At last, desperate, she waited for him to leave for school one morning and looked for answers in his diary.

"I need to touch things," one entry began.

Maggie's heart stopped. "I realized I had passed my disease on to him," she told me. "And all I could think was, 'How could I do this? How could I have the hubris to think I could have children?' It was probably the saddest moment of my life."

Maggie's own battle with obsessive-compulsive disorder had started when she was a freshman in college. Two years later, she was also diagnosed with depression. Regardless, with herculean effort, she went on to build a successful career in advertising. And today she considers it one of her life's great victories that virtually no one knows of her daily battle with what author William Styron called "The Darkness Visible."

At the news of Connor's diagnosis, Maggie's impulse was to quit her job. Every day was becoming a logistical nightmare. She'd run to the office in the morning, then rush to pick Connor up at school for a doctor's appointment, bring him back to school, then run to her office again, and finally speed home to meet Connor and her older daughter at the bus. After dinner and homework, Maggie would collapse into bed, physically drained but with her mind racing about how she was going to make it through the next day's schedule.

"I have to stop the bleeding," Maggie announced to her husband Roy one night. "I need to be with Connor all the time."

But Roy wasn't so sure quitting made sense. Maybe, he suggested, a sense of guilt was making Maggie overreact to the situation. He urged Maggie to try 10-10-10, which she had previously used in dilemmas at work, and he volunteered to join her in the process as a sounding board.

Maggie agreed, but somehow, she still couldn't get past the first 10. She was so overwhelmed that stopping work seemed like the only option.

Roy pushed her, however, to imagine the ten-month scenario. Again, the answer felt obvious. "My instinct told me quitting would be great for Connor, *especially* in that time frame," Maggie said. "I could be all over his treatment. I could be all over him. Managing things, helping."

Maggie then moved on to the ten-year picture, with Roy urging her to take it slow and keep her emotions in check. Unexpectedly, that's when Maggie began to have second thoughts, not because she dreaded the long-term impact of quitting on her family and career, but because she couldn't predict it. "I realized I had no idea how Connor would be in ten years, or ten months for that matter," she told me. "A framework like 10-10-10 is only as good as the information you bring to it. And I didn't have all the data I needed."

To move forward, Maggie and Roy arranged a session with Connor's doctors and arrived equipped with a long list of questions about how Connor's condition was likely to unfold over time. It had taken Maggie decades to get her "cocktail" of medication for OCD and depression right. She knew psychopharmacology had become more precise, but feared the same prolonged process for her son.

The doctors, however, surprised Maggie with their optimism. In ten months, given twice-weekly behavioral therapy and medication, Connor would likely be much improved, they said, although his obsessions might never completely disappear. In two years, his disability would probably be invisible to all but his family and close friends. It was fine if Maggie wanted to be at home full-time, the doctors said, but it was not crucial, as long as she and her husband had some flexibility in their schedule to accompany him to occasional appointments.

"I had just expected to hear them tell me, 'Of course, you should be with your child every minute,' " Maggie recalls. "Instead, I realized it would be unhealthy for Connor to think his problem required a crisis response when what it really needed was just daily management, like asthma or diabetes or any other chronic disease."

Maggie's decision is now a year in the past. Connor, now a seventh grader at a large middle school, has good days and bad, with many more of the former. He's even gained enough self-confidence outside the house to take up swimming and join a chess club. "Connor's amazing. He gets how he's different. He's learning to live with it," she says. "We're all learning."

STRANDS OF HUMANITY

What an apt thought. Being a parent *is* about learning every day, never giving up on the challenge of loving and raising our children. Yes, it can be tempting to disengage emotionally from child-rearing, as the consequences of so many of our parenting decisions can take years to play out. And yes, today's cultural maelstrom, with all its conflicting messages, can often make parenting feel completely confounding. Especially when your children themselves step in and say, "I know enough about the world to make my own decisions, thank you."

One winter's evening when Roscoe was a sophomore at boarding school, he noticed that Justin, the awkward freshman who lived across the hall from him, was acting strange. He looked as if he was about to cry; he kept mentioning he was going to sleep early. Roscoe wanted to ignore what he saw. Wrestling practice had exhausted him and he had piles of homework to do.

Still, something was . . . off.

"What's wrong with you?" Roscoe suddenly found himself asking Justin. "Whatever — come to my room, OK? Let's talk."

Years later, Justin described what happened that night in an essay which he read to the school and also shared with me.

"I started crying. I told Roscoe everything. I told him what I was planning to do, about the pills I'd stockpiled. I'm sure he was uncomfortable, but he didn't show it," he wrote. "He told me about how he cried sometimes his freshman year. He told me how he had felt lonely and slightly geeky too. And then Roscoe sat next to me and hugged me with his hand on my head and asked me to be happy, because he would always stick up for me. I noticed our friendship for the first time, the string connecting Roscoe and me, and then I saw them all, all the connections I had linking me to others.

"I realized that I couldn't cut all the strings from me without cutting someone else. My loneliness was tethered back by so many strands of humanity."

Sometimes our children teach us how to make decisions.

More often, however, it is our job in this noisy, complicated world to teach them how to live, so that they can come to see that each decision is a tether to humanity.

10-10-10 is our partner in that most precious duty.

Chapter Eight: Lean on Me

FRIENDSHIP LOST AND FOUND
WITH 10-10-10

Sue Jacobson and I met for the first time on a tennis court. She was Camp Clear Lake's "Director of Racquet Sports," a hilarious overstatement, given the humble reality of the place; I was to be her "aide." Any kind of hierarchical arrangement between us, however, lasted about five minutes. We just liked each other too much, and before our first week of friendship was out, we were inseparable. During the day, we'd entertain the campers by playing practical jokes on each other. At night, we'd set out in pursuit of Hyannis's greasiest onion rings, driving around for hours on end in Sue's dilapidated convertible, with Blondie and Lene Lovich at full blast.

It was during one such escapade that Sue and I accidentally rear-ended a gang of tough girls from the local high school. We jumped out of our car to apologize, but they weren't having it. They surrounded us.

223

"What's your weird problem?" the leader of the pack demanded to know, leaning ominously into Sue's face. Then, this being Cape Cod in 1978, she and her friends laughed uproariously and drove away.

The bizarre humor of the incident wasn't lost on us, though, and Sue and I immediately adopted the gang leader's question as our personal refrain. "What's your weird problem?" Sue whispered to me as I walked off the stage right after receiving my college diploma. I had the exact same question for her after she received hers.

A few years after college, still close friends, Sue and I both landed in Boston, me at the Associated Press, and Sue as chief of staff for the governor's wife, Kitty Dukakis. The concordance of our careers was serendipitous, and, as ambitious young women working in essentially the same industry, we found more things than ever to talk about. But our friendship remained primarily about laughter, even after I got married and Sue found a serious boyfriend in Michael, a surgical resident at a Boston hospital. Many weekends, we'd still steal away for a drive in Sue's car or a quick run for onion rings at the Howard Johnson's in Kenmore Square.

Then one day in 1984, Sue called me at home. "I can't be your friend anymore," she whispered and hung up. Did I think it was a joke at first? The answer is no. Sue's voice was so different and strange that I knew in the pit of my stomach that she was dead serious.

I had other friends, of course, and I filled the huge hole Sue left with more still, but I never stopped missing her, even after I met Jack, who became the dearest friend of my life. It only made me sad that Jack hadn't known Sue, and when I mentioned that, he would always frown. "There's a reason she went away," he would say. "You just don't know it yet."

A Fragile Necessity

Sue's inexplicable departure from my life was such a blow — a devastation, to be totally candid — that I told myself for years afterward that I would never trust her again, even if she came crawling back to me on hands and knees.

10-10-10 changed that. In time, it empowered me to open my heart to Sue again, and led both of us to understand why we had had to break apart in the first place.

Indeed, 10-10-10 can rescue all kinds of friendships. It can give one or both friends a framework for putting a struggling relationship into perspective, and lay out a road

map for reviving it. It can clarify values —
both those that are shared and those that
may be pulling a friendship asunder. It can
uncover assumptions and hidden expectations, which, unvoiced, can bring a friendship to the brink. And in a crisis, it can help
paint a vivid picture of what it would take
to save a friendship and what it would cost
to lose it.

10-10-10 allows you to decide what kind
of friends you need, and what kind of friend
you want to be.

Because friendship comes in so many va-
rieties, doesn't it? We have friends who have
become dear to us because our paths cross
so often that something simpatico has blos-
somed. Tanya Ntapalis has been cutting my
hair forever. In terms of background, interests, and lifestyle, we have almost nothing
in common, but we've shared every little bit
of our personal histories along the way, from
first dates to divorces. Last year, I attended
the wake of Tanya's beloved Gram. I'd never
met the departed, I told the fellow behind
me when he asked, "but her granddaughter
is a very good friend of mine."

And then there are memory friends, the
people with whom we've shared a seminal
period of our past. My husband still hangs
out with a gang of guys he played ball with

fifty years ago. They talk plenty about politics and the Red Sox, but the old days are never far from the conversation.

If you've ever said, "She's a mommy friend," or "He's a work friend," you know what an identity friendship feels like. And how important they can be. I don't know how I would have survived the early days of child-rearing had it not been for the advice of my mommy clutch — I can still hear Maria telling me, "Just put pizza in the blender, Suzy. The baby will live." Nor will I ever forget how Kim prayed with me when I had run out of hope over Sophia's adolescent antics.

But the best friendships of all, I've found, are those that combine all of the above elements. Your paths cross often enough to keep you current, you have history to ground you, and you have some form of shared identity to sustain you. In this way, good friends can become our most enjoyable and easiest relationships. They don't carry the responsibility of marriage, the stress of extended family, or the angst of raising children.

Ironically, therein lies friendship's inherent fragility. We love and need our friends. We turn to them for solace in times of crisis and rely on their unvarnished advice. But they often take a backseat to the other relationships in our lives. We're not bound to them by blood like our relatives, by legal documentation and cultural expectations like our spouses, or by a paycheck like our coworkers. Friends, practically by definition, can wait.

And when things start to go wrong in a friendship, we can walk away and pretend nothing in our lives has really changed. We can stay in the same house, work at the same job, and go about our daily business without obvious upheaval.

Besides, of course, the upheaval in our hearts.

CONTINENTAL DRIFT

Jeremy met Lucille as he stepped off the elevator on his first day of work at a Las Vegas real estate development firm. New to the job and the city, he was a bundle of nerves. The buttoned-up woman behind the receptionist station only redoubled his anxiety. He politely introduced himself and asked to be directed to his desk.

"Weren't you supposed to be here yesterday?" the receptionist snapped.

Jeremy's stomach dive-bombed — but then the receptionist broke into a huge bolt of laughter. "Welcome, welcome, new guy!"

she cried, coming around to pump Jeremy's hand warmly.

Jeremy came to love Lucille's whole earthy approach, as different as it was from his. At thirty-two, Jeremy had spent most of his life in Fort Lauderdale, living with his parents. At forty-four, Lucille was a self-described "spinster" from a large Armenian family in Brooklyn. But the pair shared a love of White House politics, gossiping each day about news out of Washington. Their rapport was so palpable that some colleagues suspected they were a romantic item, a rumor that became something of an office joke after Jeremy introduced his colleagues to his life partner, Dan.

Lucille and Jeremy's bond grew deeper when Jeremy supported Lucille through the end of a long and troubled affair with a married man. Afterward, Lucille would often spend weekends with Jeremy, Dan, and other friends, who affectionately nicknamed her "The Den Mother."

But even with Jeremy's companionship, Lucille was struggling in Las Vegas. She missed her family back East, and she felt that her job was vulnerable. As a member of the firm's support staff, she knew that if the city's economy started to cool off, she'd be among the first to be let go. And there was another question that kept popping into her mind. By spending all her time with Jeremy, was she "accidentally on purpose" keeping herself out of the dating scene?

"I basically had whiplash," Lucille recalls of that period. "Obviously, I was never going to have kids, but I still had a chance of getting married. But to get married, I would have to move away from a friend that made me about as happy as I'd ever been."

After a few years of ambivalence, Lucille decided to accept a higher-paying job closer to home, in Hartford, Connecticut. Jeremy and Dan threw her a beautiful going-away party, and Lucille cried openly during Jeremy's touching farewell toast, in which he referred to her as "a friend for now and always."

But in the months that followed her move, Lucille found she just couldn't bring herself to return any of Jeremy's calls or emails. She was afraid of missing him so much that she'd end up hating Hartford, where her new life was slowly warming up. Jeremy wrote her a few times, asking if something was wrong, but finally stopped trying.

Six months passed. Then on Christmas Eve, in church with her family in Brooklyn, Lucille found herself praying to hear Jeremy's voice again. She had so much to tell him about her new job, which was harder but more fun than she had expected; she wanted to get his feedback on a single man at work she liked and who seemed to like her. Overwhelmed by emotion, Lucille went home to her old bedroom, determined to analyze her friendship with Jeremy using the logic of 10-10-10. Could she devote herself to her new life, she wondered, and keep her old friendship too?

In ten minutes, Lucille reasoned, contacting Jeremy was sure to be awkward. She would have to explain and apologize. Would he even forgive her? And talking to him might open up emotional floodgates that would set back her acclimation to her new life. Could she afford that risk?

Lucille then tried to imagine her life in ten months. She was sure to be more settled in her new job. It was in her nature to make her own happiness; self-pity simply bored her. Wouldn't *that* Lucille — the future Lucille — have room for Jeremy in her life?

Finally, Lucille thought about the ten-year consequences of her decision, especially in light of her values. She had always put family and friends first. They were her pride and joy, her comfort and her clan. And Jeremy was among the most treasured of the lot. Why in the world would she let him go? To avoid a little short-term poutiness?

It was past midnight in New York, but still early enough to call Las Vegas. Lucille grabbed the phone and dialed Jeremy's number. "We cried for about a half hour," she told me. "It was just like old times, only sweeter."

Two years have passed since that reconciliation. Lucille and Jeremy now communicate often by email, with updates about their lives, and call each other on holidays and birthdays. Of course, without daily contact and common work challenges, their friendship has changed. It's based more on memories than office camaraderie, but they've brought it back to life.

More memories are sure to be made.

VALUES DRIFT

Jeremy and Lucille's friendship hit a rough patch because they moved apart, not an uncommon phenomenon in our mobile world. Just as often, though, friendships hit a rough patch because *values* have drifted apart. The beliefs, goals, and priorities that once brought two people together no longer match, and may even be at odds.

As college roommates in Vermont for four years, Isabelle's and Sarah's lives were so intertwined that some people on campus couldn't tell them apart. They shared clothes, wore their hair the same length, ate at the same table in the dining hall, and attended the same parties. Their only difference, really, was academic. Isabelle majored in studio art, Sarah in math.

After graduation, both women moved to New York City. Isabelle became a conceptual artist, supporting herself with part-time waitress jobs to pay the rent for the small apartment she shared with her boyfriend, a drummer. Sarah eventually became an equities analyst on Wall Street and married a trader. And yet, even with their lifestyles growing apart, a sense of history continued to bind the women. Once every two months or so, with Sarah as the organizer, the couples met for a night of dinner and drinks.

A few years in, however, Isabelle started to find ways to wriggle out of the get-togethers. The problem was Sarah's husband, Bertram. Isabelle considered him a smug control freak, and it bothered her that Sarah was absorbing his conservative political and social views.

The next time Sarah called about dinner, Isabelle waited until she knew Sarah was at work to leave a return message about being unavailable. When she hung up the phone, Isabelle later told me, she felt like "a liar and a skunk."

Isabelle had heard about 10-10-10 from me — we met through a mutual friend — and decided to apply it to her dilemma. She liked that the process could help her look at her friendship through a "values prism" to determine whether her values and Sarah's had diverged too far. She framed her question as, "Should I try to save my friendship with Sarah or let it go?"

Immediately, though, Isabelle hit a roadblock. If she and Sarah didn't share any values, could an authentic relationship exist in any time frame?

"Basically, we're connected by the experiences that made us the women we've become," she told me. "And we have a shared desire to stay lifelong friends. That's like a badge of honor to both of us. But is it enough?"

To explore the answer to that question, Isabelle asked Sarah out for a dinner, just the two of them. Probably sensing the topic, Sarah agreed reluctantly. And in fact, her concerns weren't unfounded. The conversation was painful, even with 10-10-10 as a road map.

In the immediate future, the women agreed, there was no getting around the ever-widening gap in their values. Isabelle admitted that she didn't like Bertram. Sarah blurted out that she thought Isabelle's boyfriend was a "slacker." Isabelle told Sarah that her high-paying job had made her insensitive to the struggles of the under-privileged. "My high-paying job allows me to give more to charity than you ever will," Sarah shot back.

The dinner might have ended right there had there not been a process to keep the friends at the table. They proceeded to the next step, which was a consideration of the ten-month picture. Letting the friendship go, the women conceded, would remove a source of ongoing discomfort from both of their lives. Isabelle confessed that she had lied in her phone message about dates. Sarah replied, "And you thought I didn't know?"

But then Sarah reminded Isabelle that they had a college reunion coming up. "Should we just ignore each other there?" she asked pointedly. "Like every other pair of old friends that couldn't keep it going? I thought we were stronger than that."

A long silence lingered between the women.

"Let's be real," Isabelle said at last. "In ten years, you'll be living in the suburbs driving a BMW, and I'll still be living in Astoria, scraping by."

Sarah could only nod. She and Bertram were already looking for a house in Westchester County.

"How about this? What if we hang in there for the next couple of years and see where it goes? I love you. I love what we've lived through together," Isabelle went on. "Maybe the fact that we can be friends, despite our differences, could be a source of real pride for us."

The idea gave Sarah the first flutter of hope she'd felt all evening. She too knew the relationship had an iffy long-term future, but losing it in the midterm felt premature to her.

By the end of the evening, the women had decided that they would work together to respectfully acknowledge that their sensibilities were no longer parallel. They could start to see each other once a year or so to renew the shared goal of maintaining an authentic bond. It would be a nice night out, they agreed — alone.

Since that decision, Isabelle reports, "What Sarah and I have now — it's such a relief. We don't have to tiptoe around each other. The air has cleared. We're both looking forward to making it work in a new way."

Even with new terms, however, not all friendships can be saved. There's been an injury of some kind: an unpaid loan, say, or one rude remark too many. I know two women who, after thirty years of friendship, stopped speaking when their sons became entangled in a legal dispute.

More often, though, friendships end because staying together would just hurt too much. At such a juncture, 10-10-10 can help to clarify the reasons for parting, alleviate guilt, and bring a needed sense of closure.

I first met with Angela, a social worker in Baltimore, because I'd heard she had a great 10-10-10 story about buying a house. And she did. In fact, her house 10-10-10 story was such a good example of the process that for our first two hours together, that's all we talked about. Angela described how, with her thirtieth birthday looming, she had decided that the time had come to move out of her parents' place. When two different realtors failed to find the house she was looking for, Angela's relatives kept telling her she needed to be guided in her real estate search by a midterm horizon, not a long-term one. But Angela wanted to buy a home she would live in forever.

"You know, a lot of women wait for their knight in shining armor," she told me. "I wanted to take care of myself. My dream was that no one but me was going to decide my life."

That comment was my first clue that Angela's 10-10-10 decision was not just about real estate.

It was also about real friendship.

In ninth grade, Angela had met Rebecca, and they'd bonded immediately. "We found comfort in each other," Angela reflected. "There was no explaining to do. We both had trouble fitting in, except with each other."

Each girl weighed more than 220 pounds.

Through high school, Angela and Rebecca grew into a two-person universe in which they shared all their time and an ever-darker worldview. "There have been studies of overweight friends that show how they identify with each other and reinforce one another into obesity," Angela said. "Rebecca and I were the perfect example." The young women decided to live at home after high school and attend the same community college. After graduation, both took jobs nearby.

Just after Angela turned twenty-five, her father's health took a turn for the worse.

Her sister was married and couldn't be around all the time, and her elderly mother needed help. There was no other option. Angela took a leave of absence from work to assume the majority of caretaking for her father. But her weight made every chore difficult. She was almost physically unable to feed her dad, take him to doctor appointments, or put him to bed.

One morning, Angela had an epiphany: "People need me here," she thought. It was time to dedicate her life to losing weight and becoming healthy. She immediately called Rebecca. "I'm going to lose weight, this time for real. Are you in?" she asked.

Rebecca said she was, and that afternoon, the friends drove to a local Weight Watchers center. But it was soon clear that Rebecca's heart wasn't in the project. As Angela's weight started dropping and her resolve intensified, Rebecca grew angry, frequently challenging Angela with the assertion, "I don't know you anymore."

Bit by bit, over the course of eighteen months, Angela started to let go of old patterns. For years, she had spent every evening snacking in front of the TV at Rebecca's house. Now she started taking long runs through their neighborhood and lifting weights at a local gym. Her weight dropped to 200 pounds, then 180, then 160. At the same time, she decided to pursue a longtime fascination with Buddhism — she had been raised as a Catholic — and eventually joined a temple in the next town. Still, for the sake of their friendship, Angela continued to spend most of her time with Rebecca. They watched their favorite old shows and rented movies, but conversation was becoming increasingly difficult. Food and clothing became off-limit topics, and Rebecca forbade Angela from talking about her exercise routine.

In silence, Angela reveled in how her life was changing. She reached her goal weight — 150 pounds — and ran a mini-marathon. With her new vitality, she was better able to help her father, whose health had also improved, and they started to take walks together in a city park they loved. Angela's emergent self-confidence spilled over into her job as well, and one day she asked her boss for a small promotion. To her delight, she got it on the spot.

Angela kept the news from Rebecca for weeks, anticipating a negative reaction, but even without knowing of the promotion, Rebecca's criticism of Angela continued to heighten. Then one day her phone calls stopped all together. "I knew Rebecca was trying to force my hand," Angela told me.

It was a decision that Angela had been dreading. In the immediate future, she knew, breaking things off with Rebecca would be a blessing and a curse. Gone would be the constant low-level antagonism, but so too would be the one true friend she'd ever had. There were many wonderful things about Rebecca she would miss — her witty sarcasm and the way she never judged Angela's family, in particular her emotionally remote mother.

In ten months, the picture wasn't much more promising. Angela worried about her ability to make new friends; she still thought of herself as the "fat girl" in the room. Without Rebecca, there might be months or years of nights and weekends alone.

But it was the more distant future that most captured Angela's imagination. "When I thought about the ten-year time frame, and I saw the life I was working so hard to create, I knew Rebecca wasn't going to be in it," Angela said. "She couldn't be; her whole set of values was too different from mine. She was right. I had changed."

The next evening, sitting in Rebecca's familiar kitchen, Angela urged her friend for the last time to join forces with her, but Rebecca instantly grew disgusted. "You're making me hate you," she warned. Not wanting to end their long friendship in acrimony, Angela quietly left the house.

In the aftermath of that parting, Angela endured some lonely times. There were moments when the comfort of Rebecca's friendship and their old lifestyle beckoned. But a fragile bond had been broken, and there was no chance of repair.

Angela poured her energy back into house-hunting, and finally her journey came to an end. She found a small condo that needed some repair, but reinventing the place from the boards up appealed to her. Today, she has built an active life around her new home — a "sanctuary," as she calls it — and often entertains her nieces and nephews there.

"Thinking about Rebecca still makes me very sad sometimes," Angela told me recently. "But my life went on."

Of course it did. When a meaningful friendship dies, just as when a marriage ends, eventually we all pick ourselves up. We can be damaged. We are invariably changed. But if we can make some kind of sense of the past, it is in our nature to face the future again, believing we are stronger and wiser for what we have experienced.

STARTING OVER

I too tried to move forward when my friendship with Sue Jacobson ended. But instead of feeling stronger and wiser, I mainly felt confused.

Then one summer day in 2002, I received a letter. I recognized my old friend's handwriting on the envelope immediately and ripped it open. "Dear Suzy, I don't know if you will remember me, but if you do, I want you to know that I am sorry," the note read. "Please let me explain." At the end was an email address.

I rushed to my computer. "Well, well, well, what a surprise," I typed. I wanted to sound cool, invulnerable.

But Sue's reply was open and direct. She told me that she had married Michael, the surgical resident, and that they had had two children. Over the years, she said, she had watched my life through the media, often reading my articles in *HBR.* "I was always rooting for you," she wrote.

Five minutes later, we were on the phone.

"I'm going to tell you what happened," she began, "but you have to promise not to hate Michael."

I couldn't imagine what Sue was talking about. When I had known Michael — albeit briefly — he had been a very square, very mild-mannered guy.

"All right," I assured her.

"Because Michael is a great man and a great husband, and I don't want you hating him."

"I said OK —"

"But back when we were dating, our friendship scared him. I would jump whenever you said jump, and we spent all our time together, and we had all those inside jokes too, like —"

"Our friendship *scared* him?" I interrupted her to ask.

"Listen, he told me it was him or you, Suzy," she said. "And I chose him."

For a long time, I was silent. Then Sue asked, "Are you going to hang up?"

"No!" I cried. I wasn't angry — I was relieved. Of all the explanations I had imagined, Michael feeling threatened by me was not among them. Yet it made perfect sense. He had been trying to build a meaningful relationship with Sue — a sacred, authentic thing, the kind of "third force" I spoke of earlier in this book — and I was interfering.

"What a good husband Michael must be" was all I could think of to say.

I asked Sue if I could think about her proposal to rekindle our friendship. She said sure, I could take all the time I wanted, as long as I didn't take enough time to do something stupid, like not call her back. "I am assuming you still have a weird problem," she ventured.

"Not one as big as yours," I replied, laughing despite myself.

Over the next few days, I thought about Sue nonstop. My gut was all over the place. Even with her good explanation — she'd made a values-driven choice I truly respected — I didn't think I could trust her anymore. On the other hand, I loved her zany personality and her smarts about everything from politics to family relations. After eighteen years, the idea of having a beer together was completely thrilling.

I turned to 10-10-10.

In ten minutes, I knew that trying again promised daunting unknowns. We would have to catch up. We would have to heal. And perhaps hardest of all, we would need to learn to trust each other again. Yes, *each other*. Did I forget to mention that in our phone call, Sue asked, "Why didn't you ever try to call *me?*" It was a legitimate question. Perhaps our friendship could never get over an injury as deep as the one we had inflicted on it ourselves.

In ten months, though, the awkwardness

might be fading. We might even find common ground once again.

And in ten years — well, imagine that, I thought. We would be in our fifties. Our kids would be grown and we'd have plenty of time to tool around in my red Jeep looking for greasy onion rings. Our summer haunts, it turned out, were an hour away from each other.

I had nothing to lose by reconnecting with Sue, I decided, and an inimitable friendship to regain.

Our reconciliation ended up being remarkably swift. We arranged a visit and then another and another. We laughed as easily as ever and still shared many of the same sensibilities, but we had a new bond too. We both had happy marriages and demanding children, and we both spent the better portion of our days trying to figure out how to balance them with our active careers.

Our reunion, to be sure, was made easier when our husbands hit it off swimmingly, as did our kids. But at the center of our renewed friendship, it's still just the two of us, helping each other live with joy, not to mention perspective. Not long ago, when my son, Roscoe, and Sue's daughter, Elizabeth, were both applying to college at the same time, we pinged emails back and forth probably twenty times a day. "The guidance counselor won't look me in the eye. He knows she's not getting in. We're screwed," Sue would write, to which I would respond, "*We* are screwed. Roscoe just got a B-plus in Chinese. These stupid colleges only take kids with all As. I hate them. They don't deserve my son." And Sue would swiftly click back to me, "Let's kill ourselves together tonight."

In person, we've had even more fun. Last winter, we took our kids — all six of them — Christmas shopping at the mall. At one point, I steered the entourage into a dress store. But Sue was on to me in an instant. "Oh no, you don't," she whispered. "Not again. You can't make me do it."

"Oh come on, Sue," I pleaded. "Just try this." I pulled a tight little beaded number off the rack.

"Stop it!" she cried, grabbing the dress out of my hand and hanging it back up. "For God's sake, what is your weird problem?"

I took a long look at Sue's sensible shoes, and made a face that she knew all too well.

"What is *your* weird problem?" I naturally replied.

ALONE OR TOGETHER

Ah, friendship. The great, fragile, voluntary necessity of our lives. Ralph Waldo Emerson was right. A good friend is a "masterpiece of nature," rare and wondrous. The songwriter Bill Withers, perhaps a poet of lesser distinction, was on to something too. We all do need somebody to lean on.

Some friendships of course find their natural ending, like that of Angela and Rebecca. Others hum along without a blip for decades, like Jack and his high school pals. But in most every life, there are meaningful friendships that hit a crossroads, and we must decide whether to go forward alone or together.

It is at those turning points that 10-10-10 helps us see how our friendship's underlying dynamics have shifted, and as important, whether those changed dynamics can, and should, be overcome.

As soon as I finish writing, I'm going to give Sue a call.

I have a question to ask her.

And I know she has the same one for me.

Chapter Nine:
The Mistletoe
Dart

SOME THOUGHTS ON 10-10-10
AND THE CIRCLE OF LIFE

There have been two times in my life when I've felt as if I've just fallen through a trapdoor, my eyes blurry, my heart in my throat, my whole everything suddenly tumbling into a vast unknown.

The first occurred fifteen years ago when, with my marriage long gone in all but pretense, I saw a little "+" sign on a pregnancy test stick, and the second more than a decade later, when my mother's surgeon called to say, "Suzy, I'm sorry, but something has gone very wrong."

Beginnings and endings are petrifying.

Sure, some people greet a baby's arrival with serene composure and face the loss of a loved one with sage equanimity. But for most of us, most of the time, the seminal experiences of birth and death can bring us to our knees, even literally. They can rob us of our equilibrium; they can fill us with fear and confusion.

And our decisions often show for it.

The day I found out I was pregnant with Eve, I made one of the most costly judgment calls of my life — to keep on keeping on, chirpily, as if nothing was the matter in my house. If my beautiful baby was going to be born into a "regular" family, I told myself in a private panic, I had no other choice.

For the next five years, we all paid the price of my stubborn decision to stay married, as our family painfully unwound in slow motion. Today, a lot older, somewhat wiser, and finally the authenticity adherent I should have always been, I know that 10-10-10 could have intervened on our behalf.

Because 10-10-10 surely has a special role to play at beginnings and endings, when our emotions are at their most attenuated and our reasoning at its most vulnerable. When a baby is born or a dear one dies, sometimes all we know for certain is that nothing will ever be the same again. At such times, 10-10-10 can guide us through to that new future — a future that we purposefully build.

To Have or Have Not

The roller-coaster emotionality of having a baby can actually begin long before conception.

It can start, in fact, with the very decision to have one, a topic that has the power to surface (or at least aggravate) every suppressed issue in a relationship. How committed are we? What kind of life do we want? Which one of us will work and how much? What role will our families play in our lives? How much freedom does each of us want?

A few years ago, after speaking about 10-10-10 to a group of MBAs, I was approached by a woman in her late twenties named Pam, who was working as a manager at a computer company and earning her degree at night. Pam's bearing was serious and intense — crisp blue suit, hair in a tight bun — but her expression betrayed more than a little free-floating anxiety. She needed an answer, it seemed, and soon enough, I found out to what. "Should I have a baby now," she asked me urgently, "or wait until after I'm promoted in two years?"

Pam's voice dropped and, in whispers, she gave me a quick rundown of all the circumstances complicating her decision. Her husband, a partner in his family's Greek restaurant business, wanted a baby immediately and believed it was a mother's duty to stay home with the children. But Pam loved her job, dreamed of a high-powered career, and wasn't sure she wanted a baby, *ever.* "I wish we had discussed this before we got married, but we were too in love," Pam said. "Guess I just figured it would work itself out."

She exhaled in a way that made her desperation palpable. "What does 10-10-10 say?" she wanted to know.

I reminded her that every 10-10-10 process starts with a survey of our personal values.

"Well, I know *mine,*" she blurted out in response. "They're just not the same as Theo's — or his mother's. Or his father's. Or his sister's! I am not pumping out babies for ten years and then going to work behind some cash register."

And at that moment, Pam knew, as did I, that the baby debate in her household was a symptom of a larger problem.

We both knew too that her 10-10-10 decision was already made. She only needed the courage to live by it.

IT'S ALL IN THE TIMING

Obviously, many couples are in sync about their values. But even then, they can disagree about when to bring a baby into their lives.

Ajitha and Rohan, you might recall, were eager to have a second child once their marriage was restored by Ajitha's 10-10-10 decision. But another 10-10-10 analysis, conducted together, suggested that they needed to wait.

"In ten minutes, we both felt that a new baby would be like a symbol of our renewed strength," Ajitha told me. "That whole feeling really got us going, 'Let's just do it! Let's have a baby right away.'" When the couple looked at the ten-month and ten-year scenarios, however, their enthusiasm was tempered by their professional challenges and goals. "A baby in the next few years, frankly, would be very hard," Ajitha said. "Neither of us wants to sacrifice our career."

10-10-10, ultimately, has impelled the couple to come to terms with the fact that, at some point, one of them will have to bend if their daughter Laya is to have a sibling. They haven't decided which one of them that will be yet, or when, but 10-10-10 has kept the dialogue open and focused on their shared purpose: a welcome addition to their lives.

GOING IT ALONE

Sometimes a 10-10-10 decision not only helps us decide when to have a baby, but with whom.

Divorced twice and nearing forty, Jerri, a dental hygienist I've known for almost ten years, thought she was dating the perfect man. Nick was also divorced, with custody of his two teenage boys and a steady job in construction.

But after a year, the couple started bickering. At first, it was about little things like scheduling, but soon the fights started to extend into larger issues, like the boys' behavior.

Finally, the relationship came to a crossroads you might not expect. Nick asked Jerri to marry him. A solid commitment, he said, would solve their problems.

Excited and flustered, Jerri agreed.

Yet the quarreling continued.

One day Jerri asked me if I could 10-10-10 a question with her: Should she marry Nick right away or wait a year to give herself more time to plan the event?

We had barely made it through the consequences of the ten-minute scenario, though, when Jerri threw up her hands. "Forget it, we have to get married *now*," she pronounced. "I can't wait any longer for a baby.

I need to be a mother. I'm ready. It's all I want in life."

I pressed her to think of the ten-year implications of that value. She looked surprised for a moment, then answered, "Not good."

Fiercely independent, Jerri had always been a person with a high need for "alone time," as she put it. Moreover, disappointed twice in marriage, Jerri basically didn't trust the institution or the commitment it demanded. "I want to be in charge of my own life, with no one owning me," she said as we continued our 10-10-10. "Nick has one picture of marriage and I have another. I can't bring a baby into that." The realization was especially poignant for Jerri, as she had been raised by parents who had warred incessantly.

With both sadness and relief, Jerri soon ended her relationship with Nick, and today is exploring options to become a single mother through adoption.

"No fancy dress and bouquet," she says, "but I think I'm on my way to my own version of a family — a family that could really work, because it's the family I know that I want."

I had been working as a management consultant at Bain & Company for six months when my boss Andy Wasynczuk called me into the conference room for a performance review. Along with being a great mentor, Andy was a great friend, and I knew before the meeting even began that he was generally happy with my work.

The first half of our conversation went as expected, but then Andy turned to the ways in which I could improve my performance. For instance, Andy suggested, it wasn't a particularly good use of my time to fixate on the aesthetic quality of my PowerPoint slides.

"What's it to you?" I muttered in response. "I'm not paid by the hour."

Stunned, Andy took my comment as a joke and moved on.

"Another thing to think about is your reliance on using regression analysis," he said. "There are other computer tools that work as well and are often more appropriate —"

"You have a *problem* with regression analysis?" I cut him off. "I find that very odd for a person trained as an engineer."

"I don't have a problem with regression, exactly," Andy replied patiently, but then, taking in my petulant expression, he stopped dead in his tracks. "Let's continue this conversation later," he said, sounding mystified. "You're definitely not in receive-mode today."

"Get used to it," I snarled. "This is the *new* me."

Well, it was the *pregnant* me. And while my mood did eventually right itself, my meeting with Andy was my first glimpse into the evil hormone genie that invades your body with conception.

That genie can become positively demented after the baby is born too, especially after it bumps into its best friend and soul mate, exhaustion.

Now, I'm not talking about anything clinical here, like the kind of severe postpartum depression that can lay some new mothers low. Such situations most certainly require professional counseling or pharmaceutical intervention.

No, I'm talking about standard-issue new-baby madness. The kind that makes you say hurtful things to people who care about you and forces you to make decisions as if there is no tomorrow. The kind of baby madness that operates from the assumption that there is only right now, this minute, and you are tired and fat and the house is a mess and no one is helping you and the baby isn't

pooping right. And you are tired and fat —
very tired and *very* fat.

That kind of madness.

AND BABY MAKES THREE

Bethany had wanted a baby for as long as
she could remember, and she spent her
pregnancy in a state of blissful expectation,
readying the bassinet, preparing homemade
organic baby food, and picking out adorable announcements. She and her husband
Juan were especially excited about having
their birth experience at home with the help
of a midwife, avoiding all medical intervention.

But the couple was to learn the first lesson of parenthood when Bethany went into
irregular labor three weeks before her due
date: Babies have their own plans. Santiago
was delivered by an emergency Cesarean
section.

Once she was home from the hospital,
Bethany found that nothing continued to
go as she'd planned. She couldn't get Santi
to latch on during breastfeeding and had to
resort to bottles. Nor did Santi "find a
schedule" as Bethany's baby books had said
he would. At six weeks, he slept all day and
wanted to play all night. And then, when
Bethany thought she couldn't feel any more

exhausted, Santi got a head cold that required medicine dispensed with an eyedropper every two hours, around the clock.

Bethany called Juan at work to report what was happening. "I need you to come home and let me sleep," she said. "I'm begging you, so I can stay up with him all night."

Juan was silent for a long minute. "I guess this means you aren't coming with me," he answered quietly. "Remember, this weekend? It's Julia and Greg's wedding."

Bethany slammed down the phone, practically shaking from fury. Of course she remembered the damn wedding. Julia was *her* cousin after all. But given the circumstances, she had just assumed Juan wouldn't go.

She grabbed her cell phone and typed Juan a text message: "I will never forgive you" is all it said.

Bethany was still in a rage when her mother came by later in the day to drop off groceries. While she was sympathetic to her daughter — Bethany had never looked more bedraggled — her mother urged her to 10-10-10 the situation. They formulated the question as, "Should Juan attend the wedding?" and got started.

In ten minutes, handling Santi alone during the weekend struck Bethany as a burden too heavy to bear. Her mother offered to help, but as Bethany told her, "You cannot be here twenty-four hours a day. Papa needs you."

But Bethany's mother urged her daughter to imagine the weekend without Juan, regardless. Wasn't there any scenario that made his absence tolerable?

"No," Bethany stated flatly, rolling her eyes. "None."

In ten months, her mother asked next, "What will it be like around here if Juan stays home this weekend?"

Bethany caught the drift of her mother's question immediately. As husbands went, Juan didn't demand much. He'd been a great help with Santi, forsaking all of his after-work activities, including going to the gym, his favorite way to unwind. If Bethany demanded he miss the wedding as well, his resentment might linger indefinitely. By contrast, if he went to the wedding, he might find renewed energy to help Bethany in the coming weeks and months.

Bethany and her mother turned to the ten-year picture. "That's too far off to matter," Bethany dismissed the notion. "Santi will be going to school. We'll have other kids. I'll be sleeping again. Everything will be normal."

All at once, she laughed at her accidental eureka. "And this crisis will be a distant memory," she said. "I must be making it into something so big because I'm so worn out."

An idea occurred to her just as the phone rang. It was Juan, calling to plead his case again. "I have a better idea," Bethany replied, surprising him with her sudden brightness. "Why don't we go with you? Everyone wants to meet Santi, and God knows he can stay up all night dancing with us."

Just hearing the plan out loud thrilled Bethany. "Santi is managing us," she told Juan. "We have to manage him. We have to bring him into our life, instead of the other way around."

"I love it," Juan cried.

In her changed physical and emotional state, Bethany had been living in the moment, every moment. But with 10-10-10's help, she began to see how things could change if she took it upon herself to forge the shape and feel of those moments, for the days, months, and years ahead.

FROM SNARKY TO SUBLIME

Maybe I sound like I have amnesia. My oldest child is twenty now, the youngest fourteen. It could be that I've forgotten how hard caring for a new life makes it to think about creating a deliberate one for yourself.

Or maybe I've just earned my perspective.

When Sophia was a baby, she was so easygoing that we called her our little Buddha. She never fussed, she never cried. She slept through the night when she was two weeks old. When she was done nursing, she used to look up at me with a dreamy smile, as if to say, "Nice going, Ma."

But she made up for lost time as a teenager. Of course she did. Once, at age fifteen, she was so errant — she has forbidden me from sharing the specifics — that I sat on the living room sofa for two hours and cried nonstop. Big, heaving stuff too. It wasn't the last time. By seventeen, though, she was back to being the Buddha again, a poised and thoughtful student, a constant friend, a mature and loving daughter.

Eve was the surliest baby you've ever seen — so grouchy, tough, and snappish it was as if the word "snarky" was invented for her. Even Abby, the sweetest dog in the world, couldn't take her constant pestering. In her only moment of canine misbehavior ever, she bit Eve on the face. At the emergency room, as we awaited stitches, a nurse asked if the dog was a problem.

"No," I told her, "the baby is."

But at Eve's last parent-teacher conference, I was informed that "Eve fills every room with light. She's kind and friendly to everyone. She's pure goodness."

"If you only knew her when," I thought to myself.

My friend Marybeth Turner used to fret that her daughter Caroline was sweet but very ordinary. "I'm afraid Ryan got all the talent and brains," she used to say, referring to her older son. "Caroline just sort of floats along in life. I worry about her."

A few years ago, Marybeth put Ryan and Caroline into tennis lessons — Ryan because he showed athletic promise, Caroline because she had nothing going on after school on Thursdays.

One day, waiting in the parking lot for the lessons to end, Marybeth looked up from her magazine to see the tennis teacher frantically tapping on her car window. "Are you Caroline's mother?" he asked. "We've been waiting for you to come in."

"Is there a problem?" Marybeth replied, her heart sinking. "Is Caroline being moved down to beginners?"

The teacher looked aghast. "Have you ever *seen* your daughter play tennis?" he cried.

Today, Caroline is ranked the sixtieth-best tennis player in the United States in the under-twelve category.

Babies have their own plans for you.

But because it's only natural not to think so, 10-10-10 is there to help.

DARKNESS FALLS

One spring day last year, I was driving Roscoe to an eye doctor appointment north of Boston — I will never forget how we were both belting out a Coldplay song along with the radio — when my cell phone rang. It was Jack, and he was weeping. A close friend, far too young and full of life, had died of a heart attack.

At the next exit, we swung around and sped home. I was running up the stairs to find Jack when my assistant intercepted me. "I have very bad news, Suzy," she said softly. Her expression was grave.

"I've already heard," I cried. "Jack called —"

She grabbed my hand. "This isn't about Tim. It's about Valerie," she said. The mention of my old friend's name stopped me in my tracks.

"What?"

"There's been a terrible car accident. Valerie was driving and — I'm sorry, I'm sorry — they're not sure she's going to make it."

The news was too much. "She'll make it," I asserted automatically. "She's my age — and my God, she's strong."

Tragically, Valerie wasn't strong enough.

For the months after that terrible day, our house was filled with the stages of bereavement that, sadly, many of us know too well — shock, denial, anger, bargaining, and finally acceptance. Although the truth is, I still cannot drive by Valerie's house without feeling awash in a wave of disbelief. Her garden is still there — why isn't she?

Death — unfair, unwanted, and so often unexpected — rarely gives us good answers. That is why when it steals away someone we love, we need our family and our friends to help us sort through the confusion in our hearts. And we need a framework for moving forward.

Alice and James met in New York in the late 1980s, she a struggling musician, he a struggling artist. They never expected to get married — James had a severe case of anxiety that took much of his energy — but when Alice found herself pregnant, they took the subway to City Hall and exchanged tinfoil rings. Soon after, Hugo was born, and two years later, a second son, Leo, arrived. Alice took a job teaching music to keep the family afloat while James devoted himself full-time to sculpting.

A shotgun wedding and financial hardship aren't usually harbingers of a happy marriage, but they were for Alice and James. They scraped together enough money to buy a dilapidated loft in the Meatpacking District and delighted in making it their own, fashioning bolts of cheap gauzy fabric into a tent for the boys' bedroom. Alice grew to love her job and began to give private guitar lessons on weekends, taking enormous pride in her role as breadwinner. "I believed the world would someday discover James's talent," she told me.

She was right. After a decade of obscurity, James was signed on by a respected gallery and his work began to sell steadily. Alice quit her job and the family, with the boys then ten and twelve, moved to Greenwich Village. Even with their improved circumstances, however, James's anxiety remained, and his success seemed to exacerbate it. As the pressure to produce more pieces heightened, he started to medicate himself with a mixture of prescription drugs and alcohol.

He died of an overdose one day while Alice was at the supermarket.

For weeks after James's death, Alice felt like she was sleepwalking. She took the boys to school in the morning, watched TV all day, prepared dinner, and made sure the entire family was in bed by nine. "I was filled with rage, I think," Alice recalls, "but I blocked everything just to get by day to day. I had to stay centered for the boys."

About six months after James died, Alice lifted her eyes enough to look at the couple's bank account. The balance shocked her — there was barely enough left to make mortgage payments for the rest of the year.

"What do I do?" Alice found herself asking as she stood outside the bank, the winter's first snow coating her shoulders. She imagined running away to Jamaica, leaving her sons in her sister's care, or maybe taking the boys with her so they could all start over from scratch. Both plans were crazy, she knew, but what plan made sense? Alone in the cold, Alice dropped to her knees on the sidewalk and started to cry.

An elderly woman walking by rushed to her side. "Are you all right?" she exclaimed, lifting Alice by the elbow. "Should I get an ambulance?"

"I need my sister," Alice finally managed

to say, and, handing her phone to the woman, hit speed dial to place the call.

The next morning, Alice and her sons sat in their living room, and with Alice's older sister as a facilitator, considered their future with 10-10-10. Their question: Where do we go from here?

In ten minutes, no one in the family could abide the thought of upheaval. The boys didn't want to leave their friends at school or the home they had known with their father. And Alice insisted that her current emotional state made moving or working impossible.

Softly, Alice's sister injected a dose of reality. The family's financial situation, she said, was precarious.

"How can we stay in our apartment and at our school?" one of the boys wanted to know. Alice wracked her mind for answers. "I could try to sell the sculptures Dad was working on when he died," she said, surprising herself with the idea. "Or we could look for a smaller place to live."

For the next half hour, the family bounced ideas off each other, and for the first time since James died, Alice felt present — in the room and in the moment.

When the conversation started to slow, Alice's sister raised the ten-year scenario. What kind of life, she asked, would the family want then?

Both boys spoke at once. They had already agreed between themselves that they would attend the same college somewhere — maybe in Boston, maybe on the West Coast — and they hoped to backpack through Europe one summer.

As they chatted away, Alice saw something new. Her boys were growing up and moving on. That wasn't wrong. It was inevitable; it was necessary.

But what did that mean for her own life?

She would need to become self-sufficient, Alice knew; that much was obvious. She needed a job. A career.

She had her decision. "It's not a question of if we should change our life," she told her sons. "We have to."

Over the next year, Alice sold some of James's art to shore up the family's finances and returned to her old teaching position. But she was most excited about a new "side" job, consulting to an online music service, a start-up venture.

Just after the first anniversary of James's memorial service, the family sold its apartment and moved to smaller quarters back in the Meatpacking District. The proceeds of the sale, Alice told the boys, would pay for their education for many years to come.

Of course, every loss like Alice's reverberates for years. Even with the help of 10-10-10, Alice and her sons experienced untold hours of sadness and struggle. But Alice no longer allows herself to dwell only on the challenges of the present and the unknowns of the distant future. She keeps her sights on the near horizon, a place where grace and hope seem to mingle.

REGRETTING REGRET

After my friend Valerie's funeral, I was touched by the number of people who came up to thank me for my eulogy. But what most of them really wanted to say, I discovered, was how sorry they were for never telling Valerie how much they loved her while they still had the chance.

One of the hardest parts of living within the specter of death is processing our own feelings of regret.

Jack and I were in Europe on business when my mother's surgeon tracked us down. His call was unexpected to put it mildly; knee replacements are usually pretty straightforward.

My mother had come out of the operation with flying colors. She had chatted with my father and eaten a small meal. But sometime during the night, a blood clot had left her knee and traveled to her brain.

After the surgeon called us with the news, my sister Della took the phone. "Suzy, I'm putting the receiver up to Mom's ear," she wept. "I think she can hear you. I think you . . . may need to say your goodbyes."

With Jack holding me tight, I too wept. "Mama, I love you, I love you," I said, "and I am so sorry for not thanking you more for everything — for everything you did for me. I never thanked you enough."

When Jack and I arrived at the hospital the next morning, my mother was still hanging on. Curled in her bed, overwhelmed by machinery, eyes fastened shut, she already looked gone. My father sat in a chair in the corner, stunned and motionless.

Our vigil was to last three weeks. My mother came and went, and when she came, she was so vague that my siblings and I could only hold her hand to comfort her. She was unreachable.

There were no decisions to be made in that terrible time. The decision would be made for us.

My mother was a fighter.

She still is.

Today, at eighty, she's back playing tennis.

"My knees make me superwoman," she likes to say.

Her knees, and what they almost wrought, taught me about all the decisions I should have made, and didn't, as a daughter. They taught me about all the times I should have factored the irrevocable pain of loss — and the agony of regret — into my thinking. When I use 10-10-10, I think of those things now, when I need to. When decisions involve letting go. When they involve estrangement and forgiveness. 10-10-10, one moment at a time, helps us prevent regret. I know now how hard saying goodbye can be if you live and make your choices as if goodbye will never come.

Thank you, Mom, also for that.

FROM MY BOW

One summer's day when my children were young, I took them to the beach with my older sister Elin and my friend Lori. At the time, Elin's children were already teenagers off doing other things, and Lori was pregnant for the first time. So understandably, the two women could plop themselves down on a blanket to chat and read in the sunshine as if they hadn't a care in the world. Meanwhile, I stood by the shoreline having a heart attack as I watched four little bodies frolic in the choppy surf. "Someone's going to die," I kept thinking. "Right here on my watch, one of my kids is going to be washed out to sea, and then I might as well go in after them, and allow myself to be sucked up by the undertow and die too."

An hour later, when at last I had managed to coax my kids back to the blanket for lunch, I slumped down in a heap to recover for a few minutes.

"What's the matter?" Lori asked. By the sweet tone of her voice, I could tell she was oblivious about the hours of happy torment that awaited her.

"Suzy gets a little nutty when she thinks her children are going to drown," my sister reported.

"Have you no memory?" I snapped.

"I remember it all too well." Elin laughed. "But don't worry. You'll be reading magazines at the beach before you know it."

"I won't know how," I informed her. "I haven't had time to read a book in four years."

Suddenly Lori brightened. "Read poetry," she suggested. "Just as much pleasure in a fraction of the time. I'll send you a few books."

It is to Lori's great credit that she actually did so, and it is thanks to her encouragement that poetry did come to carry and comfort me through the next several years, as my children learned to swim, in more ways than one.

Somewhere in that period, I came upon Marilyn Nelson's poem "Mama's Promise." Lori was right. In the moments it took to read its scant sixty-three lines, I finally knew I was not alone in feeling the bittersweet irony of parenthood: that by giving our children life, we also give them danger, heartbreak, and loss.

"From my hands the poisoned apple," Nelson writes, *"from my bow the mistletoe dart."*

Were it not so. And yet beginnings and endings are part of the human condition. They *are* the human condition.

We are all living; we are all dying. In between, we have the gift of deciding how.

CONCLUSION:
THE HAPPINESS LIST

Three years ago, Jack and I attended a beautiful New Year's Eve party. The host's home was decorated with dozens of twinkling lanterns, waiters swished around topping off glasses, and a jazz band filled the air with sparkly music. Around 10 PM, a bell tinkled for dinner, and we were swept into a grand tent lit by candelabra and festooned with flowers. If there was ever a moment to think "Ain't life grand?" it had arrived.

But then a strange thing happened. As soon as we sat down with our friends — there were eight of us at our table — instead of the oohing and aahing you might expect, one couple shushed us.

"It's crazy, I'm telling you. We've been trying to make a list since last week," exclaimed the wife. "And we can't come up with a dozen people who are really happy." She grabbed a piece of notebook paper out of her shiny evening purse and held it up for all of us to see. It was indeed a list of names, all but two or three scribbled out. "We've been dying to see you guys tonight because we can't believe this," her husband added to explain. "Can any of you name a dozen people who qualify?"

"As *happy?*" Jack asked, incredulous.

"Yes — just that," the wife replied, shaking her head as if she couldn't believe the answer herself. "I dare you. Name twelve people who are actually living the life they want. Come on."

At her invitation, each couple around the table entered into a sidebar conference. Jack's and my list came quickly, but just as quickly, we crossed names off it for one reason or another. Then, just as we were closing in on our quota, a man at the table cleared his throat to get everyone's attention.

"Well, people, I know this will come as a shock to you, but please scratch me off your lists," he said. "I'm not happy. I can't be. I'm Irish." We burst into laughter, but no one disagreed. The speaker was a wonderful person — funny, smart, and dear — but a true cranky-pants, committed to the Hobbesian notion that life is nasty, brutish, and short.

"I'm occasionally happy," his wife offered next, "but I won't be *fully* happy until the kids are settled." She paused as we all nodded empathetically. "And I'm not stressed out about my job. And I've lost fifteen pounds."

The two other couples at the table threw out a few names for consideration, but most were dismissed.

"Too bitter."

"Hates his wife."

"Living the picture."

"Jack's happy," I finally volunteered, to general concurrence. "Yes, he was on our list," the first wife said, waving her little piece of paper.

"And I am," I added meekly, getting the sense that maybe I hadn't made the cut.

Apparently I had. "You're a little intense," the wife said, "but a lot less than you used to be."

In the middle of all this, the soup was served, but none of us seemed to notice. We were engrossed — stymied — by the task of compiling our happiness lists.

Most of us were able to summon up a name or two; one friend volunteered a yoga teacher she knew who lived with her funky artist-husband in a converted barn on her parents' estate north of Boston. But others harrumphed at the choice. Another guest picked himself for the list, but his wife interjected, "When was the last time you slept through the night without the help of a little white pill?"

His sheepish reply: "I have to — otherwise I get up every hour to check my Black-Berry."

Amid the laughter, I suddenly felt Jack straighten. "Jim and Linda are happy," he whispered to me for consideration, naming a couple we knew well. We had just attended the husband's sixtieth birthday party, in fact, a celebration right out of a Norman Rockwell painting.

"OK, we have two contenders!" I announced to the table.

And so it went for yet another half hour or more, each couple struggling to come up with a list of a dozen certifiably contented people. Candidates didn't need to be without battle wounds; they didn't even need to be successful by society's standard measures. They just needed to be, we all agreed, at peace with themselves.

So here's the kicker. By the end of the evening, we'd collectively come up with eleven names. Eleven happy people — out of the hundreds of people we knew from our varied walks of life.

"What a disturbing piece of data," one of our friends summarized as dessert came out and, incongruously, the dance floor started to fill with happy-looking people. "What's going on in this world?"

"Too much pressure," someone said with a shrug. "Technology — it makes everything so fast."

"It's the media," another friend suggested. "You turn on the TV and you see everyone's better house, better car, better job, and better life." He sighed. "The media manufactures envy."

There was a brief lull while we all gazed at each other helplessly.

"Too many decisions, too little time," a voice finally piped up.

"That's it!" I heard myself cry.

Just then, Jack grabbed my hand. "Enough already!" he declared. "I'm officially happy and so's my wife. Come on, everyone, let's dance."

And dance we did until the clock struck midnight and we did what people do at big parties, which is kiss and hug and blither about new beginnings. I'm not complaining; it was a wonderful night. The band was great; my strapless dress stayed up. And when it came time to say goodbye to our friends, we all knew we'd never forget the astonishing conversation we'd shared.

But that night carried extra meaning for me. At the time, I'd shared 10-10-10 with my family and friends; I'd shared it with coworkers and with the readers of my magazine column. But the Happiness List — or, should I say, the difficulty in compiling one — galvanized me to offer 10-10-10 more widely. After all, if complicated decisions were responsible for the scarcity of happiness that we'd hit upon, I had an answer. I knew of an approach to dilemmas that empowered people to create more deliberate, centered, and authentic lives. It wasn't a magic pill or a silver bullet. It required emotional work; it took commitment and candor. But with its simplicity and clarity, 10-10-10 worked.

I'd seen it; I'd lived it. I knew more and more people who were using the idea and seeing their lives transformed.

That night driving home, I resolved to tell their stories.

And so here we are, technically at the completion of that pledge. But this moment hardly feels like an ending to me. If I've learned anything in the process of writing this book, it's that once 10-10-10 is in your life, it's your companion as long as you allow it to work within you and for you.

10-10-10 is still with Antoine, as he continues his life's dream to spread compassion, one welfare client at a time. It's with Ajitha, who recently stopped by my house to tell me how happy her marriage remains. It's with Nancy, who makes decisions every day that allow her to be a wife and daughter in proper measure. It's still with Angela, who recently painted her living room her favorite shade of sunny yellow; and with Maggie, who not long ago welcomed Connor home from three weeks at summer camp, where he had a blast, just like a regular kid.

10-10-10 is of course with me too, helping me live with increasing insight and understanding. It's with my children, as they learn and grow without a magic wand in sight.

In Hawaii, the last thing I ever could have imagined was that sunrise would bring a new idea to change my life. On a strange and wondrous New Year's Eve more than a decade later, I realized that new idea was meant for everyone seeking a way out and a path forward.

If transformation beckons, 10-10-10 is meant for you.

ACKNOWLEDGMENTS

An old friend of mine in publishing once told me, "No one ever finishes a book and says, 'Wow, that was easier than I thought.' "

How right she was. Writing a book is not only harder than you imagine, it requires the guidance, patience, and love of more people than you could ever dream of.

I would like to thank those people here.

First, this book would simply not have been possible without the generosity of spirit, humanity, and candor of the many 10-10-10ers who shared their stories with me. I will forever be grateful to the friends, coworkers, and relatives who opened their hearts to describe how 10-10-10 changed their lives, and to the many strangers who became dear friends in doing so.

This book was shaped, nurtured, and improved immeasurably by the superb editorial team at Scribner: Susan Moldow,

Roz Lippel, Nan Graham, and Samantha Martin.

The chapter on decision making is in debt to the psychologist and author Daniel Goleman; Nigel Nicholson, a professor of organizational behavior at the London Business School; and Stephen Martin, formerly of the department of philosophy at Tufts University. The chapter on values was enriched by the wisdom of Ken Shigematsu, the pastor of Vancouver's Tenth Avenue Church.

Several friends listened to me think aloud as this book came into being, offering invaluable insights and reading drafts of the manuscript as it went from mind to page: Nancy Bauer, Chris Daly, Liz Feld, Bronwyn Fryer, Sue Herera, Betsy Lack, Joe Tessitore, Marybeth Turner, and Rebecca Wasynczuk. I am especially grateful to Tina Brown for her keen feedback and encouragement, and to Rosanne Badowski for her meticulous copyediting and enduring companionship.

Other friends provided great tidings of comfort and joy along the way: Jeremy Bromberg, Brenda Buttner, Pam Goldman, Susan Krakower, Elaine Langone, Linda Robinson, Linda Tullis, Kim McKown Walters, and Jackie Welch. I thank also Sue

Jacobson for sending a constant stream of text messages to keep me centered, and Skye Swett for being my life-support system for the past decade.

My sisters, Elin Kaufman and Della Cushing, blessed me with their unceasing love and support.

My agent Robert Barnett was a steady source of strength and guidance.

I am immensely thankful for the forbearance of the "bosses" at my other jobs as I attended to the work of this one: the *BusinessWeek* editors John Byrne, Ciro Scotti, and Barry Maggs; my good friend and editor at the *New York Times* Syndicate, Michael Oricchio; my editor at *O, The Oprah Magazine,* Mamie Healy; my rock of ages, Janelle Shubert, director of the Center for Women's Leadership at Babson College; and the living saints at Boston Health Care for the Homeless, Cheryl Kane and Linda Wood-O'Connor.

My children, Roscoe, Sophia, Marcus, and Eve, also endured their share of my distraction with all things 10-10-10, but still managed to love me every day, checking in all the time, being funny and good, and bringing me iced coffee exactly when the iced coffee bell went off in my head. I thank them also for letting me share their stories in these pages without too much hysteria and drama.

Finally, I could not have written this book — full stop — without two people.

When I first met my editorial assistant Megan Slatoff-Burke I knew she was smart, but I had no idea how intensely and wonderfully smart she would be. Nor did I know how much I would come to depend on her cogent push back, deft touch with language, and tireless commitment. Megan read every word in this book — a thousand times — and made every sentence and chapter incalculably better. Thank you, Megan, for everything you have done, and will do, in your brilliant career.

Which leaves my husband, Jack.

There wasn't a day — not an hour — during the writing of this book that Jack was not my best friend, most fanatical booster, and toughest critic. As I traveled around the country to interview 10-10-10 practitioners, Jack would always be the first to hear their stories, usually retold by me over a bad cell phone connection, and his enthusiasm never waned. Later, when I locked myself in a little room to write, Jack abided me like no other. He listened to me ruminate; he encouraged me when it felt too hard. He asked the best questions. And he read everything I wrote, red pen in hand. The truth is, he should have been an editor.

It is the greatest blessing of my life to have him as mine.

The employees of Thorndike Press hope you have enjoyed this Large Print book. All our Thorndike, Wheeler, and Kennebec Large Print titles are designed for easy reading, and all our books are made to last. Other Thorndike Press Large Print books are available at your library, through selected bookstores, or directly from us.

For information about titles, please call:
  (800) 223-1244

or visit our Web site at:
  http://gale.cengage.com/thorndike

To share your comments, please write:
  Publisher
  Thorndike Press
  295 Kennedy Memorial Drive
  Waterville, ME 04901

"Raegan Moya-Jones shows entrepreneur hopefuls that it's okay not to know it all—as long as you're willing to do whatever it takes to make your dream a reality."

—Whitney Port, television personality, fashion designer, and author

"Raegan Moya-Jones is a force to be reckoned with. Funny, creative, and full of gumption, *What It Takes* gives you the tools you need to create your own success story." —Tiffani Thiessen, actress

"Raegan Moya-Jones is the definition of a 'girlboss.' I am so inspired by her story!"

—Amanda Saiontz Gluck, creator and writer of Fashionable Hostess

"You might think Raegan Moya-Jones is special: After all, she did found aden + anais (the $100-million baby blanket company) from her kitchen table . . . as a mother of four . . . with no previous entrepreneurial experience. You'd be right. But what makes her special is not just her surprise success story. It is her ability to help her readers seize on the thing(s) that might make us special, too. Take the advice of this outspoken, no-filter, hilarious entrepreneur and she will empower you to see that her secret sauce—no fear, no expectations, grit, and vision— is available to all of us. Drink up!"

—Daphne Oz, author and television host

"In *What It Takes*, Raegan Moya-Jones shares an inspiring story for anyone who wants to change their career, play by their own rules, and build a successful business in the process."

—Rebecca Minkoff, founder and creative director of Rebecca Minkoff LLC

"From the kitchen table to a global stage . . . Add a little determination, sass, Aussie grit, self-belief, and a sense of humor, and dreams come true. Congratulations on achieving enormous success, giving back, sharing the journey, and inspiring others to do the same . . . And, most important, enjoying the ride."

—Deborra-lee Furness, actress and founder of Hopeland

"Raegan Moya-Jones is an outspoken, no-filter, hilarious entrepreneur who will empower you to finally make that leap you've wanted to in your life."   —Beverley Turner, television and radio presenter

"Moya-Jones will inspire you to greatness with a kick in the ass, laugh-out-loud saga of overcoming adversity, and instill in you a renewed belief in yourself that only someone with her energy and vision is capable of. Pour a glass of wine, read this book, and go out and conquer the world."   —Geralyn Breig, founder and CEO of AnytownUSA

"Forget what you think you know about women in business. Raegan is here to surprise and inspire you to write your own rules to achieve your career dreams. She is a remarkable woman with a remarkable story everyone can learn from."   —Rosie Pope, founder and creative director
of the Rosie Pope Maternity clothing store
and lifestyle brand

"Moya-Jones is a force to be reckoned with. Funny, creative, and full of courage and charming sass. *What It Takes* will give you the tools you need to create your own success story."
—Sarah Kauss, founder and CEO of S'well

WHAT

IT

TAKES

WHAT

IT

TAKES

———————

How I Built a

$100 Million Business

Against the Odds

RAEGAN MOYA-JONES

PORTFOLIO | PENGUIN

PORTFOLIO/PENGUIN
An imprint of Penguin Random House LLC
penguinrandomhouse.com

Copyright © 2019 by Raegan Moya-Jones

Most Portfolio books are available at a discount when purchased in quantity
for sales promotions or corporate use. Special editions, which include personalized covers,
excerpts, and corporate imprints, can be created when purchased in large quantities. For more
information, please call (212) 572–2232 or e-mail specialmarkets@penguinrandomhouse.com.
Your local bookstore can also assist with discounted bulk purchases using the Penguin
Random House corporate Business-to-Business program. For assistance in locating
a participating retailer, e-mail B2B@penguinrandomhouse.com.

Library of Congress Cataloging-in-Publication Data

ISBN 9780735214644 (hardcover)
ISBN 9780735214651 (ebook)
ISBN 9780525542865 (international edition)

Printed in the United States of America
1 3 5 7 9 10 8 6 4 2

Designed by Gretchen Achilles

Penguin is committed to publishing works of quality and integrity.
In that spirit, we are proud to offer this book to our readers; however,
the story, the experiences, and the words are the author's alone.

To my family: Anais, Lourdes, Arin, and Amelie Rose,
thank you all for driving me mad, and keeping me sane. The
four of you are my reason for being—my earth angels who make
complete sense to me when most other things around me don't.
Markos, I could not have done any of this without you, despite
the fact that you drive me the most mad of all. Thank you for
being my biggest champion and for putting up with me.

I love you all.

I wrote this book for all the women
who were told they can't
by people who knew they could.

CONTENTS

├────────┤

WHAT
IT
TAKES

INTRODUCTION

──────

Y ou just don't get it!" my boss hollered, cutting me off midsentence. "You don't have an entrepreneurial bone in your whole body!"

My boss—let's call him Jack—and I were having a heated discussion about some restructuring of the divisions within the company. Among other changes, Jack had just replaced a longtime editor—I'll call her Jill—at one of the magazines and given her a new, far less prestigious title (not unlike letting an ousted CEO call herself an "honorary chairwoman" in order to save face). What killed me as I sat there listening to him ramble on was that he kept talking about how "thrilled" Jill was with her new position, what a "great opportunity" this was for her future.

As if anyone has ever been thrilled about getting demoted.

Any other day, I might have been offended by his comment. On that day, however, I had to bite my lip to keep from smiling. Because there was something else I knew that Jack didn't: I had secretly been running a business at night (actually, in the wee hours of the morning, long after I'd put my daughters to bed) for two years. I was only a week or two away from announcing my resignation to pursue the business full time.

And at the time of Jack's dressing down, my fledgling company had just hit revenue of $1 million.

Today, aden + anais, the swaddling blanket and baby-goods company I cofounded with a friend and just $15,000 in initial start-up capital, is a thriving global business. Beyoncé, Jennifer Garner, DJ Khaled, Chrissy Teigen, Priscilla Chan, Channing Tatum, Pink, Gwen Stefani, Neil Patrick Harris, and the Duke and Duchess of Cambridge are customers. aden + anais has offices in New York, the UK, and Japan. The company sells more than two thousand products in sixty-eight countries around the world, with revenue in excess of $100 million.

I'll also go ahead and mention that aden + anais was named to the *Crain's New York Business* "Fast 50" list in 2013, 2014, and 2015. Guess who went on to become a C-level executive at *Crain's*? My old boss, Jack, the man who basically told me I had no idea how to run a business. (Oh, and one last jab at Mr. You-Don't-Have-an-Entrepreneurial-Bone: In 2014, I was named an Ernst & Young Entrepreneur of the Year.)

As much as I love telling that story because the irony is fabulous, there was a time not so long ago when I would have agreed with Jack. Until a few years ago, I'd never thought of myself as an entrepreneur, either. At the time of this conversation, in the spring of 2009, I was celebrating my tenth anniversary working as a sales executive in the research division of The Economist Group. Although, to call myself an executive is perhaps a bit of a stretch—I was more of a midlevel salesperson. I didn't have a single employee working under me until I'd been on the job for more than eight years. And *celebrating* isn't really the right word, either. It's not that I disliked my job, which was to enlist corporate sponsors to fund our industry research reports. I was pretty great at sales. My little two-person division was earning the company upward of $2 million a year. What I was having trouble with were the people. Namely, Jack, who could not understand why a longtime editor might not want to be given a new role.

I had never been quite so forthcoming with Jack before, mind you. I just figured he might want to know that one of his most senior employees was unhappy and, at that point, I had nothing to lose by being honest.

Unfortunately, Jack did not appreciate my honesty. In fact, he was pissed.

"She's an entrepreneur, Raegan," he said, his voice rising. "She knows where we're taking the company. *She* understands."

I have never been good at holding my tongue. That's probably the Aussie in me; I have always given my opinion primarily when asked, but on this occasion I did so freely. In this case, I happened to *know* that Jack was way off. When it comes to office politics, lower-level employees often know more about what people really think and feel about a company than the people barricaded behind closed doors in the C-suite. And, as a lower-level employee at the time, I happened to know that Jill was evaluating her options. Clearly, she was not thrilled. But Jack refused to listen—he didn't think I could possibly understand, not being an entrepreneur myself. To him, I was just stirring up trouble.

He wasn't totally wrong about that part, though—I do have

a penchant for troublemaking. I was a bit of a party-girl mess in high school: skipping class, staying out late, drinking. I had more than a few (albeit minor) run-ins with the local police. I dropped out of university midway through my first semester and spent the early part of my twenties dancing on tables (fully clothed) to encourage the tourists to visit the bar on the island of Santorini in Greece to support myself while backpacking around Europe. As my mum would no doubt tell you (because she's been telling this story to anyone who will listen for more than forty years), I once locked her out of the house when I was two years old because she told me "no." Because I knew what I was in for once she got ahold of me, I absolutely refused to open the door. She had to crawl through a window to get back inside . . . while she was seven months pregnant with my sister Paige.

Only later did I realize that the traits I was seemingly born with—a tendency to push boundaries and question authority, plus a fiery independence—are fairly typical for an entrepreneur.

After running out of money from gallivanting around Europe, I came home to Sydney and went into sales, working for a professional hair-care brand, then at pharmaceutical giants SmithKline Beecham and Pfizer. At every job I was the top salesperson. But despite my track record, I was held back, especially at The Economist. I was repeatedly passed over for promotions and constantly told to stay in my box, to focus on what I was good at. I refused to agree with the boss simply because he was in charge, and it quickly became obvious that my bosses, almost all of whom were men, did *not* like having their leadership or decision making questioned by a junior-level, outspoken woman.

I started to dream about what "my" company might one day look like—all the things I'd do differently, all the ways I'd value and listen to my employees regardless of their position in the company, how much fun it would be to throw the hierarchical nonsense and bureaucratic bullshit right out the window. I didn't think of myself as an entrepreneur, but I knew that I wanted to do something on my own. Open a coffee shop, maybe, or a restaurant, the venture itself didn't much matter. I didn't get joy out of going to work for someone else and was drawn to the freedom I'd have doing my own thing. Part of me wanted to stick it to all those bosses who didn't think I had it in me, and another part was waiting to find the nerve to make a go of it on my own. What I wanted most, however, was to prove to *myself* that I could do it.

But I had stayed at these jobs, unfulfilled and unchallenged, because I had yet to come up with the right idea that I felt had real substance and a bloody great chance of being a successful business. And it was really thanks to Jack that I realized, even though I had a lot of pressure at work and at home, having started a family, that I needed to take a risk, to not only dream but also go for it—to make the leap and not hold myself back.

It seems I'm not the only one who has the dream and the drive to go it on my own. More and more, women are leaving the corporate world to do exactly what I did—which is exactly why I'm writing this book. I knew so little when I started my company, and I've accomplished so much in spite of that. I have never considered myself the smartest person in the room, and I don't have an Ivy League education. I really am a very average person, I promise. If I can do it, you can, too.

And you won't be alone—so many women are making this leap. Between 2007 and 2017, the number of women-owned businesses grew 114 percent, compared to a 44 percent increase among all businesses. Women make up 40 percent of the new entrepreneurs in the United States, a number that has been steadily climbing since 1996. Women of color have founded businesses in stunning numbers: from 2007 to 2016, the rate of firm ownership grew at more than four times the rate of all women-owned businesses (467 percent). Not even fifty years ago, women were routinely denied the right to open a line of credit or secure a mortgage in their own name, to say nothing of qualifying for business loans. Hillary Clinton was famously denied a credit card back in the late 1970s, at least two years *after* passage of the Equal Credit Opportunity Act. She was already a graduate of Yale Law School by then, not to mention a practicing attorney and a professor; she made more money than her husband. Still, she was told to use Bill's credit card instead.

In the span of just a few decades, we have made remarkable strides, in part thanks to incredible role models who have paved the way, such as Anita Roddick, creator of the Body Shop, which was recently valued at over $1 billion, and Michelle Phan of Ipsy, a subscription beauty sampling business she cofounded in 2011 in her early twenties, reportedly valued at $800 million in 2016.

Despite this progress, most female entrepreneurs will never experience that kind of success. In fact, women-owned firms receive only 2 percent of venture capital funding. Men are still 3.5 times more likely to hit the million-dollar mark; only 27.8 percent of firms with $1 million or more in revenue are owned by women or women in equal partnership with men. In fact, according to a 2014 report, more than 75 percent of women-owned firms won't reach $50,000 in annual revenue. Nearly half won't even make $10,000. Those stats, by the way, haven't budged in about two decades. In other words, women may be starting more companies than ever before, but many of those companies aren't reaching the levels of success of those of our male counterparts.

Women must really be messing up, eh? That's the common narrative in our society, and of course the explanation for this depressing problem has always fallen on women. We need to be more confident and less emotional, to worry more about "scaling up" and less about "work-life balance." To act like a lady but think like a man. Research and media focus on what's "wrong" with women entrepreneurs, and how to "fix" the companies they run. The prevailing wisdom, for example, is that female entrepreneurs are more cautious and risk-averse than men and are more reluctant to grow their businesses. Female entrepreneurs are said to have difficulty coming up with the resources to grow their businesses to the levels that men do, and underperform as compared to male entrepreneurs. You might have heard those myths before. You might even believe them. If that's the case, you might be surprised to hear that some of the latest research indicates there is no statistical difference between male and female performance in these areas. (Don't worry, we'll go into this in more detail later on.)

Consider a recent study in the *Harvard Business Review* analyzing venture capitalists' conversations with male versus female entrepreneurs. If a man was young, he showed promise; a woman, inexperience. Men were congratulated on their aggressive stance, while women were told to remain cautious and unemotional. When men were cautious, they seemed levelheaded and sensible, where women seemed not daring enough. You get the point—men were praised for their seemingly entrepreneurial potential and rewarded, but the same qualities in women were viewed as downfalls and reasons not to fund them or their ventures.

Which illustrates exactly why women want to start businesses in the first place. Unlike men, women often pursue entrepreneurship because they've been faced with fewer opportunities for advancement (true in my case), little to no flexibility (yep), and systemic discrimination (sad but true!) in the corporate world, even when, according to the Women in the Workplace study and Sheryl Sandberg's *Wall Street Journal* article, "Women and men stay with their companies at roughly the same rate . . . [and women] seek promotions at the same rate as men." So it seems to me that the very last thing we should do is encourage women to create businesses that mirror the very companies they abandoned, or shove them into a one-size-fits-all approach to success—much less perpetuate the systematic sexism they've faced inside a corporation.

And in fact, there is a lot of research that runs counter to these beliefs and proves how women are good for and good at business. When women are the direct beneficiaries of credit, their repayment rates are higher than men, both in the United States and worldwide. Women-led private tech start-ups achieve a 35 percent higher return on investment dollars; when venture-backed, they also earn 12 percent higher revenues. Women who invest tend to trade less and hold less-volatile portfolios, but they actually make slightly higher returns; since 2007, women-owned and -managed hedge funds have had annualized returns of 5.64 percent, as compared to the HFRI Fund Weighted Composite Index with annualized returns of 3.75 percent. So shouldn't we be empowering women to see that our unique perspectives, skill sets, and life experiences, far from being liabilities, might actually be . . . assets? Highly relevant, profitable, productive assets at that!

Empowering women lifts us *all* up; and when women entrepreneurs aren't properly supported, *all* of us are held back. The McKinsey Global Institute estimated that if women reached their full economic potential worldwide, "as much as $28 trillion, or 26 percent, could be added to global annual GDP by 2025." The US economy has benefited from the increase in participation among women—estimates suggest that the economy is 13.5 percent, or $2 trillion, larger than it would be had women's hours remained at their 1970 levels.

To grow the economy and help those in it, we need women to participate and lead. We need to end the sexism pervasive in America and entrepreneurism. We need women to take the leap into the unknown to benefit themselves, their families, the economy, and our society at large.

One of my favorite quotes has always been "Leap, and the net will appear" by the American essayist John Burroughs. More than that, it's been my guiding principle—it was the first quote I added to our conference room wall at the office in Brooklyn. When I started aden + anais, I knew nothing about textile manufacturing or supply chain management, or about anything other than sales. When I pitched the owner of a baby boutique in the early days of the business, she told me she was interested and asked if I would send over a line-sheet. "Sure," I said. Then I hung up the phone and immediately Googled *line-sheet* to find out what she was talking about. What I knew was that if I didn't go for it, if I didn't leap and follow my dreams, I'd regret the decision forever.

Only now am I beginning to understand that decisions like these have made me something of a rarity in the business world. Several years ago, a journalist from a prominent business publication asked me to explain the "secret" to my success. So I told her: Believe in yourself, work really fucking hard, and never ever give up, no matter how tough it gets. You might be a working mum, thinking about escaping the confines of an unfulfilling job. You might be on to a huge idea, with the determination and eagerness to try it out. Perhaps you're dreaming about the opportunities and ideas you come across on a daily basis, as a stay-at-home mum or a recent college graduate. You might have the desire for the kind of financial freedom for yourself or your family that a nine-to-five career could never create, or you might just have the desire to see a brilliant idea brought to life. Or like me, you might be ready to burst out of the confines of bullshit corporate red tape and hierarchy to set your own direction. No matter your circumstance, if you're feeling trapped and want more, I encourage you to take the leap.

I can't offer you step-by-step instructions to building a business or a road map to success, because, I'm sorry to say, there *is* no magic formula. There is no one "right" way to become a successful entrepreneur (lord knows I am proof of *that*). But I can tell you that I've succeeded only because I leaped even though it was scary and people thought I was nuts. Hear me when I say that if I can do this, anyone can. You can. I hope that my story inspires you to blaze your own path forward. I truly believe that every woman, if she so desires, has the potential to reach a leadership position, start a business, and hit (and surpass) $1 million in revenue, not by emulating men or abiding by the status quo, but by embracing yourself as a woman, and having the courage to leap.

CHAPTER 1

TRUST IN YOUR IDEA

I was sitting on the floor of my friend's nursery in Los Angeles when the idea came to me.

"Claudia, we *need* to go into the muslin wrap business!" I said. "And we should call it 'Aden and Anais,' after the babies!"

It was May 2004, and I was holding my infant daughter Anais, who was swaddled in a sheet of gauzy muslin. A second muslin blanket was stretched out on the floor; it was "tummy time" for my friend Claudia's newborn son, Aden.

Claudia was one of my closest friends. When my husband, Markos, and I moved to New York in 1997, we knew no one. Actually, Markos knew one person: the ex-girlfriend of his best friend. Awkward. But Claudia and I hit it off the moment we met and became good friends; she even lived with us for a time. When she met her husband she settled in California and we remained close despite the distance. I was a bridesmaid in her wedding and, should the worst happen, a legal guardian to her children. Because we were Australian, we both knew about swaddling, but had struggled to find swaddling blankets for our babies stateside.

Muslin swaddling blankets—"wraps," as we called them back home—had been a parenting staple in Australia for as long as I could remember. In fact, for Aussie mums-to-be they're as essential as nappies (that's diapers if you're American). We used them as burp cloths and nursing covers and stroller shades, as changing pad covers and security blankets, and, obviously, to swaddle our babies. One of the great things about muslin—which is really just a gauzy, open weave cloth, a fabric that's been around since biblical times—is that it's lightweight and breathable. When used for swaddling, it keeps babies warm while reducing the risk of overheating. It also gets softer with time, rather than falling apart after a few dozen washings. So I was pretty much blown away when I started shopping for baby gear during my first pregnancy, and I couldn't find a single muslin blanket anywhere in the United States. I asked shopkeepers at trendy boutiques and chain stores alike, and they all looked at me like I was crazy. I tried searching online and still found nothing. Eventually I phoned my sister Paige, also a new mum, and had her ship over some of the Aussie stuff, which is what Claudia and I were using that morning in L.A. Without even trying, I'd identified a gaping hole in the market. I knew that if Americans were introduced to the product, they'd soon find it as indispensable as we did. Going into business just seemed sort of . . . obvious.

Well, it seemed obvious to *me* at least.

Claudia, on the other hand, wasn't so sure at first. "Maybe we should just reach out to one of the Australian companies instead?" she suggested. "Maybe we could become a distributor in the States?"

She had a point. Certainly, it would be easier to become a distributor for an existing brand than to make and manufacture a product ourselves. But as I looked again at her son on the floor and at my daughter in my arms, I thought: *How hard can this really be?* We weren't talking about much more than a large square of cotton cloth. And besides, the Aussie wraps I'd grown up with were boring, predominantly white, and sold in cellophane packaging. I knew I could make them beautiful. I could design them with vibrant colors and patterns. I could take white cotton muslin and turn it into something people coveted.

It was not the first idea for a business that had popped into my head. I'd had loads of them over the years, in fact, and I can tell you that not one of them had anything to do with babies. I didn't have a burning desire to make a product for mums. I didn't have a burning desire to make a *product* at all. My motivation was to be the master of my own destiny, to work for myself rather than "the man." The baby blanket idea just happened to be the first that, upon further inspection, seemed viable. The more I thought about it, the better and better it sounded: Here was a practical product for a proven market that I could actually improve. Better still, the potential for growth—blankets! clothes! sleep sacks! bibs!—was exponential.

The thought of improving swaddling blankets was intriguing, but it was more than that—I knew it was an industry-changing idea. The swaddling blanket would be a unique product in the multibillion-dollar baby industry. It would solve a problem for mothers and create a completely new market segment in the US.

I felt within every bone in my body that—finally—this was a great idea to pursue.

It didn't take much convincing to get Claudia on board—she saw the hole in the market as much as I did. It was just a matter of agreeing on the right way forward. What's more, while we had our big idea, we still had much to learn. I figured that first on the to-do list was signing up a manufacturer. I thought (naively) that I'd be able to find one somewhere in New York (the garment district was less than two miles from my apartment, after all) or at least somewhere within the lower forty-eight states. So, in my spare time, I started doing research. I made calls. I asked around.

At first, this was not an all-consuming project. I was already busy balancing the demands of my full-time job at The Economist with my responsibilities as a new mum. I wasn't in much of a hurry to get to market, but no matter how many calls I made or how much research I did, it felt as if I wasn't making any progress—at all.

This was incredibly frustrating. Muslin was available everywhere in Australia, in the usual boring prints and colors, with its typical stiff feel, so I couldn't figure out why I couldn't find it anywhere in the US. Every time I visited a store, the salesperson had to ask me what muslin was. In retrospect, I think part of the reason there was such a hole in the American market was that the very few individuals who knew what muslin was thought of it in its true, raw form: scratchy and stiff, almost like cardboard. They couldn't easily make the connection between a cheap workhorse fabric and a luxurious, extra-soft baby blanket.

Another part of the problem, I would soon discover, was the collapse of the textile industry in the US. A flood of cheap foreign imports and the growing strength of the dollar—along with advances in technology and the higher cost for domestic labor (compared to foreign labor)—had driven pretty much everybody to use offshore mills just a few years before I started my search. Further complicating matters was the fact that none of the few remaining manufacturers seemed to have any idea what I wanted or, to my total surprise, even understood what I was talking about.

Before long, I resorted to cutting up pieces of my Aussie muslin. Whenever I found a potential manufacturer, I'd send or show the sample to them: *This! This is what I mean! Can you produce this fabric?* None of them could.

Actually, a few of them could, but only at a ridiculous price point.

Think: $150 and up. For a four-pack of muslin baby blankets.

Over the next nine months or so, my enthusiasm waxed and waned; for a few weeks here and there I'd be laser focused and looking for leads, but then I'd get busy with work and my daughter and not think about the business at all for a while. I had a lot on my plate, as any new mum knows. I was being pulled in multiple directions and living the reality that there are only twenty-four hours in a day. But I truly believed in the idea of aden + anais so I gave it all of the little free time that I had.

One morning I went into work and struck up a conversation with Brenda, our receptionist at The Economist. Somewhere between talk of our kids and bitching about work, the mail carrier came around to drop a huge stack of letters, magazines, and packages on her desk. Right on top of the pile was an issue of *Women's Wear Daily*. Since I love a sample sale and a five-inch heel as much as the next woman, I asked Brenda if I could borrow it. As I was flipping through the magazine, I came upon a full-page ad for an Asian manufacturing textile show happening in New York just three days later.

I couldn't think of a reason not to go. I figured I might as well take my sample of Aussie muslin over there and check it out.

There must have been fifty vendors in that showroom, each of them milling around in their little booths. I started going up to them one by one and asking the same question I'd been asking for a solid year now—"Can you produce this fabric?"—but the answer was always a version of what I had already heard:

No.

I don't know what that is.

We can't make that.

After a half hour or so, I was discouraged. After an hour, I was ready to head home. The entire exercise had been such a waste of time that I almost didn't bother approaching the man in the very last booth by the exit. But I decided to show him the muslin just for the hell of it. His name was David Chen. Like the other vendors, he wasn't familiar with the fabric. Unlike the others, however, he offered to take the sample back to the factory he worked for to take a closer look.

It would turn out to be one of many serendipitous moments in the history of aden + anais. Because two weeks later,

Chen emailed me with good news. For the first time, the answer was yes.

Claudia and I were in business.

We still had a long way to go. Finding a manufacturing partner at that textile show in New York had been lucky, but we weren't ready to launch a real business yet. My goal from the beginning had never been to simply replicate the Aussie muslin products. What that muslin lacked was softness and beautiful design that would make people want it. I wanted to make it better, so the manufacturer and I set about making the fabric softer by upping the thread count and pre-washing the blankets. He was a creative, persistent partner who was willing to work with me and engage in a lot of back and forth to get the product right—mainly, him sending me samples of muslin and me promptly returning them to China with lots of feedback on how to improve them.

Ultimately, it took us more than a year to get the quality of our muslin where I wanted it, above the quality and softness of the blankets I could find in Australia, but it was worth it. I knew our little company would live or die based in no small part on quality. If we had a chance in hell of succeeding, the product we brought to market had to be perfect.

And we weren't just entering the market—we were creating a new category in it. Because people in the US generally hadn't heard of muslin, we had to educate our customers as we built our business. Despite the fact that every maternity ward swaddled, American parents generally didn't. As a mum, I'd found that swaddling was essential to soothing my babies and keeping myself sane. It calmed them down and helped them sleep, and I felt other parents were missing out on these major benefits of the practice. I didn't realize that I was becoming a swaddling evangelist; I just came at it from the experience of a mother who believed in the product and wanted it for her own children.

While I was figuring out how to make our blankets, Claudia was busy with the paperwork, filing our articles of incorporation, and looking for a design outfit to help with our logo, packaging, and branding. I'd had a vision for the look of our product, too, and it was largely a response to the existing market. When we launched aden + anais, baby products primarily came in pastel colors, with traditional, whimsical prints: think chickens, ducks, teddy bears. We threw that right out the window. (I am *so* not a chicken and duck girl.) I wanted vibrant colors and bold patterns, simply because that's my personal taste and that's what I wanted for my daughter and my future children. We wanted high-quality, well-designed products that didn't feel like typical baby goods.

In one sense, our designs were a bit polarizing in the beginning. If you play it safe and go with basic designs any grandparent would choose, you may do OK, but no one will love your product. No one will say, "My *god*, I love that design," because it's status quo. I wanted to create eye-catching patterns that made people stop and notice. I wanted people to love them.

Unfortunately, I am the world's worst artist—you do not want my "artwork" adorning anything in your baby's nursery. While I've never called myself a creative person, I love design and have been told that I have an eye for it. Coupled with a strong opinion, I used those qualities to guide me while working with professional designers who were willing to take direction from a mere salesperson and run with it.

In September 2005, in the midst of all of this, my second daughter, Lourdes, was born. I brought my prototypes with me to the hospital and gave them to the nurses so they could wrap Lourdes in muslin. They went gaga over them, asking, "What is this fabric?!" As they wrapped my beautiful, healthy baby girl in one of our blankets, I was thrilled. I had trusted my initial instinct, but now I was even more sure that my idea would work out. Soon, all my samples disappeared, swiped by the Mount Sinai team of very excited nurses. I knew American mums would have the same reaction.

But I didn't know anything about textiles. Or fashion design, the retail industry, manufacturing, or the baby product business. I didn't have a warehouse or a factory or a workspace or a salesroom. I couldn't sew anything to save my life. But while I didn't know anything about launching a brand, I did know a thing or two about mums and their babies. I also knew deep down that this was an idea to follow, and that if I could just take one step after another, I could turn this into a success. I didn't stop to wonder if this was the "right" kind of business to start. It's a good thing, too, because if I had listened to the most common beliefs around women and their businesses today—that it's too hard to start a business, that women struggle because they only start "girly" companies—I might never have moved forward.

There's a lot of discouraging stuff out there. In the fall of 2011, a young reporter headed to Santa Clara, California, to cover the DEMO technology conference, an annual event that spotlights new technology and provides entrepreneurs with a platform from which to debut their products and services. As this reporter wandered around the space, she noticed that the majority of the women-led start-ups were positioned in traditionally "female spaces," rather than fields that were considered to be more reputable, like science and tech. Taking her frustration to social media, she tweeted:

> Women: Stop making startups about fashion, shopping & babies. At least for the next few years. You're embarrassing me.

As you might imagine, this did not exactly go over well. In fact, the tweet pissed off a whole lot of people. They called it "crass," "confusing," "ignorant," and "badly worded." It inspired a slew of rebuttals and think pieces, the general consensus of which seemed to be that women should support other women; that we should applaud any and all women entrepreneurs, regardless of the industries they're in, just on principle.

What very few people bothered to ask, however, is why "girly" companies are looked down on in the first place. Could it be perhaps that our society, especially in the business world, deems "women's work," and feminine traits in general, as inferior?

Evidence supports this; you just need to look at the strides women have made in business. In 1982 we started earning 50 percent of bachelor's degrees. Today, that number is closer to 60 percent. As of 1987 women earned more master's degrees, and since 2006, more doctoral degrees than men, too. And yet, even in 2017, women as a whole still earn only 80 percent of what the average white man earns. The numbers are even more dismal for women of color: African American women earn 63 percent of what white men earn, while Hispanic women earn just 54 percent. You're likely familiar with the common reason given for this gap: that women choose to enter professions where they are paid less in exchange for more flexibility, that women "opt out" en masse to take care of their families (ideas I'll discuss further in chapter 5). But a recent study indicates that virtually every field experiences a corresponding drop in wages once women move into it. This report, in the academic journal *Social Forces*, shows wages between 1950 and 2000 fell precipitously—for everything from designers to biologists—once women started showing up in larger numbers. As one of the study's coauthors explained to the *New York Times*: "It's not that women are always picking lesser things in terms of skill and importance. It's just that employers are deciding to pay it less."

Entrepreneurship is no different. Just look at headlines like "Are Women Starting the Wrong Types of Businesses?" in *Forbes*, "Why are Women-Owned Firms Smaller than Men-Owned Ones?" in the *Wall Street Journal*, and "Are Women Starting Too Many Fashion and Baby Businesses?" on Jezebel. Not only are we criticized for starting the wrong kinds of businesses, but critics also claim that ours underperform, partly due to the fact that women tend to start service-based companies. More than half of women-owned businesses are crowded into the healthcare/social assistance, professional/science/technical, administrative support, and retail-trade service industries. Services, while important to our economy and viable as a business model, are not typically positioned for *scalable* growth. A small, local daycare center, for example, will find it more difficult to hit a million dollars in revenue no matter who's running it. A self-employed tax-prep professional might not crack seven figures, either.

However, these service businesses are not all inherently feminine; salons and daycare centers certainly are a common example, but law, accounting, and architectural firms, medical centers, repair outfits, and science organizations also fit the bill. And the fact that so many women's businesses are in the service sector doesn't mean these companies *underperform*. In fact, one of my closest friends, Leslie Firtell, founded Tower Legal Solutions, a legal-services company, which she scaled to $80 million. And through both the EY Winning Women and Women's Presidents' Organization (WPO) networks, I have met women who have scaled their service-based businesses to over a billion dollars. That's billion with a big fat capital *B*.

Women should be able to start whatever businesses they want, with support and without judgment. I happen to have a vagina and, having had four children, I happen to know a thing or two about babies. Naturally, my focus as a woman tends to be on things that are female-focused, so I see no problem with starting a business aimed at women. Leslie, the founder of that $80-million legal-services company, is a woman who is also a take-no-prisoners, hardcore lawyer. That was her world and what she knew, so she started a company that matched her expertise. Like her, I was uniquely positioned to understand the opportunity that was in front of me, and it would have been absurd for me to say to myself, *You know what? I'm not going to start a baby blanket business—that's too girly.*

The simple truth is that plenty of traditionally feminine businesses *are* scalable, and in fact go on to make millions: Skinnygirl, Birchbox, Ipsy, The Body Shop, Build-A-Bear Workshop, Polyvore, Rent the Runway, Stitch Fix, IT Cosmetics—all are wildly successful, "girly" companies created by and for women.

Quite a few men have gotten in on the action, too, including the founders of Etsy, Diapers.com, ShoeDazzle, and Pinterest. I don't hear anyone complaining that they should start a more male-focused business instead. Are they getting paraded around because they're selling baby products and women's shoes online? No. They're just building successful businesses and being lauded as smart, savvy entrepreneurs.

Furthermore, we've known for years that women control a majority of global consumer spending, both through influence and direct buying power—estimates range from $18 trillion to roughly $30 trillion annually. The market for female-centric businesses isn't likely to shrink, so it's demonstrably untrue—stupid, even—to suggest that women are a niche market not worth pursuing.

So let's take a moment to think about that—our power. These are the issues I was grappling with and fighting against when starting aden + anais. I was trying to come up with a more useful way to frame the discussion around success in business when I ran across marketing guru and bestselling author Seth Godin's post about the difference between entrepreneurs and freelancers. Godin explains that a freelancer is someone who gets paid for their work, charging by the hour or project. Entrepreneurs, on the other hand, build a business bigger than themselves, focusing on growth and on scaling the systems they build. While a freelancer is looking for a steady stream of clients, the entrepreneur's goal is to "sell out for a lot of money, or to build a long-term profit machine that is steady, stable, and not particularly risky to run."

You might evaluate your current situation, decide it isn't working for you, and choose to do your own thing. In this situation, success often means earning the equivalent salary of a previous or similar role, or in Godin's words, becoming a freelancer. Or you could go into business for yourself to build a multimillion-dollar company, which Godin distinguishes as becoming an entrepreneur. People who go into business for the motivation of earning an income aren't interested in growing a business, and yet they are lumped in to the statistics with those who are.

There's nothing wrong with being a freelancer or starting a business because you want flexibility in your schedule and a steady income. It takes initiative and drive to make a living on your own.

However, the argument against any "girly" company that allegedly underperforms is impacted by those of us who leave our jobs to freelance, and we won't be able to see the full picture until we drill further down into the numbers.

All of this is to say that you should pursue what you want, without letting misleading stats or haters hold you back. Take the leap to do whatever it is you've been wanting to do, but don't shy away from thinking bigger. Imagine if you were to grow your business to a global scale, if only for a moment.

From the beginning, my dream was to build a big, successful business. Starting aden + anais didn't give me more time or flexibility with my family. In fact, I worked harder as an entrepreneur, particularly when I was still working my full-time job at The Economist, than I ever did as a salaried employee. But I was OK with that; I wanted to build a $100 million company. That big goal inspired me to work as hard as I could to make it happen.

Like that fateful morning I had with Claudia, you might have your own moment in which the seed of an idea is revealed. Listen to yourself and that little voice telling you to go for it. Don't let misperceptions about women-led businesses stop you. Ignore the criticism. Do what you know, what you're passionate about. Stop asking yourself whether you're starting the right business and start asking yourself whether your idea is viable and scalable, whether you have an existing customer base that you can grow, and whether you are filling an existing need or solving someone's problem. Then, and most importantly, be prepared to work harder than you've ever worked before.

You wouldn't be alone in doing so. I've met plenty of women over the years who think big. Women entrepreneurs regularly reach out to me asking for advice and input as to how to grow their businesses. My friends are of the same mind-set, too. Of the female entrepreneurs whom I hang with, each is interested in making their company as big and successful as they possibly can.

I had my "big idea"—right there on the floor of Claudia's

nursery—in the spring of 2004. As it turns out, a company that sold muslin swaddling blankets checked all the boxes: It was viable, scalable, had a customer base that could grow, and solved what I saw as a problem. All I had to do was figure out how in the hell to make the blankets.

CHAPTER 2

HARD WORK BEATS
B SCHOOL

I believed I had the right idea, but what I definitely did not have was an MBA—or even a bachelor's degree. Let's face it, I didn't really have any business experience outside the realm of sales. I wasn't a twenty-something technophile working out of a garage in Silicon Valley, either. I was a wife, mother, and full-time corporate cog in her thirties. Not exactly what you might consider a typical entrepreneur.

I grew up on the outskirts of Sydney, Australia, a mere fifteen minutes or so from some of the world's most beautiful beaches and about a twenty-minute drive to Sydney's Central Business District. Truly, it was an incredible place to spend my childhood—surrounded by coastline, close to the city center and all its vibrancy. Where I lived, however, was very much typical suburbia: brick houses on quarter-acre lots, rotary clotheslines dotting the backyards. (Those clotheslines, by the way, are called Hills Hoists—they look a bit like naked umbrella frames if you're not familiar—and they are *iconic* in Oz. There's not an Aussie my age who doesn't remember climbing and swinging on the clothesline as if it were a jungle gym.) I went to a very average public school, in a suburb that in many ways resembled midcentury American suburbs. But while I was born in the late 1960s, the environment in our home was perhaps more reminiscent of the early 1950s.

Dad would come home from work and my mum would immediately put a meal in front of him. Then he'd sit in front of the TV with his scotch, or he'd be out with his mates having a drink at the pub. I don't remember him doing much of anything around the house. In fact, I don't even remember him being around all that much, except for weekends when we all competed in our respective sports. My brother, Grant, was a talented rugby league player, while my sister, Paige, and I played netball (a sport best described as a variation of basketball—Paige always outdid me). We were all very athletic, and my dad was enthusiastic about anything sports related. Despite his now obvious shortcomings as a husband to my mum, I felt loved by him. He was the jokester, the fun guy. We're talking about the kind of man who thought it would be great fun to take us kids down to the local shopping center and make us belt out the Australian national anthem in front of total strangers to get an ice cream.

By contrast, my mum was the disciplinarian, and we were terrified of her. Once you were put to bed at seven o'clock, you didn't *dare* set foot outside that bedroom. I remember my brother, sister, and I peeking our heads out the doors of our rooms, rolling tennis balls to each other across the hallway that connected them in an act of defiance.

In truth, I had always been a bit of a cheeky kid.

Even at a very young age, I'd challenge my teachers. We used to have this thing called the "no-play line" in primary school. If you didn't follow the rules, you had to stand on the line—a painted stripe on the asphalt, coming off the flagpole in the middle of the quadrangle. I was constantly standing on that line, busted for something. I was a troublemaker, but I wasn't a slacker. As I got older the teachers whom I respected thought I was great, and I was always at the top of their classes. Those who I thought were idiots *hated* me, as I've never had much patience with stupidity or incompetence. I do not suffer fools gladly, a trait that is innate in me.

My mother's been saying for years that I was always defiant and rebellious, that I thought I knew more than she did, even from the age of two. I asked her once, "Do you know how ridiculous that sounds? That I was supposedly a know-it-all trying to run the house at the age of *two*?" She was adamant, though, so apparently I really was a pain in the ass—willful and determined from the very beginning.

For the most part, mine was a happy childhood. When I was nine or ten, my father, who worked as an accountant, decided to start a printing business. Long story short, his partner screwed him over, the business went bust, and my father was left holding the debt. My mum had to go back to work so we wouldn't lose the house, and she took the only job that was available: washing vehicles in a car dealership. All of a sudden, my siblings and

I were latchkey kids. As the oldest, I brought my brother and sister home from school and looked after them till my mum got home in the evening, my dad following much later from his new job at Pfizer.

What I remember most from that period was how hard my mum worked, both inside and out of our home, and the incredible amount of tension in the house. My parents were always fighting and from what I could tell as a young child, it was mostly about money. Like a lot of kids who grow up around that kind of anxiety and stress—tiptoeing around in anticipation of the next blowup—I was determined that I was never going to find myself in the same situation. As far back as I can remember, I knew that I wanted to have money as a result of my upbringing. Apparently, I used to prance around saying that one day I'd have enough to buy a pink Lamborghini. Thank god my tastes have changed (although I wonder what my childhood self would think about the fact that my husband and I drive a very functional black Honda Pilot to cart around our four girls). Watching my parents attempt to dig out of the hole they'd found themselves in was an education in itself. Their mistakes taught me that nothing is handed to you, that you have to work your ass off to get what you want in life.

It wasn't until years later after their eventual divorce that I realized their problems had never just been financial. It turns out my dad had been far from the ideal husband. They finally split up because he left my mum for a woman only two years older than me, and I was in my twenties. I was so angry with my dad that I didn't speak to him for a year, and I never did meet his girlfriend.

And my mum, though she was the enforcer with us kids, had been a bit of a pushover in her marriage. I was blown away when I found out that she'd never known how much money my dad earned. Worse still, she wasn't *allowed* to know. That's when all this stuff I'd never known about the nature of their relationship spilled out. My mother was consumed with anger: Your father did *this*, and your father did *that*. At some point, I snapped: "If you hated him so much, why did you stay?"

She gave the answer that many, many women (too many women) give: I had you kids. I had nowhere to go. I wouldn't have survived on my own financially.

I understand things better now, but at the time, I, as a woman, was disappointed that she had put up with as much shit as she did to get by—for me and my siblings. The months immediately following their divorce were especially bad, partly because my dad put me in a horrible situation: the middle. The night he left, he called and explained that he wasn't coming back and that I needed to go over to my mum's house and make sure she was OK. At the time, my sister was backpacking through Europe and my brother didn't want to deal with it. (Great, thanks, Dad.) My mum, understandably upset, ended up taking a lot of her frustration out on me, straining our relationship further.

The thing is, my mother and I have never been close. What I needed most was to feel as though both of my parents really loved me, and, right or wrong, I never really felt that from my mum. No matter what I did, whether it was excelling in school in my younger years or in sports, in my mind she never noticed or acknowledged any of it. That really hurt. I was too young to understand that she'd been preoccupied with her own shit, like raising our family mostly on her own. So at fifteen, I went from being a mischievous kid to being a rebel. I mean, I went totally off the rails. I was sneaking out and lying about where I'd been; I had a fake ID and was heading out to the pubs and spending way too much time with boys. Believe me, *then* I had my mum's attention. Trouble was, it was the wrong kind of attention, and my acting out only worsened our relationship. In contrast, my brother and sister were the apple of my mother's eye. It didn't help matters that she could be cutting and cold; she once let slip that she wished she'd only had *one* daughter. We had a lot of arguments, which sometimes turned into physical, knockdown, drag-out fights.

Now that I'm a mum, I see the situation a little differently, and I understand the stresses that come with parenthood. I guess I knew deep down that my mum loved me in a way that a mother "has to" love a child, but I never understood why she didn't like me—until recently, thanks to an episode on the show *This Is Us* ("The Fifth Wheel," season two, episode 11, if you're curious—and caution, spoiler alert if you aren't caught up!). In it, a mother and her three adult children are in a therapy session together to support one of the children, who's in rehab. That character expressed anger that their mother had treated the other two siblings better, and that one of them was their mother's favorite. After hearing this, the frustrated mother jumped up, yelling, "I didn't love him more! He was just easier!" Even at fifty years old, it hit me hard, and I thought, *OMG, I was the difficult child.*

Some kids are easier than others to raise, and as a result, the "easier" children appear to have all of the love and affection, and the one who causes the grief seems to have none of it. I love all of my girls the same, I do not have a favorite, but I am absolutely different with each of them because they are different people. I can look back now and see why my mum might have treated me differently. I was not an easy kid.

But I digress. Back to the story. By seventeen I'd had enough and moved out.

I was listless and aimless for the next few years. I'd gotten into university, but it just wasn't my thing. I only lasted about six months before dropping out for good. I worked a string of odd jobs, shared an apartment with a bunch of flatmates, drank too much, and got into a decent amount of trouble. (For example, I may or may not have kicked in the side of a girl's car after I found out she'd been sleeping with my boyfriend.)

Which makes it all the stranger that I almost became a police officer until I hit one of the least proud moments in my life. A friend of mine was a cop and I didn't know what the hell I wanted to do with my life, so when she suggested I join the force, my response was: "Sure. Why not?" I went through all the training, the psych tests, the physicals. I'd been accepted into the academy and was waiting for my notification to start training. Everything was in place. I felt as though I might finally have a bit of direction in my life—until a long night of partying with my best friend, Sue, led to a late-night run for pizza and me totaling my flatmate Charlie's car by smashing it into the side of a garbage truck. I'm extremely lucky that no one was hurt and that the only casualty that night was the car. To make an already fucked-up situation worse, Charlie had no idea I even had his car. I spent the night in jail and was fingerprinted, so my law-enforcement career was over before it had even started. I was once again directionless and going nowhere fast.

If you're an Aussie and a university dropout, it's not long before you might find yourself on one of the islands. I ended up on Hamilton, the tourism and commercial center of the Whitsundays, off the coast of Queensland in the Great Barrier Reef. Except for a fleet of golf buggies, Hamilton is a car-free island, and it's exactly what you might imagine when you think of a tropical paradise: white sand beaches, clear blue water, broad blue skies. I was a bartender and a waitress for about a year and partied like a rock star—my flatmate there was a *Playboy* centerfold model. But at some point, my desire to wait tables and get people drunk for a living started to wane.

Then I got a phone call from my dad: "Raegan, it's about time you come back to civilization and get a real job." As rebellious as I was, when my father called to point out that I couldn't spend the rest of my life shot-gunning beer and partying with *Playboy* centerfolds, I thought he might have a point. I didn't really know what I wanted to do for the long term and I was still having fun, but I knew I didn't want to be a waitress or bartender for the rest of my life.

When I returned home, I had an idea that I wanted to go into advertising. Back then you didn't need a degree to work at an ad agency—it was expected that you would work your way up. The only job openings I could find were for receptionists and assistants. The work didn't engage me, so it wasn't long before I was dreaming of traveling yet again. Once I'd saved enough money, Sue and I left Australia and went backpacking around the world.

After almost a year away, I was once again faced with the reality that I had no money left and had to go home and get a job. The second time around, I was right back where I started and didn't know what I wanted to do. Contrary to the typical American mind-set, I didn't have a clear career path or a direction. I had a need for money and I was willing to throw myself into whatever work I could find that would help me earn it.

I remembered that my dad had once said he thought I'd be a natural in sales. Like him, I'm a people-person and (obviously) anything *but* a wallflower—I presume that's why he thought I'd be good at it. Heading back to Sydney, I scoured the newspaper (really showing my age here, since that's how you used to find job openings). After bouncing around at a few advertising firms and again working as an assistant and a receptionist, I landed my first real sales job, selling outdoor advertising space—by which I mean billboards. It turns out that my dad had been right—I *was* good at it. Soon I switched to selling consumer goods for the hair-care brand Schwartzkopf and then moved into pharmaceutical sales with SmithKline Beecham. I worked hard and became one of the top salespeople at SKB.

Because of my success as a salesperson, my boss at Smith-Kline Beecham gave me the opportunity to spend a day in the field with the global CEO, who had come in from the head office in the UK to visit the Australian office for a series of management meetings. He was a lovely man and I spent the day showing him the business from the sales front—he tagged along to a dozen pharmacies that I called on regularly. Spending eight hours in the car with someone leaves plenty of time for conversation. He asked my opinion on multiple areas of the business, and I gave it willingly.

After our day together, he asked me to join a management committee, which was controversial, as I was a junior salesperson at the time. This seemed implausible to the other senior managers on the committee, all men, and it didn't take long for the rumors to start. I must have been having an affair with the CEO—in their minds, that was the only way I could have secured a seat at the table.

At the end of the second meeting, which took place about a month after my appointment to the committee, I felt the need to address the elephant in the room.

"I just want to address the rumors. I never slept with [said CEO]. I only blew him once."

Obviously, I did no such thing. I was trying to make a point. Some of the managers put their heads down, while others laughed, realizing the point I was trying to make, but in the end, they could never accept that I was there because the CEO thought I could add value with my perspective of the business. I couldn't take it, and I resigned from the committee.

Not long afterward, Pfizer came calling. In the years after his printing business failed, my dad had turned to sales, too. He was the national sales manager at Pfizer Australia. This should have prevented me from coming on board, since Pfizer had a nepotism policy. Instead, my dad announced his retirement a year in advance, which meant I was lucky enough to get the job and we had the chance to work together, albeit briefly. Because of my success at SKB, Pfizer had come looking for me.

At a business conference in Vanuatu, someone at the long

conference table said something that I strongly disagreed with. True to form, I called him on it: "Listen, that's ridiculous," I said, "and here's why . . ." One of the senior managers couldn't help but smile. "Oh, my god," he commented. "Like father, like daughter."

Things were going well for me in sales, and I was happy to have settled on an actual career path, so I surprised myself when I decided to go for an MBA. Back then, anyone could get into sales—there was no barrier to entry. As a result, it wasn't considered a very noble profession. I thought that if people knew I had an MBA, they would know I had a brain, so I went for it. Even without an undergraduate degree, I was accepted at Macquarie University in Australia, based on work history and an entrance exam. I continued working at Pfizer while I went to school. Unfortunately, I wouldn't end up finishing that program, either, because I left a little more than midway through to move to the States with my then-boyfriend, now husband, Markos. Luckily, I didn't have to walk away entirely empty-handed; I didn't have enough credits for my MBA, but I had enough to earn a postgraduate diploma.

Still, for a long time, I figured that I probably wasn't cut out for anything other than sales, which I had more or less lucked into (thanks, Dad). I thought that my rebellious childhood, the decisions I'd made about dropping out of school, my lack of direction when I was younger, or that I'd never have Harvard alumni connections or a McKinsey consulting gig to slap on my résumé, might prove to be liabilities, or at least things I'd have to overcome, especially when trying to start out halfway around the world. It wasn't until I started my business that I realized all the ways in which those early experiences and my rebellious attitude had set me up for success. No, really!

Time after time, I've found that real-world life experiences, the kinds of things they just don't teach you in business school, have mattered far more than the fact that I dropped out of university or that I never got that high-priced MBA. I wanted the credibility that I thought an MBA would give me. But I can honestly say I have used nothing from my eighteen months of business school in the creation of my business. I can't tell you one impactful thing I learned, despite earning top marks in every subject (except for accounting, which is not my forte). Every accomplishment is a direct result of my determination and strong will, the very traits that seemed to cause me so much trouble in my younger years.

I so strongly believe this that I say this to would-be entrepreneurs on a regular basis: It is your hard work and commitment to your idea that will determine your success, not your pedigree.

I didn't grow up with much. My parents had their flaws, like all humans, but they instilled in me an incredible work ethic. They taught me that if I wanted anything I would have to work for it—nothing was ever handed to me. I watched them have to work hard just to cover the basics like food and shelter. I very clearly remember the day my father told me that the only thing you start at the top of is digging a hole. He knew I wanted to be the boss from day one and he wanted me to know that I would have to work hard to get there.

While a solid work ethic is important, having a master plan for your life is not. Even the most wayward of people, people like me who partied their way through their twenties, can find their purpose eventually. I certainly didn't have the typical climb up the corporate ladder setting me up for success. But I figured out what I didn't want while starting to discover, act on, and test out what I *did* want. I began to see that I wanted to start my own business, but it took me a very long time to get there. Although I'd had many ideas over the years—importing jewelry from Indonesia, starting a juice bar business, opening a restaurant—none of them ever felt right enough to take the ultimate leap. When I finally set out to build aden + anais, it isn't as if I was suddenly a different kind of person who had a clear direction in everything I did. All I knew was that I wanted to create a big, successful business, and I let that dream be my guide, and for the first time I had a business idea that felt as if it could work. My hope for you is to know that you don't have to strictly follow every bit of advice, you don't need to graduate from Harvard Business School, and you don't need to have everything planned out to launch your business. Whatever your path, your age, your experience, you can take the leap, and that could make all the difference.

For example, when we launched our diffusion brand, aden by aden + anais, in 2009 (I'm jumping ahead in time here for a bit, but bear with me), I met with a buyer from Target. I pitched her six stock keeping units (SKUs), hoping she'd take two. Instead, she took all six products, and we immediately launched in all seventeen hundred stores. It wasn't luck or pretty PowerPoint slides that made the sale. It was all the hard work I had done up to that point that paid off, and my ability to connect with her as a mother.

Sure, I had sales experience when I started this business, and that counts for something. Selling a product, even a product you deeply believe in, can be one of the scariest aspects of business for a new entrepreneur; the fear of rejection can be difficult to overcome (and I'll talk about that more in the next chapter). But everything I learned about sales I learned on the job, not in a business-school classroom. And that's all I had—I knew how to sell and I had drive, but I had no other business experience.

I'd never want to argue that education isn't important. It is— and as I mentioned earlier, you'll find plenty of women (more women now than men!) who find MBAs and other advanced degrees to be extremely valuable. In the United States, not having a degree has potentially negative consequences that can't be ignored. My husband is now an executive recruiter and his clients tell him that if a candidate for employment doesn't have an MBA, their application goes into a separate pile, removed from those submitted by the "highly qualified" candidates. In his experience, if you want to ascend to higher levels of leadership in the corporate world, you must have an MBA.

But traditional MBA programs are simply not well-suited for those of us who want to be entrepreneurs. MBA programs focus on technical skills and strategy, as opposed to the soft skills and execution that entrepreneurs need to lead their companies through the inevitable sticky situations of day-to-day business. Vivek Wadwha, an academic and entrepreneur, expressed this idea in a *Wall Street Journal* business blog post. Despite having earned an MBA and finding value in it, he now dissuades wannabe entrepreneurs from pursuing them, because he noticed "a growing mismatch between the skills that business schools teach and what fast-paced start-ups require. And corporate management isn't the best path to entrepreneurship anymore—the best way is to work for a start-up."

I'm going to take it one step further than Wadwha. If you get your MBA and then go straight into your chosen industry, you'll start with a higher salary, sure. And maybe you really would learn a lot by working for a start-up. But if you build a business, the amount of experience you'll gain from the time you spend in the trenches is far beyond anything you could learn in a business-school classroom or under the wing of another employer. In other words, no one can teach you how to be an entrepreneur; you learn by doing it. Only 3 percent of graduates from over a hundred US and international MBA programs ventured down the entrepreneur's path. And let's not forget the price tag of this degree. The burden of six-figure student loan debt may also prevent many MBAs from becoming entrepreneurs. It's definitely not easy to take on the stress of starting a business, especially when you're worrying about making your student loan payments.

So don't fall back on not having a certain background or degree or skill set as the reason you don't make your leap. Four years of building your business from scratch, being in the weeds of all of it, will teach you more than years of sitting in a classroom learning theories and skills ever could.

Remember, I knew nothing about running a business, other than sales, and it wasn't like I had ever sold baby products before. I didn't even know the most basic aspects of retail. Everything I know, I learned on the job (and from Google). I realize I may have had a leg up because of my sales experience, which I don't take for granted. But that notwithstanding, I worked hard to make my idea a reality and learn what I didn't know. Even if you fear that you lack what it takes to create a business, I believe that if you want something badly enough, you'll find a way to make it happen. No matter your situation, you definitely have some life experience that you can draw from, and it's OK not to have all the answers. It's OK to tap your network for help and to cold-call strangers who have the experience and knowledge you lack. I will never tell another person not to go to college or pursue higher education; I'm just saying that when it comes to jumping into your own business, an MBA or lack thereof does not determine your success as an entrepreneur. It's your willingness to learn and work hard that does.

CHAPTER 3

DON'T LET DOUBT STOP YOU

Although Claudia and I had our big idea in 2004, it wasn't until 2006 that we were finally ready to go to market. While it might seem as though we were in the background doing a lot of heavy lifting to get our product off the ground, that isn't the case. We spent the majority of the time just trying to find someone to make it. Neither of us was all-consumed by the fledgling company—we weren't working sixteen-hour days to make it work. We were just plodding along, patiently going from one manufacturer to the other to see if they could make the blankets the way we wanted them. There wasn't a lot going on, but there was a lot of frustration at the slow pace of our progress.

It would have been easy to get discouraged, but the voice in my head insisted that this was a good idea worth pursuing. Still, I can admit that if I hadn't found our manufacturer when I did, we might have given up too early.

In the summer of 2006—two full years after that first conversation on the floor of Claudia's nursery—we were finally ready to launch. Determining how much merchandise to stock turned out to be a fairly easy decision: our manufacturer's "minimum order quantity"—a typical requirement in the manufacturing world—required an outlay of about $30,000.

When I first explained to Markos that I wanted to take $15,000 out of our savings account to launch the company, the conversation went something like this:

"What are you, insane? Where's the business plan?" he asked.

"It's in my head," I said. "I know this is going to work. Can you please trust me?"

"Well, you need a business plan," he said, as if that was that.

My husband is an academic and an engineer; he's a numbers guy and his mind works in a pragmatic, linear fashion. I, on the other hand, am a fly-by-the-seat-of-my-pants, get-in-there-and-get-shit-done type of woman.

"No, *you* need a business plan because you're a fricking engineer and that's how *your* mind works," I retorted. "I don't need a plan. It'll all work out. Trust me."

Back then, it didn't make any sense to spend time putting together massive presentations and bulleted business plans with pretty graphs and images. I preferred to take action to move the idea further along instead. There is so much pressure on entrepreneurs to prove an idea, to have it all thoughtfully written out so that it makes sense to someone else, that it can stop you before you even begin. We have this belief that unless you're a genius with a well-thought-out business plan and the background to make it work, you shouldn't bother starting a business. Don't get me wrong, I had done loads of research and spent considerable time and energy thinking through the business proposition; I just didn't feel it was necessary to record it in a twenty-page document to convince anyone else that my idea was a good one.

I'll admit that as the business grew, so did our need for business plans. In order to scale, plans and forecasts are important, especially because they can keep you focused and on track to meet your goals. But it was a number of years into the business before we implemented real planning; for the first few years after the launch of our product we were acting on instinct, teaching ourselves as we went along, flying at a million miles an hour to make things happen.

Markos could tell just how determined I was at this moment and thought it best not to fight me, since I was clearly on a mission. That may seem like a flippant statement, but I was truly dead set on my direction. I was going to do it no matter what anyone said, even my husband. We hadn't talked much about it up to this point, so I could see why Markos was somewhat alarmed. I had spoken to very few people about the idea—had barely even mentioned it to Markos until it was time to place the initial order. He had seen the samples, but we didn't discuss it as a business idea; it was simply a side project I was working on.

You might be wondering how (or why) I kept it from Markos. The few people I'd told hadn't been supportive, and I didn't want that kind of feedback clouding my decisions. It also felt as if it wasn't real yet, as if there wasn't anything to talk about. The work Claudia and I had done to that point was leading up to the moment when we would see the product on the shelves. To me, it wasn't a real business until the merchandise entered the market. When I finally felt it was a real thing, that Claudia and I were actually going to make a go of it, I talked to my husband about the initial investment.

Although Markos and I disagreed initially, we talked about it in depth. I knew that it was a lot of money, but it wasn't an amount of money that would ruin us financially—I was sure we could recover from a loss if things went pear shaped (or, for the Americans, if things went awry). Claudia and I had done the research, found the manufacturer, perfected the samples, and we were finally ready to place our first order after two years. I don't want to give you the impression that I was supremely confident all the time—I always had doubts and fears. But my belief in the idea was just as great, and I simply had to learn how to manage the doubtful moments. Nothing was going to stop me.

Clearly, I'm the kind of woman who doesn't feel she needs her husband's support—or permission—to do what she wants in the world.

While Markos wasn't completely OK with me taking the money out in the beginning, he got on board as soon as the business started taking off. He was supportive when we needed more money and when we had to make some hard decisions down the road. He never wavered after deciding to support me. That's not to say he had a big smile on his face every time we had to withdraw money—of course not—but he never questioned me again. On the contrary, he was my biggest champion and encouraged me to keep going every time I came to the next hurdle. On the other hand, Claudia's husband was not convinced we were going to be able to make it a meaningful business. He was a trust fund baby, so their financial situation was the polar opposite of ours. It quickly became clear we had completely different support systems at home.

Despite our husbands' initial misgivings, Claudia and I each put in $15,000 from our savings accounts. It amounted to about a quarter of the savings Markos and I had been building, and while it wasn't an astronomical amount of money, it was significant to me. We placed our very first order: a four-pack of muslin blankets in what you might call "boy-friendly" prints (which we named "Prince Charming"), a four-pack for girls (we named that set "Princess Posie"—it was red and fuchsia pink), a plain white four-pack, and a towel-and-washcloth set. The bulk of that merchandise got shipped over and dumped in Claudia's garage, and I flew to L.A. It was time to start selling. Up until then, Claudia had been handling the marketing PR and accounting while I had been handling the production and manufacturing. And since Claudia was *so* not a salesperson, that was going to be my territory.

As new mums, Claudia and I were familiar with the best maternity shops and baby boutiques on both coasts—The Pump Station, Bel Bambini, and Petit Trésor in Los Angeles; Rosie Pope and The Upper Breast Side in New York—so that's where we started. We targeted boutiques because we knew boutique owners and sales people would help the customers understand the product. They would effectively be the ambassadors who would pass the word on to their customers. We loaded up the boot (that's trunk in American) of the car (or taxi, if I was in New York) and went door-to-door, giving the boutique owners and salespeople our pitch.

Creating a market doesn't happen overnight. You have to

take on the task of first getting people's attention so they know about your product and then educating your customers about the benefits of your product while convincing them they need it. Because we were bringing a product to the US that wasn't in demand, I had to educate customers on both the practice of swaddling and, more importantly, muslin. When we were ready to go to market, I had to make sure salespeople and shop managers knew that it wasn't just a blanket, it was a blanket with multiple uses. We had to get the language right, too. They're referred to as wraps in Australia, but in the States that word only makes people think of sandwiches. "Swaddling blanket" was no good, since most people either didn't know what swaddling was or didn't swaddle their babies, and that didn't encompass all of the possible uses anyway. When the blankets were finally ready to sell, we called it a multi-use muslin blanket, a hook that helped us both educate the customer and ultimately sell the product.

After we were up and running in L.A. and New York City, it didn't take long to figure out via a quick Google search the upscale boutiques that made sense for our product in other US cities. If I took work trips for The Economist (remember, I was still working full time!), I threw a few samples in my bag and made quick stops if time allowed. It was as simple as walking in, asking for the owner or manager, showing them the product and explaining how it would help their customers, and then asking if they would like to buy. Some bought right on the spot; they would often ask for a dozen of each, and we'd be in business. The sales I made gave me the momentum to keep pushing forward, and I was encouraged by the interest in and enthusiasm over our product.

But like my early foray into finding a manufacturer, I heard "no" far more than I heard "yes," and faced more resistance than I anticipated. Nine out of twelve store managers I pitched to turned me down. Such a dismal ratio might have been soul crushing, but I knew this was the nature of sales. I was never fazed when people said, "Thanks but no, it's not for us." I always knew that it was just no for now.

"Develop skin as tough as a rhinoceros hide," Eleanor Roosevelt once said about female leaders. I take this to mean not to be less sensitive, but as a reminder not to let rejection dictate how we feel about ourselves; to keep failure from meaning that we as people are failures. A recent study evaluated more than ten thousand senior executives at companies in the UK and found that women who had experienced rejection previously for a job were 1.5 times less likely to apply than men. We tend to let rejection stop us in our tracks.

And when they do land these jobs, women are subject to a different kind of criticism than men. A study published in 2014 by *Fortune* found that both male and female managers gave more negative feedback to female employees. Nearly 76 percent of the negative feedback to females held a criticism of their personality with descriptions like "abrasive," "judgmental," or "strident."

Is it really any wonder that women as a whole feel less confident?

Unfortunately, women are still treated differently in business today—it's almost a given. We are subject to criticisms in the workplace that men don't experience. If we want to make strides in the business world given the current situation, we need to show up again and again in the face of rejection, not lose the confidence to keep moving forward.

If you ask the people who know me best, they would say that I've always been an extremely confident person. The irony makes me laugh; I don't *feel* confident. Luckily, I was able to build a tolerance for rejection thanks to starting out in sales. When you're in sales (and if you're starting a business, you *are* in sales), you hear "no" a lot. If you can distinguish between "no" as a personal rejection and "no" as a business decision, you'll be able to go back again and again without losing faith in yourself. After all, the rejection likely has little to do with you and everything to do with whether the product or service that you're selling is the right fit for that person or business at the time.

It also helped that I fully believed in the product I was selling and the business we were starting. It didn't bother me to walk into a store and pitch to someone I didn't know because I felt I was doing that person a favor. The product was going to do well for them. I took the perspective and approach that I was more than selling, I was educating.

I say this all like it was easy to let rejection roll off of me, to remain unfazed. That I'm always confident and never deal with doubt. Not true. As I said, fear was ever present from the moment the idea came to me. That didn't change after we were a global success, either. Even more burdensome is the fact that as the leader, I didn't want my team to see me wobble, so my ability to manage fear and doubt became more important the more the business grew.

Unfortunately, my occasional doubt in myself leads me to question my lack of education, for example, despite knowing what I've built without it. I was sitting on a panel at Harvard speaking to their MBA students, with Neil Parikh, the COO and cofounder of the mattress company Casper. Prior to leaving medical school to found Casper, he designed bacteria and worked on robotics teams at NASA, where he coauthored three patents. As he was talking, I couldn't help but think *Oh my god, I'm sitting next to fucking Einstein. WTF am I doing here?* Over the course of the afternoon, however, I realized we built our companies from very different standpoints and neither is less valid.

Societally, our perception of entrepreneurship is that all business founders are like the Casper guy—genius level and confident every step of the way. While building a business isn't easy, it is not nearly as mystical and difficult as many people would like you to believe. And you don't need to be a genius to do it.

It's not just your doubt that you'll run into. You'll have to deal with the doubts of your family, friends, and even your own employees. The only way to combat that is to have a healthy connection with your own intuition, your own inner voice. I've relied on following my intuition to build my company, which isn't a generally accepted way of doing business. It takes inner conviction to be able to follow your instincts in the face of other people's doubts, especially when they're telling you that you're wrong to rely on something intangible, a gut feeling. What was key for me was that I was absolutely fine with being wrong and getting rejected. The only way you can have the confidence to follow your gut is to be OK with failing, because you won't always get it right. It's the fear of failure that cripples us and makes us afraid to act on something that might feel right. Take children, for example. They don't refuse to try to walk because they might fall down. No, they just want to walk, and falling down is part of the whole process.

Remember, though, that doubt can sometimes be a good thing. It makes you stop to think about your course of action and ask questions about what you're doing. It forces you to consider why you're feeling the fear or doubt in the first place—to question whether it is based on something real or whether it's just nerves getting the better of you.

Even in the face of my own doubt, making a decision despite my insecurities has always been one of my greatest strengths. I was not always 100 percent confident in my decisions, but I always felt it was better to make one than not. Years later, this was one of the traits my team would come to appreciate most.

Your job is to make sure that any emotions you have about your business—doubt, fear, even overexcitement—don't consume and cripple you. Use your doubt as a tool instead of a deterrent, and don't let anyone else see it. Sharing your doubt has a trickle-down effect on your business. I don't know about you, but if I'm experiencing turbulence while traveling on a plane, I look at the flight attendants to study their facial expressions. If they're calm, then I'm calm. But if their faces are full of fear and worry, I will feel the same. It's no different in your business. Your team notices more than you think they do.

Finally, despite the fact that I question myself from time to time, I have a surplus of determination. If I want something, I make it happen through sheer will. While I've never been the best at anything, I am always the most determined.

Besides, my prior sales experience taught me that three out of twelve stores was actually a pretty good ratio. The rest might've said no for now, but I knew they'd say yes eventually.

The very first sale I made in New York was to a woman named Felina Rakowski-Gallagher at The Upper Breast Side, a popular maternity and breastfeeding store where I'd taken nursing classes and rented my breast pump. She was a strong woman, a former New York City police officer, and when I first showed her the products she ordered six of the boy-design four-packs and six of the girl-design four-packs. Three days later, she called to tell me she'd sold out.

She wasn't the only one. Within a week, every store that had taken the product called to reorder. Suddenly, that $30,000 worth of merchandise, which Claudia and I had taken a big bet on and thought might last us a year, didn't seem like such an extravagant or risky investment after all. That initial order had lasted us just three months.

"Hang on to your hats," Felina told me over the phone when she called to place her second order. "You're in for a wild ride with these blankets."

CHAPTER 4

REDEFINE RISK

I t probably sounds ridiculous (and more than a little bit arro-
gant) to say that I always knew that aden + anais might one
day be a million-dollar business. After that call from Felina,
however, I could *feel* it. My heart skipped a beat when I thought
about the feedback from stores selling our merchandise, how
our product had sold out in a week, and the fact that people
were responding to the product instantly. What I'd imagined
might just be on the verge of happening. Of course, I still really
had no idea what I was doing, but I truly believed that if I just
kept putting one foot in front of the other, focusing on the day-
to-day tasks at hand, I'd somehow manage to figure it all out.

In the meantime, I still had a day job to do.

By the summer of 2006, my gig at The Economist Group
had settled into something pretty straightforward: The magazine editors would write about complex financial topics and
business trends—the Sarbanes-Oxley Act, implementing Enterprise Resource Planning (ERP) systems, improving Governance,

Risk, and Compliance (GRC) operations—and then I'd reach out to major accounting, technology, and professional-services firms to solicit their sponsorship. For the bargain price of, say, $250,000, a company like PricewaterhouseCoopers or Grant Thornton or Oracle could slap their name on one of our research reports to use as a way of attracting new clients through showing their expertise in the subject matter or burnishing their corporate reputation or drumming up publicity for themselves in the press.

Hell. That does sound boring, doesn't it?

No matter how much money I made for the company or how many new clients I brought in or how much I grew my little one-person division, it never seemed to be enough to be taken seriously as a businessperson. Often when someone is good at their job, it looks easy—and too often we forget the hard work that goes into making it look that way.

An opportunity to run a department opened up and I wanted the job, so I sat down with one of the managers for a breakfast meeting to express my interest and discuss my qualifications. Dismissively he rattled off why I wasn't cut out for the job, starting with, "You don't have a degree."

"I have a postgraduate diploma," I corrected him. At this point, I also had an excellent track record and more than a decade of corporate experience—more than necessary to qualify for the job. What seemed to be holding me back more than the fact that I'd dropped out of university were the guys above me with zero belief in my ability.

As much as the lack of career progression annoyed me, there was conflict, too. With two young children at home I was often knee-deep in Cheerios until a quarter-to-nine and sometimes, I'll admit it, I came in late. I just couldn't see the problem. I have never been a clock-watcher; I often stayed after hours to finish my work. I worked from home whenever necessary. And, more to the point, I was a *salesperson*. One of the things I'd always loved about sales is that it's fairly black and white: If you're hitting your quotas, you're successful. If you're not, you're failing. But if you're routinely and consistently *exceeding* your sales goals, as I was, then who gives a fuck what time you walk through the door in the morning?!

I mean, really. What possible difference could a half hour make?

Unfortunately, Jack, the boss who told me I didn't have an entrepreneurial bone in my body, did not share my opinion about this (surprise!). When he got word that I would sometimes stroll in at 9:45 or 10:00 a.m., he demanded that I move my office. I was thirty-seven, maybe thirty-eight years old at the time, but I was made to start working in an office right outside my boss's so he could keep an eye on me.

The whole thing struck me as needlessly childish. This wasn't about work ethic or job performance; this was about power. And the hysterical part is that Jack's "plan" didn't even work. I kept up the same work ethic but also the same schedule. One of my co-workers said with a laugh, "The joke's on him, then, isn't it? Now he gets a front-row seat to watch you waltz in here at quarter to ten."

What's more, I was constantly getting in trouble for challenging authority. Years before Jack came on the scene, our then-boss, "Peter," had a favorite male employee on the team, who got away with murder. The preferential treatment was so blatant that it caused a stir among the rest of the team.

People were upset by this bias, and I remember a tipping point when one colleague emailed, "How come he gets to walk in and just sit there reading the paper and nothing gets said? And in the meantime, Peter is up our butts about everything."

That set everyone off, and they all started unloading on the favorite, saying he was lazy and spoiled. (Pro tip: don't do this via work email.) I was a little surprised—why were they attacking him? He was just doing what he could get away with. So I replied: "Guys, don't be pissed at him. Be pissed at Peter for letting him do it. That's who your anger should be directed at."

Peter, who was the publisher, and his boss, who was the CEO of the division, later went into our emails and read them, and guess who got separated from the pack? Me. And by separated, I mean moved out of the open office area I shared with the rest of the team and into a new separate office that used to be the supply closet. Imagine an employee of The Economist being moved into the broom closet for challenging the manager, albeit not to his face.

Experiences like that were par for the course for me. I just couldn't keep my mouth shut when I instinctively felt we were going in the wrong direction. It was clear about five years into my career at The Economist that I was not going to be promoted in this organization.

The politics and hierarchical nonsense were mostly why I chose not to tell people at work about my fledgling company. I didn't want anyone looking over my shoulder (at least not any more than they already were). As far as I was concerned, if I continued to deliver for The Economist, what I was doing on my own time was nobody else's business.

The other, much more pressing concern was a financial one. I might have been treated like the junior salesgirl, but I was making good money; certainly, quitting my job would not have been an option. Though we could have survived on his salary alone, Markos is not what I call a "hedge-fund husband." Losing my income would have required a significant lifestyle adjustment. More important, I didn't want to put that kind of pressure on my barely-off-the-ground business. I didn't want the temptation to turn aden + anais into a slush fund if things got tight for us personally. Of all the myriad reasons to leap into entrepreneurship, money hadn't been on my list. What I truly wanted was to be challenged and fulfilled.

A ballsier person, a *braver* person, might've gone all-in, possible financial ruin be damned. Instead, I decided to hedge my bets.

Probably not the image that comes to mind when you think of an entrepreneur, right?

The way most people envision an entrepreneur, I think, is as more of a hard-charging, throw-caution-to-the-wind, take-no-prisoners badass, like a Steve Jobs or a Larry Ellison. Someone with the guts to quit his job or drop out of Harvard before going on to earn untold riches and enjoy wild success. Taking risks, after all, is just part of the job. I mean, the very definition of the term *entrepreneur*—thought to have been coined by an eighteenth-century economist named Richard Cantillon—is "a specialist in taking on risk." *Entrepreneur* magazine puts it even more succinctly: "If you aren't prepared to take risks, you have no business" launching a business.

This notion of the vanguard entrepreneur willing to risk everything is so pervasive, in fact, that it can apparently even sway the actions of *non*-entrepreneurs. In his bestselling book *Originals*, Wharton professor and organizational psychologist Adam Grant explained the reasons he chose not to invest in a scrappy young internet start-up called Warby Parker back in 2009. Most of the founders, all seniors at Wharton, had decided to line up jobs after graduation rather than pursue their business full time. Grant thought they "lacked the guts to go in with their guns blazing, which led [him] to question their conviction and commitment . . . In [his] mind, they were destined to fail because they played it safe instead of betting the farm."

If you're anything like these examples—if you, too, believe that entrepreneurship requires a willingness to bet the farm—then it's a short leap to the idea that a whole bunch of folks just aren't cut out for the task, maybe even you. Because here's the thing about risk-taking: It has long been viewed as a distinctly *male* trait. Women are typically viewed as the safe, conservative players, the ones who choose to make smaller bets and avoid risk if at all possible. We get this message from the media, from historical/cultural roles, and from some of our most lauded evolutionary theories.

The oft-used interpretation of Darwin's sexual selection theory in a nutshell is: our cavemen ancestors evolved to be daring to better woo women and father more children. It gets rolled out to explain all sorts of interesting facts about our modern world, like how men are more likely to die in car accidents, to drown, to gamble, to experiment with adverse behavior such as drinking and drug use, and to engage in "risky" bedroom behavior.

In the boardroom, too, men seem more willing to seek out promotions, aggressively negotiate salaries and pay raises, and pursue highly competitive or even dangerous work—like firefighting or entrepreneurship.

When it comes to cave*women* and risk? While men were busy developing their inner Evel Knievels, the theory goes, women were more cautious and wary. The thought is that staying close to home and venturing out to gather plants (rather than hunt for animals) is, in traditional hunter-gatherer societies (and presumably for ancestral women as well), the best way to ensure a return on that long-term investment of having children. Certain types of risk-taking just didn't pay off that much.

The idea that women are biologically, immutably risk *averse* gets bandied about so often these days that it feels like a truism.

A 2017 *New York Times* article, "Why Women Don't See Themselves as Entrepreneurs," states explicitly that women are more risk-averse than men, which discourages them from entrepreneurship and trying to build high-growth businesses. A 2009 EY report posits one way to help women entrepreneurs overcome their apparent "fear of failure" is to have them emulate "role models who exemplify risk-taking." In a roundup of inspirational quotes by prominent female business leaders in the Huffington Post, the CEO of a health nonprofit explains that "for all professionals, and especially young women, the world outside our comfort zone can be huge and scary. Until we are willing to put ourselves out there and take a risk, we will never be able to achieve professional success and realize our potential."

Faced with this kind of rhetoric, it's easy to see how even the steeliest among us might begin to internalize the message. After all, the idea that women are at a biological disadvantage "appears to be cool, dispassionate, unarguable evolutionary logic," as one scholar put it.

But what if our ideas about what it takes to go into business aren't remotely accurate?

Adam Grant, for one, learned that they might not be.

Unfortunately for him, Warby Parker, which he decided not to invest in because he thought it was doomed to fail, turned out to be an e-commerce juggernaut. On launch day in February 2010, *GQ* magazine dubbed it the "Netflix of eyewear." Five years later, it was crowned the "most innovative" company in the world by *Fast Company*. From the sidelines, Grant watched as the business founded by his careful, cautious former students raked in $100 million in revenue and rocketed to a valuation of more than $1 billion.

Failing to invest when he'd had the chance proved to be the worst financial decision of Grant's life, so he set out to determine where he'd gone wrong, why he'd been so convinced that the founders wouldn't succeed. Part of what he discovered is that a growing body of research suggests that entrepreneurs—contrary to popular opinion—*aren't* any more fearless or fancy-free than the rest of us.

The key to entrepreneurial success, in fact, might just *be* an aversion to risk. Crazy, right?

If only I had Adam Grant's book back when I was at The Economist, I wouldn't have felt so conflicted about staying while starting my business on the side. Because reading *Originals* later blew my mind, especially the studies Grant references to show how the risk-taking behavior of successful entrepreneurs differs from what we commonly perceive. Take, for example, a study published in the academic journal *Strategic Organization*. More than eight hundred Americans, both entrepreneurs and folks with regular full-time jobs, were asked a simple question. Which of the following businesses would you prefer to start: (1) one that made $5 million in profit with a 20 percent chance of success, (2) one that made $2 million in profit with a 50 percent chance of success, or (3) one that made $1.25 million with an 80 percent chance of success?

The entrepreneurs, those crazy, risk-taking gamblers, were significantly more likely to choose the safest option. This finding held true regardless of income, age, entrepreneurial experience, marital status, education, household size, and gender. The study's authors concluded that entrepreneurs aren't just risk averse, they're even more risk averse than the general population.

Grant provides plenty more examples of steady-as-you-go businessmen and -women (the very opposite of risk-takers) in his book, but he's far from the first to challenge the stereotype. In a 2012 article, *Inc.* magazine declared that it was time to "shelve one of the most common stereotypes about entrepreneurs . . ." after a study of 250 British entrepreneurs found that a mere 3.6 percent reported having "adventurous" characteristics.

(Compare that to 12.8 percent of two thousand people from the general population.) Two years before that, in 2010, Malcolm Gladwell wrote at length about the risk-*mitigating* tendencies of successful businessmen for the *New Yorker*, showing they

> are all successful entrepreneurs, businessmen whose insights and decisions have transformed the economy, but their entrepreneurial spirit could not have less in common with that of the daring risk-taker of popular imagination. Would we so revere risk-taking if we realized that the people who are supposedly taking bold risks . . . are actually doing no such thing?

One of the most common tropes of the successful entrepreneur is that one must quit one's job to show dedication and have the time and energy to build a business. Aside from the fact that this is clearly not true based on my experience alone, some of the most famous entrepreneurs in the world, including Steve Wozniak of Apple, Pierre Omidyar of eBay, and Phil Knight of Nike, practiced hybrid entrepreneurship, choosing to leave their day jobs only when their start-ups had evolved enough to become much safer bets.

I'm going to go out on a limb here and suggest that when it comes to women entrepreneurs, an aversion to risk might not be the problem.

On the contrary, it's the *myth* of entrepreneur as risk-taker that has the potential to do far more damage—whether by deterring women (and men!) from starting businesses because they don't fit the stereotype, or by discouraging potential investors (like Adam Grant) because they wrongly perceive caution, discretion, and risk aversion to be negative traits. Pushing women, in particular, to take more risks willy-nilly or to emulate "role models who exemplify risk taking"—whatever the hell that means—seems like particularly misguided advice.

Even scientists, psychologists, and academic researchers can be guilty of bias, of misinterpreting the data, of seeing patterns in behavior where there aren't any. A growing body of research suggests that risk-taking can't be reliably linked to any one thing like gender, but is instead attributable to a wide variety of factors: socioeconomic status, worldview, political leaning, personal values, cultural norms, societal pressure, emotions, age, and more.

When you think about it, it makes sense. Which is the more likely scenario: That women, just by virtue of being women, are so averse to risk that we just can't hack entrepreneurship, or that each and every one of us has a unique set of goals, gifts, limitations, and circumstances that shapes not only our choices, but also the course of our lives? The assumption that women are so averse to risk flies in the face of the numbers that indicate women are starting businesses at 1.5 times the rate of men.

Perhaps we should stop focusing on why women are allegedly risk averse, and instead consider what risk-taking means in the first place. What one person deems risky—based on a million little factors, from the size of their bank account to their place in the social order—another might view as harmless. Some of us think starting a business is inherently risky and that finding and keeping a full-time job is the safe bet. However, counting on your employer to be the sole provider of your income is a huge risk. Most people don't understand that they can be fired at any time, or the company could fold—they falsely believe they have security. Starting a business might be enormously risky for someone with $200,000 worth of student loan debt (and no guarantee of immediate income), but for someone like me, who had income in the form of a full-time job to fall back on, it wasn't particularly risky at all.

It's ridiculous to chastise women for being too cautious because they are women. It would make much more sense for aspiring entrepreneurs—men and women—to identify the specific risks they face and then determine how best to mitigate them.

As a new mother—someone for whom childcare was both indispensable and an enormous expense—the single biggest risk I faced in launching aden + anais, outside of the drain on my time, was financial. I knew next to nothing about the science of risk back then; indeed, I presumed (wrongly, it turns out) that entrepreneurs were more often daredevils. True, it was a risk to put in that initial order of $30,000. The orders that followed, however, were not risky to me—they were logical. Demand was through the roof and we couldn't keep product on the shelves. Any risk that existed, in my eyes, was only the risk of slowing down, of not filling those orders fast enough.

Likewise, spending my free time on a side hustle was not a risk. Yes, I had limited time given that I had a job and a growing family, but it was a greater risk *not* to act on an idea that could eventually provide financial freedom for my family. In my eyes, depending on my employer for a paycheck to support my family for the rest of my life was the greatest risk of all, because it was based on the false idea that employment is safer.

But what I most wanted—aside from the opportunity to be my own boss and define my own future—was a chance to prove to myself that I could *do* this. Keeping my job was just a way of mitigating the risks. More than that, it alleviated virtually all of the pressure I might otherwise have put on myself to be successful: I had not put my family in financial jeopardy by quitting my job. I had not invested more than we could afford to lose. It allowed me to (as I like to say) make peace with potential failure, which means that I really, truly internalized the notion that it was OK to fail. It was much more important to me to *try* and fail, in fact, than to sit back, wait ten years, and watch somebody else find success exploiting the very same idea that I'd had. To me, the risk was greater in not trying, in not taking a chance on something that would help me free myself from my dependence on a paycheck written by someone else. Even if the whole thing went up in flames, I'd be able to walk away knowing I'd given it my best shot.

I'd been at The Economist for eight years and my division had grown so much that I just couldn't handle all of the opportunities on my own anymore. They finally let me hire someone. Nobody, however, wanted me to hire David Suk. He was young, twenty-two, and didn't have any sales experience. (He'd worked in marketing but had never sold anything in his life.) He was very opinionated and not particularly . . . *tactful*. He had no tolerance for stupidity and just told it like it was—so of course I liked him. More important, David is brilliant. I knew he'd be a quick study, and I don't mind saying that I am, most of the time, an excellent judge of character.

About six months after I started my side company, David stuck his head in my office and asked what I was working on. Because of the time difference with China, I'd just finished up a call with my manufacturer there, and David was curious about whom I was talking to. (Ninety-five percent of the work I did for aden + anais happened in the wee hours of the morning, after I'd put my girls to bed. But, yes, sometimes I did take a phone call or shoot off an email during office hours when absolutely necessary.)

"Don't ask," I initially said, feeling guilty about the fact that I'd made a call about aden + anais during my day job. But then I took the risk and filled him in, anyway. David became the sole co-worker to know about my side business. Luckily for me, he kept my secret.

CHAPTER 5

MUM GUILT

When I was pregnant with Anais, I attended a party during which I ate the better portion of a wheel of brie cheese. If you've ever had a baby, are thinking of having a baby, or know someone who's had a baby, then you might know that soft cheeses are strictly verboten when you're expecting—according to most Western doctors, at least. (It's a pasteurization thing. Raw milk ups your chance of ingesting harmful bacteria.) But what can I tell you? The notion that cheese can be dangerous just seemed ridiculous to me, especially given that when my mum was pregnant with me, they expected I'd be born with a brandy in one hand and a cigarette in the other.

I ate the brie.

An hour or so later, though, when my stomach started to hurt, I became hysterical: *Oh, God. Something is wrong with my baby! What have I done?!*

I called my doctor, Jonathon Scher, a lovely, sane South

African man who would go on to deliver all four of my children. He listened and then very patiently explained to me that my baby and I were fine. What I had, he told me, was a case of mother's guilt.

"Let me tell you," he said, "it starts the minute you conceive that baby and it will not stop until the day you die."

Truer words have never been spoken.

As our little company continued to grow, so too did the size of my family. And though I'd always been a working mum, even before I started my company, the struggle to manage work and family life did *not* get any easier.

Once while I was out of town on business, my husband decided to take the girls out for ice cream. He stepped up to the counter, flanked by four little girls, giggling and chattering and ogling the display case. The cashier looked down at them, looked back at my husband, and in a small voice asked, "Do they have a mother?"

My husband took it in stride: "Of course, mate. She's just traveling for business."

But when Markos recounted the story to me later, instead of scoffing at this person's ridiculous question, it was like someone reached into my chest and ripped out my still-beating heart. Once again, I wasn't there. Once again, I had been away from my girls because of the business. It should go without saying the obvious and insidious double-standard at work here: I have never once been asked, on the days when I'm out and about alone with the girls, if they have a *father*.

Women share a common anguish over juggling their responsibilities. No amount of starry-eyed optimism over the things that women can accomplish in the business world will soothe the guilt of the mum who feels she should be in two places at once: at home, with her children, and at work, doing what earns her a paycheck and what she (hopefully) finds meaningful. Each of these—children and work—can feel like a calling, we can feel devoted to both. But which one takes precedence moment to moment? What is the cost to our children when we give our career priority in a given moment? These are questions all parents grapple with on a daily basis, even if unconsciously.

Consider this hilarious and on point post from blogger Lauren Cormier over at Scarymommy.com:

> I didn't spend enough time playing with the kids.
>
> I didn't get the house clean because I was playing with the kids.
>
> I cleaned the house and now I won't let the kids play because they'll mess it up.
>
> I didn't bring them outside to play and it's beautiful out.
>
> I brought them outside to play and now they have bug bites.
>
> I'm not strict enough.
>
> I'm too strict.
>
> I let them eat candy.
>
> I don't let them eat candy.

I hide candy from them so I can eat it.

I don't plan educational activities for the kids to do on a daily basis.

Who am I kidding? I don't plan educational activities for the kids to do ever.

I didn't breastfeed long enough.

My pregnancy diet is probably to blame for my middle child's food allergies.

I let them watch too much TV.

Sometimes I use the TV as a babysitter.

I yell too much.

Mummy guilt shows up in different ways for different women. It can show up at the grocery store when our kid starts screaming in aisle seven and we think we should have it all under control. It shows up when we work nights or weekends to finish that project—the one we worked so hard to land—which takes precious time away from them. It shows up when we don't know how to make the changes they need or we lack the emotional energy to do so. It's there when the "perfect birthday party" doesn't go as planned and ends in tears and tantrums. It shows up when we don't have the space to be emotionally available to them, because, well, shit happens. For many of us, it starts at pregnancy with pressure to give birth naturally like some heroic warrior goddess, surrounded by candles and people chanting.

It starts with the phrase "breast is best," which brings with it a heavy load of guilt for those who physically can't produce milk (I couldn't, despite trying for months), or have to return to a workplace with no lactation rooms, or—god forbid—simply prefer not to breast-feed. It's there when we crave time to ourselves but feel as though we should be giving time to our families, because to do otherwise is considered selfish.

Instead of seeing the conundrum for what it is—a Chinese finger trap which keeps us struggling instead of accepting our reality—we strive to do it all. We think we can be superhero mum and superhero career woman all the time, every day. Not surprisingly, this leads to an incredible amount of burnout.

Take Markos and me, for example. Until about four years ago, Markos would wake up in the morning and get himself ready for work while I'd be running around like a madwoman, making breakfasts, packing lunches, brushing teeth, combing hair, checking homework, stuffing backpacks, planting kisses, and finally shoving all the girls and Markos out the door at 8:30.

For years, I did all this without ever asking for help. I thought I could—and should—be able to do it all myself. But my anger and resentment grew. And when it became too much and I felt on the verge of a nervous breakdown, I started yelling and complaining, but that didn't seem to do much, either.

The tipping point came one morning when I was running around the apartment on a particularly rushed day, trying to get the girls ready. Markos was doing his usual routine: showering, getting dressed, watching the morning news on TV. I stormed into the bedroom and looked at him enjoying his leisurely morning and thought *What the fuck*. I said, "Would you mind getting your arse out here to help me get the girls sorted and out the door?" and his response was "Of course, what do you need me to do?"

Later, Markos and I sat down and made a list of our respective chores and duties. It turned out that my husband had never been unwilling to help; he just wasn't sure how best to be helpful. Still, some of the worst fights Markos and I have ever had were over the fact that I think a forty-eight-year-old electronic engineer with two MBAs should be able to work out what needs to be done without having to be told, but I digress. He needed a list, so we made one, and that was all it took.

So, not only do we try to do it all, but we try to do it all *alone*.

Why do we feel this enormous pressure to perform? And why is this special kind of guilt reserved for one half of the parenting equation? Women and men judge women and their career choices to no end. We judge women who work outside the home for not being there for their children. We judge stay-at-home mums, meanwhile, for not having a "real" job or not realizing their "true" potential. We judge women who choose not to have children as somehow defective or less feminine. And some of the worst judgment is an inside job. We keep a mental tally of who's doing what and who's doing it better. We are often deeply insecure about our own choices, so much so that we are racked with guilt about them. We heap this guilt on one another.

I'm not immune to this either. As a mum of kids who go to school in Brooklyn, I encounter my fair share of stay-at-home mums whose lives are focused solely around their kids and family. I admire that, but I know myself well enough to know that it isn't for me, and by default, isn't the best choice for my girls, either. I firmly believe that I would be a worse mum if I stayed at home with my children all day. But because I don't drop my girls off at school every morning (Markos takes them to school on his way to work), I get backhanded comments from women at school who say, "Oh, you're never here. What brings *you* in today?" A friend once said to me casually, "I don't see the point of having children and not actually raising them myself." (Lovely.)

Even my own mother judged me. We were home in Australia and I was making dinner for the girls. She told me that one of them was not going to want to eat what I was cooking and suggested that I make something just for her. When I insisted the daughter in question would like the food, she cut me off: "Well, how would you know? You never cook your children's meals anyway."

It was like a sucker punch to the stomach. She said it with such obvious disdain and venom that it was difficult to find the words to say in response. "Seriously, Mum? Then what am I doing right now? OK, so I don't cook them dinner Monday through Friday, but any time I'm not at work, I cook for them." But then I just stopped, knowing it wasn't worth it to argue. She wouldn't have believed me anyway. (Of course, Markos never has to deal with this type of criticism. It was perfectly OK in my mum's eyes that Markos didn't cook the girls dinner every night.) That moment still stings.

What I struggled with, especially trying to juggle a full-time job, growing a side business, and raising an expanding family, is the societal belief that working mums are somehow failing because we choose work, rather than to be with our kids day in and day out. Women are up against commonly held beliefs that we don't *want* to work, that we value our careers less than men do, and that huge swaths of us will ultimately leave our jobs to care for our children. (I would guess that every mother reading this was asked at least once during her pregnancy whether she would be returning to work after she gave birth.) Perhaps you've heard of this phenomenon, commonly known as "off-ramping" or "opting out." It's often given as the reason that so few women have snagged boardroom or C-suite spots.

In a 2014 study of more than twenty-five thousand Harvard Business School MBA graduates, 77 percent of respondents cited "prioritizing family over work" as the number-one barrier to women's career advancement. That number climbs even higher—up to 85 percent—when you ask *only* women. So almost everyone thinks this, and in fact, women are even more inclined to believe in the perception that women "opt out" than men are. Scary and disappointing.

While the opt-out story line points to the pull of family life as the main reason why women quit, studies have shown that 86 percent of women cite workplace issues, like inflexible jobs, as a key reason for their decision to leave. Recent studies have also found that despite perceptions to the contrary, reentering the workforce after having children is more difficult than women typically expect.

Overall, the study found that women are *not* actually increasingly likely to stay at home with their children. It did find, however, that both men's household contributions and women's work hours have stalled.

Remember that survey in which 85 percent of female HBS

grads cited family as the number-one factor holding women back? Based on results from the very same study, only 11 percent of women in that group had *actually* left the workforce to care for their children full time. That number drops to just 7 percent for women of color; for black and South Asian women, in particular, it plummets to 4 percent.

Furthermore, for the women who did leave to care for their children, opting out was a poor description. Researchers wrote that the survey results suggested

> [W]hen high-achieving, highly educated professional women leave their jobs after becoming mothers, only a small number do so because they prefer to devote themselves exclusively to motherhood; the vast majority leave reluctantly and as a last resort, because they find themselves in unfulfilling roles with dim prospects for advancement. The message that they are no longer considered "players" is communicated in various, sometimes subtle ways: They may have been stigmatized for taking advantage of flex options or reduced schedules, passed over for high-profile assignments, or removed from projects they once led. One alumna, now in her late fifties, recalled, "I left my first job after being 'mommy-tracked' when I came back from maternity leave."

"There is no truth. There is only perception," Gustav Flaubert once said. Despite the commonly held belief to the contrary, it doesn't appear women are opting out in droves because they prefer to be home to raise their children after all, does it? Instead, perhaps women opt out when the pressure to perform as the heroic mother and career woman collides with the lack of flexibility, adequate parental leave, and access to affordable childcare; dwindling opportunities for advancement; systemic discrimination; and a general hostility toward mothers in the typical American workplace. In other words, we're all tired and just want off the crazy-train. The danger in our shared cultural perception that women choose to opt out is that it perpetuates the status quo and obscures the evidence that factors in the workplace often conspire to *drive* women out.

Ouch. Especially because those factors are well within reason for businesses, government, and society to address.

This has very real repercussions for the entrepreneurial world. In chapter 1, we looked at the criticism that women-owned businesses don't typically grow as big as men-owned businesses. Sarah Thébaud, an assistant professor of sociology at UC Santa Barbara, surveyed data on women and entrepreneurship from twenty-four different countries, and found that "some women see a business opportunity and want to capitalize on it," whereas other women are drawn to self-employment out of need. That need could be more family income, but it's more likely a need for better work-family balance. Thébaud's study shows a correlation between the availability of paid leave, subsidized childcare, and part-time employment opportunities, and whether or not women will start businesses. In other words, women often find themselves driven out of the workplace and into entrepreneurship out of need rather than passion.

Without much flexibility or required paid leave, combined

with the expense of childcare, it's "hard to justify remaining employed or, at least, employed full time. So a lot of women try to manage childcare with a small home-based business, or maybe [try] offering childcare services themselves," says Thébaud.

The problem? These types of businesses don't tend to generate high revenues. In other words, these are typically the kinds of companies that *don't* scale—and now we're right back where we started, telling women they launch the "wrong" kinds of businesses. That is one hell of a catch-22.

Consider the cost of all this to fathers, too.

Perpetuating the opt-out myth doesn't just hurt women, it ignores the wants and needs of men, many of whom *also* care about flexibility, childcare, and work-life balance but are working longer hours for stagnant wages. Paternity leave is linked with higher retention and productivity, which keeps companies competitive. It offers a surprising benefit: A 2016 study of nearly twenty-two thousand companies in ninety-one countries found that places with the highest percentages of women in corporate leadership roles offered fathers eleven times more paternity leave than countries with fewer female leaders.

Based partly on my own experience, aden + anais has always offered six months of maternity leave. The company offers paternity leave, four weeks total, two of them paid. (We're part of a small group of employers that do so.) This is still not enough—I'd like to have offered more as we continued to grow—but already that policy costs a whole lot of money. So that's the crux, right? Offering time off is expensive. I confronted this business decision head-on when our global financial controller was gearing up to deliver her first child not long ago. She is an integral part of the business; it's not like we could just do without Desiree for six whole months. (We could not.) So not only did we have to pay Desiree's salary, but we also had to bring in a very expensive consultant to cover her job.

This is undoubtedly the right thing to do from a moral perspective, but what many people don't realize is that *not* doing it would be an incredibly bad business decision, more so than the short-term additional financial burden that it puts on the business. Congress's Joint Economic Committee prepared a fact sheet showing that paid-leave policies bolster economic growth in part by keeping employees in their jobs; they also increase the number of people working overall, while lessening the need for public assistance. Offering paid parental leave is a win-win.

Consider the cost to a company when a woman leaves her job in search of less discrimination or more balance, when she wants to work but is instead pushed out. It's estimated that the cost of replacing a midlevel employee can be 150 percent of that employee's annual compensation. Consider the cost to the economy when a woman's need for flexibility causes her salary to drop or stagnate, when a leap into entrepreneurship *doesn't* end up panning out, when a worker is left with no other choice than to opt out. That's one less worker contributing to the economy every time this happens. And, unfortunately, it happens all too often.

All of this addresses the issue of whether women *will* leave the workforce to care for their children, but we haven't addressed the long and quietly held belief that they *should*. Which brings us right back to the idea that some women *choose* to work, while others *choose* to stay at home. Meanwhile, do we ever ask men if they "choose" to work or stay at home?

The judgment about women's career choices probably won't stop anytime soon. Most of us would say our choice to work is not, in fact, a choice. Most of us either need to work to support ourselves and our families, or we need to work to feel fulfilled. Was it a *choice* to work, or to start my business? Not so much. As I said, working was not only financially important to my family, but it was important to me. When I moved to New York, I learned that I could not be idle for long without suffering the consequences of lethargy, depression, and a total lack of interest in life. My career is fulfilling, and I'm convinced I would be a terrible mother if I were a full-time stay-at-home mum. Even though I once had to use my whole salary to pay for quality childcare, investing in my career has always been worth it.

And for those of us who worry about the effect of their desire to work on their children, take heart. Research out of Harvard Business School found that

> Women whose moms worked outside the home are more likely to have jobs themselves, are more likely to hold supervisory responsibility at those jobs, and earn higher wages than women whose mothers stayed home full time . . . Men raised by working mothers are more likely to contribute to household chores and spend more time caring for family members. The findings are stark, and they hold true across twenty-four countries.

"There are very few things that we know of that have such a clear effect on gender inequality as being raised by a working mother," says Kathleen L. McGinn, the Cahners-Rabb Professor of Business Administration at Harvard Business School, who conducted the study with Mayra Ruiz Castro, a researcher at HBS, and Elizabeth Long Lingo, an embedded practitioner at Mt. Holyoke College.

All that said, I'm still in search of the proverbial "balance" that just doesn't exist. It took a couple of years before I learned how to handle my dual roles better. I needed to draw a line in the sand: When I'm at home, my mum hat goes on. I don't take calls from the office or sneak off to check my email when the girls are still up or on weekends; I focus exclusively on my family. When I work, my entrepreneur hat goes on, and I focus solely on running the business.

But that is easier said than done, and we all know it's much more nuanced than this. It took a heartbreaking moment of being pulled in two directions at once, between work and family, and a major slap in the face that forced me to prioritize. In 2011 I'd been invited to pitch Babies"R"Us when they were still the big player in the juvenile products space. On the morning of the meeting, Anais (who was about eight years old) woke up with a 104-degree fever. Markos had already called out of work, but like many sick kids, my daughter wanted her mum. She looked up at me with her big brown eyes and pleaded: "Please, Mummy. Don't leave me."

I felt sick.

The meeting had taken months to set up. I didn't think it was possible for me to back out at the last minute. So I left her with her dad. I traveled from Brooklyn to New Jersey and sat down in the waiting area outside reception, feeling like the absolute worst mother in the entire world. I waited, stewing, agonizing, anxious, for forty long minutes, until an assistant buyer came out to inform my colleague Brian and me that there had been a "change of plans" and that we'd need to reschedule.

I am not exaggerating when I tell you that Brian (aden + anais employee number six, so we were like family) had to put his arm across my chest to keep me from tackling this woman. I couldn't believe they hadn't had the courtesy to cancel the meeting earlier, couldn't believe they had left us sitting there for forty minutes when I could have been—should have been—at home with Anais.

And I realized *right then* that everything, even the really "important" stuff, can be rescheduled.

I mean, sure, I still had to miss an occasional swim meet or gymnastics performance on behalf of my business. And sometimes, seeing one of the girls spit out two lines in a (pretty terrible) school play really *isn't* as important as securing a million-dollar end cap at Target. But when one of my children looks me in the eye and says, "I need you," I drop everything, and I don't feel bad about it, either.

I could fill pages with the fact that as a working mother, entrepreneur or not, you are constantly doing battle with yourself. In fact, I think the search for balance is a bit of a joke, or like I said, a Chinese finger trap. If I didn't have aden + anais or a career, I would dedicate more time to my children. And if I didn't have children, I would be able to dedicate more time to my career. It's a constant compromise, a give and take that is always changing. What I've made peace with is the fact that I am one person and there are only twenty-four hours in a day; I'm comfortable with the amount of energy I give to the business and to my family, and I wouldn't have it any other way.

That doesn't mean I don't have my moments of doubt. Once, I was telling a friend of mine that I was worried that I was going to fuck up my children for being the kind of mother who loves going to work. I'll never forget what she said to me: It's not *whether* you're going to fuck them up; you *will* fuck them up. Because that's what parents do—it's just the degree of fucked up that you need to worry about.

I took her words to heart. I realized that I didn't want to try to be the person who raises these perfect, well-rounded children, because it's impossible and life isn't perfect. It can be hard and unforgiving, so I wouldn't be doing my girls any favors anyway. We all need to learn to give ourselves a break.

Aside from easing up on the judgment about ourselves, we need to ease up on one another. If you've read the news lately, you might have seen the study from the World Economic Forum saying that we won't reach gender parity until 2133. That's not even within my children's lifetimes. It's just not good enough, and if we as women can't come together and lift one another up, then that's probably an optimistic timeline. If we supported one another instead of dragging one another down, we might all find it easier to establish the right balance for us as individuals. It's hard being a working mum, and it's equally hard being a stay-at-home mum—for different reasons of course. Drop the judgment of other women and their choices, regardless of whether you would have made a different choice. And most important, extend the same kindness to yourself.

Finally, you know that saying "It takes a village to raise a child"? Well, sometimes you have to let that village help you raise your child. As hard as it was to have the conversation with Markos and come to an understanding, it's even harder for me to understand why I didn't ask for help sooner. There were mornings where I got to the point that I wanted to stab him in the face with the knife I was using to cut the girls' apples for lunch, but why didn't I just say, "I need help"? Like most women, I bought into the bullshit belief that these were *my* kids, and I should be the one getting them fed and dressed and out the door; rather than these are *our* kids and we need to figure out a system to take care of everyone as equally as possible.

Let the village help. Let their father spend time with them all by himself, without doing the prepping or planning for them. Let their grandparents come for the weekend so you and your husband can have a getaway for yourselves. Trust the babysitter to care for your children and engage them in novel ways. Ramona has been a nanny to our girls for ten years now. Amelie Rose, our youngest, has never known life without Ramona in it. She is truly like a second mother to our girls and I don't feel guilty about that—I feel incredibly grateful. They love and respect her and see Ramona as part of our family. Because I know that our girls are being loved and cared for when Markos and I are not able to be with them, I can focus on the "other stuff."

We were never meant to do this alone. The first step is to dig deep within yourself to find what it is you truly want; that will help you avoid the influence of other people's opinions. Only you and your partner (if you have one) know what's right for you. Second, talk to your partner. It's important that you have those conversations with him or her, and early. Don't accept the societal pressure that says it's all on you—it's both of you together, figuring it out. Remind yourself that you're really a very good mother, and wanting a successful career or a business of your own doesn't mean you love your family any less.

In the end, it helps to know my four girls have learned one hell of a lesson watching their mum run a global company that she started at their kitchen table, while clearly seeing that when push comes to shove, they are always, without a doubt, my number one priority.

CHAPTER 6

CASH IS QUEEN

In the summer of 2006, two weeks after going to market, I got an urgent call from a friend.

"Raegan," she said, "go buy *Us Weekly*. Now!"

Her tone was so serious, I dropped what I was doing and ran to a newsstand. As I flipped through the pages of celebrity sightings and fashion faux pas, there, on page eighteen, was a full-page photo of Adam Sandler and his wife, Jackie, strolling along Malibu beach with their bulldog and new baby. The foamy white water was washing over the sand and . . . holy shit. My jaw dropped as I looked more closely at the picture. The baby was draped in a blue-starred aden + anais blanket.

By chance, we had just landed prime placement in a national magazine. Practically overnight, our tiny business exploded.

After our *Us Weekly* debut, the celebrity press did not stop. In fact, we became a fixture in the gossip pages, as more and more actors and artists—from Gwen Stefani and Fergie to Channing Tatum and Neil Patrick Harris and Kate Hudson—found and became fond of the blankets. I hadn't intended to court celebrity customers or the celebrity press, but it was serendipitous that so many A-listers used our product to shield their babies from the paparazzi. aden + anais merchandise was front and center in all those photos. And I certainly wasn't complaining.

These celebrity photos certainly helped us launch the brand and put aden + anais on the map. I believe we would have sold as many swaddles to regular mums whether Beyoncé was photographed with one of the blankets or not, because it's a really great product. That's why celebrities were using it—they want great products for their babies like the average Joe does. Of course, we didn't just rely on *Us Weekly* for free press. When the photos came out, we had been working hard on all fronts, and we had already started to see results. We didn't stop working just because we got lucky. Our insistence on quality at an affordable price point (or as affordable as we could manage)—from the beginning—resulted in mums telling other mums that it was a great product. We also had only four products on the market, but we made sure those four products were everywhere. Solidifying ourselves in the high-end boutique space (the kind of stores frequented by Adam Sandler and Gwen Stefani) enabled us to build an aspirational brand. We wanted it to have a luxurious aesthetic, but we never wanted it to be a luxury that only wealthy people could afford.

The celebrity press helped, since we had virtually no money for marketing. Despite our very limited budget, I was adamant about hiring a PR agent from day one. I knew PR was a necessary expense and investment; we needed long-term exposure in addition to those quick wins from the celebrity photos. Our initial agent, Elyssa Sanders, and Kristina Junger-Godfrey, who still works with aden + anais today, steadfastly reached out to editors and bloggers in the baby space to introduce the product to them. PR is still a principal part of a launch for every new aden + anais product.

Meanwhile, our $30,000 worth of merchandise sold out within three months. We were experiencing out-of-control, exponential growth. It was wonderful but so chaotic to try to stay ahead of demand and fulfill the incoming flood of orders. We weren't prepared for this to happen. It wasn't long before we started experiencing problems with cash flow. We may have been generating revenue, but there were times when we didn't have enough cash to purchase the inventory we required to meet the demand.

Because the product was immediately picked up, Claudia and I didn't hesitate to put more of our own money into the game. It didn't feel like a risk given the instant success of the product and the overwhelming demand—customers wanted more of what we were selling, and we just needed to find the capital to make it possible to give it to them. And because we had the resources, we didn't have to go straight to OPM—"Other People's Money."

Access to capital or, more accurately, lack of access to capital, was the single biggest hurdle in the journey to build aden + anais. Truthfully, it's difficult for *any* entrepreneur to get funding, regardless of gender. While one study found there are differences in approval ratings, they weren't huge: 32 percent of women business owners were approved for credit, while 35 percent of men business owners were approved. However, women entrepreneurs are more likely to pay higher rates and receive less overall funding than their male counterparts. In other words, we're paying more in interest rates and given less access to capital. Women also tend to ask for less investment money—which is interesting, given that we also tend to ask for less money when discussing hiring and promotions with a prospective employer.

In 2017, female founders received only 2 percent (!) of venture capital dollars. This 2016 study by Columbia University's Dana Kanze sheds light onto what's behind women not getting more VC (venture capital) backing. A team of researchers watched over two hundred hours of video of entrepreneurs pitching to investors at a TechCrunch competition in New York. They tracked the words investors used when asking questions and found significant differences in the way women and men were addressed. When questioning the male entrepreneurs, investors used words like "gain," "ideal," "accomplish," "expand," and "grow." When questioning the female entrepreneurs, they used words like "afraid," "anxious," "avoid," "careful," "fear," "loss," and "pain." Men were asked questions like "How do you plan to monetize this?" Women were asked "How long will it take you to break even?" Further, men were more likely to be asked about their aspirations to make money for the investors, while women were asked how they would avoid losing investors' money. In other words, women end up playing defense from the very beginning. This is a huge problem, and no doubt a massive deterrent to female entrepreneurs.

The numbers are even less encouraging for African American women. Less than 1 percent of venture capital-backed founders are African American, which isn't surprising given that the percentage of black decision-makers within VC isn't much better.

If it's not subtle discrimination, it's overt. Kathryn Tucker is the founder of RedRover, an app that helps parents find local events for kids. When she pitched her idea to an angel investor at a New York tech event, he told her he didn't invest in women. Of course, she asked why. "I don't like the way women think," he said. "They haven't mastered linear thinking." As evidence, he went on to tell her that his wife could never prioritize her to-do list. As if to compliment her, he told Tucker, "You're different. You're more male." How fucked up is that?! All this discrimination is a waste of potential, because when women do qualify for investment, they far exceed expectations. A Women 2.0 conference report in 2013 found women-led tech start-ups achieved on average a 35 percent higher rate of return. When women-led tech companies are venture backed, they bring in 12 percent higher revenue than male-owned ones. Outside the tech world, you find similar numbers.

I personally didn't work with investors until much further down the road (we were doing about $8 million in revenue). I skipped the VC route and my first investment came from private equity, which is unusual given our size at the time. I just so happened to hit it off with a private equity firm, and they decided to invest in my small company, which didn't fit their usual model.

But I'm getting ahead of myself, because at this point Claudia and I were just trying to get the business off the ground, with lots of promise and interest but a very immediate need for capital—without an obvious source. We rallied to bootstrap our business—that is, to self-finance—and put in more of our own money at first, at least temporarily. We were profitable, but not enough to meet the demand we were receiving. Shortly after our initial order, we each put in another $30,000, more than doubling our initial investment into the company. We kept going on like that until we had each put in $70,000. By that time, Markos and I were tapped. I'd put in every spare cent I could without mortgaging our home and jeopardizing my family's financial future and could do no more.

That sum of money was an insane amount for Markos and me, and it felt scary but right, because we believed in the business. Claudia, on the other hand, had a slightly different situation. She had married into a wealthy family. As I understood it, her husband's father was a psychiatrist who started a psychiatry newspaper and then sold it for many millions. Claudia's husband and his brother each received a meaningful sum in the form of a trust from their father, so they and their families were set for life. While they could have invested more in the business, Markos and I had reached the end of our rope. However, taking money from Claudia's family was the last thing I wanted to do, so we started shopping around for bank loans.

Our timing was terrible. We had started the business at the beginning of the worst recession since the Great Depression. Although we had initial meetings with about half a dozen banks, they said no almost right away. We were profitable and growing, but they all said the same thing—they just weren't making loans at that time.

After courting the big banks and getting turned down, we sought out small-business loans. Needless to say, I'm now convinced that contrary to the public sentiment, this country does not support small-business loans at all, well, at least not back in 2007. Everywhere we turned, it was impossible to get money. Our lack of access to capital almost closed us down. Now, when I run into some of these same bankers at social events, they practically crawl over one another to shove their business cards down my throat. I delight in saying, "I don't need your money," and remind them that when I did, they'd said no.

But at that moment, I really did need their money. And getting rejected time and time again may not have been only due to the recession. Women are still likely to hear no far more often than men when applying for small-business loans. The Senate Committee on Small Business and Entrepreneurship (it's a mouthful, I know) prepared a report in 2014 that found that despite the fact that women owned 30 percent of small businesses in the US at the time (today the number is closer to 38 percent), for every dollar they received, twenty-three dollars went to men. At the time that I was applying for loans, it never dawned on me that we may have been turned down because we were women. But having done the research for this book, I now suspect that may have been a contributing factor.

So, what is a woman to do when she can't get funding? It's been frequently reported that women tend to start companies using more of their own money and less capital from outside investors. That was certainly true for me. Oddly enough, inability to secure funds is often a criticism of women-owned companies, or at the very least it's used as a prediction of future failure. (Interesting how that works, isn't it? We can't get the money to fund our businesses, often because of unmitigated gender bias, and then we're told this is a fault of women-owned businesses.) What sometimes goes underreported, however, is that more than 57 percent of *all* businesses—whether started by men or women—are launched with personal funds or credit, and another 38 percent are funded by family and friends. They're self-financed. It's generally thought that "bootstrapping," at least in the beginning stages, is actually better for the health of a business in the long run.

When entrepreneurs bootstrap their businesses, they are forced to be clever in how they build and market their products or services. They have to think carefully about how they use their money, squeezing every last drop out of all of their available resources. In contrast, those who receive large amounts of money early on might be tempted to spend carelessly, letting the luxury of having it get the best of them. Perhaps most important, when first starting out, entrepreneurs should primarily focus on building their businesses by generating as much revenue as they can and running the business as leanly as possible. Once you have truly reached the point where your growth is hindered because of a lack of capital, then look for investment, as courting investors is a major distraction from running the business.

In the process of bootstrapping their businesses, women reportedly are also more likely to turn to friends and family for the funds to grow their businesses. And again, this is portrayed as a negative, which is misleading. Friends and family are one of the primary sources of funds for *all* entrepreneurs—male or female. They also spend more as investors in the aggregate. Friends and family contribute roughly $60 billion to start-ups every year, compared to $22 billion from venture capital firms and $20 billion from angel investors.

There is no shame in borrowing money from family and friends when the deal is drawn out and explained in a clear-cut contract. This is no place for a handshake deal or for sentimental feelings about the trust you think you share with your family members or friends. Make sure they understand the risk they're taking in investing in you and your company, and make sure everyone understands the repayment terms and timelines. Finally, don't neglect to have a lawyer review your agreement just because it could feel awkward. You'll be glad you did later if questions ever arise.

And although it's a common expectation that an entrepreneur will raise funds from friends and family, this is a biased expectation, however unwitting it may be. The average net worth of a white American is $144,000, compared to an average net worth of $11,000 for African Americans. A lack of capital and generational wealth in their communities leaves the black American population with far fewer options for funding, no matter the strength of the idea.

This is where you must be resourceful and creative. Susan Petersen, founder of Freshly Picked, a baby-goods company, had no access to capital whatsoever. She was pregnant and unemployed, and her husband earned just enough to support their family. Susan funded her business by banging the glass panes out of old windows and selling the metal for scrap. She then put the funds directly into her business, which quickly went from a small side hustle on Etsy.com to a company that earned $120,000 in the first year. Now, less than ten years in business later, Freshly Picked is generating millions in sales. Susan didn't have a financial leg to stand on, but she grew her business from nothing into a multimillion-dollar brand through sheer determination and will.

There is hope for those who don't want to or can't turn to friends and family for money; in recent years, more and more options have emerged for entrepreneurs who need funding, including alternative and online lenders, crowdfunding, and grants, not to mention female-led funding groups like SheEO, private equity and venture capital firms that focus primarily on women-owned businesses, and angel investors that work with women.

For Claudia and me, we were taking the business to a new level and needed cash fast. It started to feel inevitable that we would have to borrow money from Claudia's family. Eventually, Claudia and her husband loaned the business $50,000. At 10 percent interest and full payment within a year, this wasn't a casual arrangement. While borrowing from them was the easiest and potentially the only option at the time, it made me uncomfortable. I didn't want the scales tipped. With Claudia having more money invested in the company, it made me feel as if we were no longer equal partners.

I remember the exact conversation we had that made me realize our discrepancy in financial situations might cause problems. Claudia called me to talk about the fact that we needed still more money. We were burning through cash in a good way, and the merchandise just kept selling. Every bit of money we had went right back into inventory to support the exponential growth we were experiencing. We didn't take salaries for ourselves, we didn't have anyone working for us, and everything we needed that we couldn't handle was outsourced. All of the money went to the basics of running a rapidly growing business. "I'm going to go to my husband's family and ask for more money," she said. My stomach dropped. "Do we really want to do that?" I asked. I got the sense that he was already pissed off that he and Claudia had contributed more money.

"Well, we don't really have any choice," she said. "He has what we need in a shoebox under his bed." *Oh, god, there's got to be another way*, I thought.

But there wasn't. The stress ratcheted up, and in late 2007— little more than a year after going to market—Claudia's father-in-law loaned us $200,000. The stakes were getting higher.

It wasn't just the stress associated with the cash flow; the workload was also stressful. We divided tasks according to our abilities. From L.A., Claudia handled the accounting and marketing. Back home in New York, I took care of sales and managed our China supply chain. Even with a business partner, however, the demands on my time were overwhelming between my husband, my children, and my full-time job. I was staying up half the night, every night. I started to realize that our division of labor was uneven and that Claudia's contribution was falling more in the design and publicity arenas, which didn't require her to fly all over the country to do. Her job included choosing colors and patterns of our products and meeting with our PR agent, while mine involved a lot of travel to boutiques to sell merchandise. I grew frustrated trying to figure out how to increase our distribution, while Claudia was spending time having photo shoots in her backyard with Aden. I was heavily pregnant and felt like I was alone solving the larger strategy questions, and on foot, handselling to boutiques. I don't want to imply that Claudia didn't work hard, too—she did—but I did not feel that the division of labor was even. No doubt it was made worse by the fact that I was also working a full-time job and Claudia was not. But because I carried so much guilt over their funding the business, I sucked it up and kept working.

I spent most of my time just figuring out how to do my job. I was such a novice, so I had to Google everything. Every time I came up against something I didn't know how to do, which was often, I'd fake it. I really didn't have a choice. I had to figure this stuff out (and quick!) if we were going to make this business work. At my most stressed and sleep deprived, I had an aha moment. I had read an article about Ellen Diamant, the cofounder of Skip Hop. Like me, she'd launched a baby-goods company out of her New York apartment. She made the first diaper bag that clipped onto a stroller, which was so innovative. *This is someone who's been where I am now and could offer me a few pointers*, I thought.

So I called her. When she answered, I said, "You don't know me, but I'm starting this new business just like you did and was wondering if I could ask you a few questions."

Ellen was so gracious. She gave me ten minutes, which doesn't sound like much, but she didn't owe me anything. I hadn't scheduled this call with her, and she had no idea who I was. I was so appreciative. (By the way, this is why when anyone asks for my help these days, I give it to them, no questions asked.) Ellen was also extremely forthcoming with her advice.

"Stop filling orders out of your home," she told me. "You need to work with a fulfillment house."

More important, she told me to hit the trade show circuit. Those two pieces of advice proved invaluable and set a whole new level of sales for aden + anais in motion. Though I was hugely pregnant with my third child at the time—in my eighth month, one nervous flight attendant almost refused to let me on the plane—trade shows became a major part of our early success. I'd set up a booth and all the boutiques looking for new products would tell me that they had never seen anything like our blankets. At the very first show, aden + anais picked up nearly a hundred stores. I still have retailers approach me now who remember seeing our booth for the first time and knowing instantly that our products would be a hit. While the trade shows helped us grow, there was a ton of travel, and this was one more area of the business that fell to me. After tearing down and building up trade show booths while I was uncomfortably pregnant, I finally reached the end of my rope. On a call one day, I told Claudia that it really wasn't fair that I was doing the majority of the trade shows. And that's when the truth came out: Claudia's husband didn't want her to go. It seemed to me like she had to ask his permission, which I didn't understand at all. I asked her what was up.

"Well, he doesn't like it when I travel because he isn't comfortable looking after the baby on his own," she said.

"I have kids, too, and I still do it," I pointed out. *And a full-time job*, I thought.

But there was no moving her; her husband was adamantly opposed to her traveling. I just had to suck it up, and I justified it to myself because of their larger financial investment, even though I felt like I could collapse at any moment. These red flags should have warned me, but I was too excited about the growth of the company to see the inevitable cliff we were rapidly approaching.

CHAPTER 7

EXPECT SURPRISES

The tension only continued to increase as we grew, and at the end of 2007, Claudia and I had just had our first major disagreement. We were a year and a half into our business and had already reached over $500,000 in revenue. It was humming along at its extraordinary pace, but instead of sunshine and rainbows, we couldn't see eye to eye about whether to incorporate in Australia. Claudia wanted to keep the business within the US, and I wanted to dip our toes into the international markets. I figured that my mother, being a bookkeeper, could run the books, while my sister could handle sales in Australia. Claudia was adamant that it was not the way to go. I thought she was being shortsighted, and I told her so. We hung up the phone after that argument and didn't speak until a week later.

Tension was already high between us over money to grow the business. Like any business partnership, we had had our disagreements, but up until now we'd always been able to sort them out after a healthy debate. There was the time we argued over whether to take direction from showrooms about our designs. Claudia thought we should listen to them when they asked us to do this color or that design. I told her we know what we like and we're creating *our* brand and design vision—that we shouldn't allow ourselves to be dictated to by the head of a showroom who thinks it should be green instead of yellow. Claudia reluctantly agreed and we stayed true to our design vision.

We had even briefly argued about changing the company name. As it turned out, aden + anais (pronounced ay-den and uh-nay) was being referred to by some customers, rather inelegantly, as "add-un and anus." At that point, a name change wouldn't have been a particularly rash or unwise decision. And yet, I was steadfast. There are plenty of wildly successful brands with names that people once butchered—Louis Vuitton, Hermès, L'Occitane. You could call it obscene confidence on my part, but I felt that our name was in some ways integral to our success; it was high-end and aspirational without being fussy, and it had authenticity and emotion attached to it, given we'd named it after our children. I didn't want to lose that. Our customers just needed time to figure it out. It was worth it. Although it's become apparent that no one can pronounce aden + anais, the distinctive name has become a point of conversation in the media.

I didn't win every argument. We had a major dispute over a design that Claudia felt strongly about. It was not to my taste, and I felt it was too "cutesy" for the aden + anais brand. Well, I couldn't have been more wrong. The designs in question ended up becoming our Jungle Jam collection—the best-selling print in the history of the company, and the design that was on the blanket that wrapped baby Prince George when he first left the hospital. When you have a business partner, learning to compromise is crucial. Arguments are bound to happen, but how you deal with them will affect the success of your business. Claudia and I had been able to resolve most of our conflicts in a healthy, constructive way by discussing the problem and finding common ground.

In January 2008, we had a disagreement that proved to be different. Less than two months after the birth of my third child, I got an out-of-the-blue email from Claudia. My business partner, my *friend*, was giving me thirty days to come up with the money—$400,000, according to her estimation—to pay back all the outstanding loans to her family, plus an amount to cover her contribution to date to the business, to buy her out of the company. If I couldn't come up with the money, she would exercise her right to buy me out. If we couldn't agree to those terms, she would force me to dissolve the business.

I was devastated. I tried calling and emailing her to ask why she would do this. All in all, the business had borrowed about $300,000 from Claudia and her father-in-law. My share was $150,000. I wrote to Claudia, "This is $150,000. You know that I would never just walk away from that debt to your family if, God forbid, the business went under. You know who I am, I would never do that to you." She said very little in return except to reiterate her demands.

I was in total shock. First, denial—it took me a week to accept that this was actually happening because I was so surprised. I wanted to work it out, but when Claudia wrote in one of her emails that she didn't believe in the business and it was over, my attitude changed. Once I realized there was no convincing her that she was making a bad decision, I wanted her out.

But then came the double-whammy.

In the middle of all of this, my mother visited me. We were chatting one day when she asked me if I had had my skin checked recently. I told her yes, and that I had an appointment scheduled the following week. I bitched to her that every time I went, my doctor took a skin sample to biopsy, but it always came back OK.

To which my mum replied, "Interesting you say that, because there was a big scandal recently in Australia about dermatologists taking unnecessary biopsies to make money."

My wheels were turning. "You know what? I'll have to think about that, because she's got her instruments laid out every time I go in there, ready to chop me up."

Although I'm an Australian, I'm of English and Welsh descent—light of eyes, fair of skin. Throw in the thinning of the ozone layer over Australia (you can get badly sunburned just driving around in your car with the windows up), and the fact that I used to slather myself with an insect repellent called Aerogard (more effective than baby oil) and spread myself out like a starfish for hours on end (different times!), and you've got a recipe for disaster. When I was nineteen, a doctor said to me, "Raegan, if you keep doing this, you're going to look like a wrinkled-up old prune by the time you're thirty." And I distinctly remember thinking: *Who gives a shit what I look like at thirty? I'll be so old by then, I won't care!* Nowadays, the damage is bad enough that I diligently see a dermatologist every six months for a full-body scan. But after hearing my mother's story, I was now questioning my dermatologist's motives.

The next week, I went to see my doctor of many years, one of New York's most accomplished dermatologists. She's a take-no-prisoners kind of woman who makes me look like a shrinking violet. I adore her. As usual, she did her check and found a questionable area the size of a pinhead, right on the upper portion of my chest, where open necklines tend to fall. So of course she wanted to carve that bit out to do a biopsy.

"Seriously, Dr. Gendler? It's right there and you're going to cut me? I'm going to have another scar," I said.

"I have to insist," she said. "It really doesn't look good."

"But you've never found anything on any of the biopsies," I said.

She was on to me. "What's this all about?" she asked. So I went into my spiel about the dermatology scandal in Australia.

"Raegan. Seriously? You think I need to take unnecessary biopsies to make money? Don't be ridiculous! I promise I will be very careful, but there is no way I'm not taking a biopsy of this."

She had a point, and in the end she took the sample. I went home, assuming that it would be normal like every other biopsy.

The next day she called to tell me it was melanoma, the deadliest of skin cancers. She had already scheduled me for surgery.

"I'm sending you to a plastic surgeon tomorrow because of where it is," she said.

I was still stunned, so all I could say was, "What the fuck is happening here?"

"Yes, this is no joke. You need to get in there and get it out."

I went. Though the mole in question was minute (located just under my clavicle), the surgery was far more invasive than I'd realized it would be. Melanoma has tentacles, and my doctor had to cut deep to get it all out. Imagine my surprise when the procedure was over and I had thirty-eight stitches. I had bloody surgical drains hanging out of me. All of a sudden, I looked like the bride of Frankenstein, and I hadn't expected any of it. But because I had just returned to The Economist from maternity leave after giving birth to Arin (and because I am stubborn, with workaholic tendencies), I went back to the office. I was standing in the kitchenette with the surgical drains hidden under my shirt when our head of marketing walked in: "How are you?" she asked.

"Not so good," I said, and burst into tears.

I spent the next two days waiting to find out if the cancer had spread, which felt like a lifetime. In the meantime, Claudia continued to pummel me with emails. I finally had to email her to ask her to stop so I could have a moment to breathe. I even resorted to taking a picture of my scarred chest and sending it to her to get her to take it seriously. She said nothing in return, but did keep quiet for a few days. It hurt to no end that she seemed not to care at all about what I was going through, but I took it as another sign that it really was over. If she could switch off that coldly, there was no salvaging our friendship, let alone our business partnership.

After the news came back that I was clear, I had to return to the plastic surgeon to get the drains removed. By that time, the stress of the wait to hear if I had to have chemo, the stress of the business with Claudia, and the stress of being at work during all of it had pushed me to the limit.

When I walked into the good doctor's office to have my drains removed, I was coming in hot.

I told him it was bullshit that I didn't know I was going to be carved up, it was bullshit I didn't know I was going to need thirty-eight stitches, it was bullshit that I had to walk around with these hideous bloody drains sticking out of me. I told him I was pissed off at Dr. Gendler, pissed off at him—

And that's where he cut me off.

"Just wait a minute," he said. "Two weeks before you came in, a young guy—he was just forty or so—came in with exactly the same thing as you but on his back. I did the same surgery. Unlike your case, it was advanced, it had spread, and we couldn't get it. He's got six months to live."

I stayed quiet.

"You need to get over yourself, Raegan, and be grateful that Dr. Gendler caught it. Six months later, it would have been a different story."

It hit me hard. Despite how bad it was, how stressful the entire shit storm was, I needed a moment to slow down and put things into perspective. It was easy to allow myself to be consumed by the details of the business, or consumed by the anger I had toward Claudia. All of it seemed so important, until I sat there in my doctor's office, being told how I had dodged a bullet. Those so-called important details were suddenly irrelevant.

I realized I had to calm the fuck down; no baby blanket business is worth dying over. Had I not had that epiphany when I did, I would have kept hard-charging forward, giving the business and my anger too much energy. While the stress didn't just evaporate, my mind-set shifted completely. A close call with cancer was my slap in the face.

Which is not to say that I miraculously walked away from all these life events unscathed. After being cleared of cancer, I faced the emotional weight from the entire month head-on. One night in the midst of all this, I was having a fetal position moment, curled in a ball, just trying to hold it all in.

"I don't know if I can do this," I cried to Markos. "It's killing me. I'm hanging on by a thread."

He paused and asked, "Do you believe in the business? Do you believe in what you are doing?"

"Absolutely, I believe in it," I said.

"Well, then fight for it. Do whatever you can to fight for it, because you will never forgive yourself if you throw your hands up in the air at this point and just go 'This is too hard.'"

His encouragement was my catalyst. I'm a fighter, but in this moment, having a champion who had my back and knew me well enough to know that if I quit, I would have lived with regret forever—which would have been much worse than the occasional moment of self-doubt and feeling overwhelmed—was priceless.

In an ideal world, I would have been able to buy out Claudia on my own. However, that was far from my reality. It pissed me off that I didn't have the money to do it, and I was reluctant to involve friends as investors again, given the circumstances. But I knew I was in a tough spot, on a mission, and also incredibly lucky to have trustworthy people in my inner circle who might be able to help. I felt I had no other choice but to turn to these very people and ask them to invest. Although it may seem as if I was entering the same kind of relationship that I had with Claudia, the difference here was that I wasn't asking them to become partners and run the business with me. I was asking them to invest with the idea that they could potentially make money. Given my determination not to dilute my equity or give away control again, I determined that a loan from friends who were able and willing to give it was the best route to go.

Several months before this breakup with Claudia, another close friend of mine, Paula, had lamented that I hadn't started the business with her: "Why wasn't it *me* sitting on the floor with you that day?" she had said. Her husband was a banker and she was a former investment banker herself; I knew she likely had the means to invest. And I figured, rightly, that she would be interested. (Although she had to fight tooth and nail with her husband, Matt, who had been planning on purchasing two cars, which in New York is a bit of an anomaly. *If you buy those fucking cars and don't let me invest in this business, I am literally going to divorce you*, she eventually told him. Ya gotta love a feisty woman!)

It was not an easy task. Claudia had stipulated that I couldn't go out and actively raise funds to buy out her share—the money had to come from me personally, something she could stipulate as per the terms of our shareholder agreement. At the time, I wasn't sure why she was asking this of me, but years later I had an answer. While I was writing this book, our long-time publicist, Kristina Junger-Godfrey, told me over dinner that shortly after sending me the email, Claudia had directed her to hold off on any PR she was doing for the moment. When Kristina asked why, Claudia told her that I would be out of the business soon and then they could resume their work together. She was telling me a story about wanting out of the business, but she actually wanted to force me out because she thought I couldn't come up with the money. I approached the people I did because I assumed they had access to $100,000 or so, and because they were my friends and I hoped I could trust them. Because of Claudia's demands, it was a bit of a tough sell: I had to get them to agree to a clause that the money would go into my bank account on a handshake, with no documentation, so I could pay her out of my bank account directly. Obviously, no one would agree to such a request if there hadn't already been a previous relationship. Even then, it required a leap of faith on their part, and a whole lot of trust.

Does it look like I just snapped my fingers and suddenly had $400,000 at my beck and call? Remember, my back was up against the wall and I was willing to do whatever it took to save my business. Still, not everyone can ask friends and come up with this type of money. I happen to live in New York City, the banking capital of the world, and I happen to know a lot of bankers. And these banker friends had been hearing about my business—and its success—over the last year or two as I built aden + anais in my spare time. I'm not suggesting that it was easy money for them to invest; they may have had comfortable lifestyles, but it was still a large amount of money and they had to analyze this business opportunity and risk carefully.

My ability to sell the business opportunity and myself helped in this moment. I didn't feel uncomfortable asking for these friends' investments; I felt I was offering them an opportunity. Of course, I told them there were no guarantees here, and like any investment in a small business, they had to be prepared to lose it all. But I had pretty compelling data and our current track record of exponential growth to offer, and it was clear that I believed in the business and was going to work my ass off to make sure they didn't lose their money.

All in all, three couples were willing to come in as investors: Matt and Paula, their friends Jules and Tim, and Cristina, whom I had worked with previously at The Economist, and her husband, Scott. For a total of $490,000, they collectively held 49 percent of the company, while I maintained the majority share.

When we eventually sold the company, that 49 percent ended up being worth tens of millions! Because I couldn't get $500,000 on my own, I lost out on that much money. But I saved the business, and that was more important. As irritated as I was that I couldn't fund the buyout myself, I was blown away that these people had such faith in me and my business that they were willing to invest on short notice under less than orthodox conditions.

When I called Claudia to confirm that I had the $400,000, she immediately asked for more. She wanted an additional $100,000 "for her time and energy." She didn't think I was going to be able to come up with the money in the first place, and when I did, in short order, she upped the ante. I didn't even argue with her—I didn't want to negotiate.

It was the right decision to keep the company on the right track. While I'm not always very good at accepting something I don't like, it came down to the fairness of it all. As annoyed as I was that she asked for the additional money, I didn't think it was an unfair request—she had worked to build the business with me, after all. I also felt fighting her wasn't worth the risk of losing it all, so I went back to the friends who had invested and asked for more.

In the middle of this drama with Claudia—just a few months after my bout with melanoma—David, my lone Economist colleague who knew about aden + anais, walked into my office. "Well," he said affectionately, "you look like shit." Over lunch that day (and two bottles of wine), I explained my conundrum. I had officially (legally) taken control of the business, and I was planning to fly out to California to shut down our West Coast office, but Claudia had been using QuickBooks for our accounting and I had no idea how to use the software. David did, though, and graciously offered to come to L.A. with me. The trip was a disaster. To begin with, I couldn't close the business account that was under both of our names without Claudia's signature. This had to happen before I could transfer the small amount of funds we had to a new business account. My bank— the one with which we had done aden + anais business, the same bank that also managed Claudia's family's wealth—wouldn't allow me to close out the accounts, on which I was a signatory. Instead, the banker called Claudia: "Raegan's here," he told her, as if they were conspirators. He refused to budge, even after speaking to her. This resulted in a screaming match between the manager and me that went nowhere. I left empty-handed.

Not to be deterred, David and I went to the aden + anais offices—nothing more than a small room in a serviced office, to be honest—to close out the books and shut things down. I figured that this, at least, would go smoothly. I figured wrong.

Someone who worked in one of the adjoining serviced offices called Claudia and told her there was someone else in the office with me. The next thing we knew, the police came around and asked David if he was an employee of the company. David said no, and they threw him out, saying it wasn't OK that there was a "stranger" in our office, accessing company information. Needless to say, we got nothing accomplished on this trip.

In the meantime, I set about reincorporating the business in New York, which was about the time I discovered that our books were a mess. Tons of people owed us money. We had also been naive in other ways. We'd been giving our customers extended payment terms, among other mistakes. In addition to the division of labor problems Claudia and I had had, it became clear that one hand didn't know what the other was doing financially. I mistakenly believed Claudia was ensuring that we collected the money our customers owed us and that our lone full-time employee (whom we hired a few months prior) was handling the day-to-day accounting. I also realized that when Claudia incorporated the company, she named herself as the CEO and me as the CFO, which is hysterical, because that is the last role you would want me to fill.

After the disastrous L.A. trip, my lawyer dealt with Claudia and her team so that we could accomplish what was needed to move forward, and Markos volunteered to make the trip to L.A. to wrap things up at the office. While he was working at the computer, Claudia came in and threw the office keys at his head, saying that we didn't need to make this as vicious as it had become. Markos composed himself before replying, "You're joking, Claudia. You're the one who made it vicious." She said nothing in reply but gave him the last of the passwords and information he needed, then left, wishing him good luck on her way out. That was the last either one of us heard from her.

As someone who frequently advises new entrepreneurs, I often meet pairs of friends who are going into business with each other as equal partners. It's no surprise that the promise of starting a business with a partner is alluring; you have someone to share the ups and downs, the unknowns, and presumably the work and the risk. There is someone there to tell you you're on the right track or, hopefully, see it when you're not. Starting a business is hard, and having a partner offsets the emotional rollercoaster of the entire endeavor. There's also the pooling of assets; one person can bring financial expertise, another might bring marketing knowledge. When I meet lone entrepreneurs, they're often looking for a partner. When I ask them why, they tell me it's because they want help and support. When I encounter pairs, rarely do I hear that any of them have taken the necessary steps to formalize the relationship with a contract, much less organize their business in a way that will protect them both. And if the business partners are friends or family, they *really* should have a contract.

Professor Noah Wasserman elaborates on this in his book *The Founder's Dilemma*:

> In contrast to their greatest hopes when they co-found together, teams of friends or relatives are the least stable of all types of founding teams, even

less stable than teams of strangers/acquaintances. Within a founding team, each additional social (i.e. friend or family) relationship increases the likelihood of a cofounder leaving the team by almost 30 percent.

After my experience with Claudia, I learned firsthand that starting a business with a friend as an equal partner can lead to trouble. That's difficult to say since it's what got me here today. However, going through what I did with Claudia was heartbreaking. And it nearly tanked our business. So this, along with some other valuable lessons I've learned along the way, has forced me to look at partnership differently. If I had to do it again, I wouldn't have gone into business with my friend as equal partners in the first place.

In hindsight, it was blatantly obvious that the difference in the amount of money my family was able to invest versus what Claudia's family was able to invest was an issue. Maybe *the* issue. Soon after I was tapped out and couldn't contribute any more of my family's savings, the cracks in the relationship started to form. While I felt that Claudia wasn't pulling her weight, she felt resentful that her family was "funding the business," as she once said to me.

The other obvious note here is that when you become partners, you must also consider that person's spouse and/or family. Whether you like it or not, they *will* affect your business. Although I was in business with Claudia, her husband factored into it heavily, too. I still don't know if he thought that we were taking advantage of him, but he was just not comfortable with the fact that they had invested more than Markos and me, despite the contracts and terms of payment. You would think that our close family ties would have mitigated that, right? Remember, I was the legal guardian of their children in the event something happened to them, and that still didn't keep them from going for the jugular when they felt threatened.

After the fallout with Claudia, I decided I wouldn't go into business with an equal partner for another reason: Leadership within a company falters when two people have strong opinions and both want to see them carried out; it makes execution difficult. Claudia and I had two different visions. In hindsight, I can see that even if she and I had stayed together as equal business partners, I don't believe the business would have been a success. It's hard to have two cooks in the kitchen with an equal say. While it can be done, a partnership where your vision and execution are exactly the same is very rare.

Also, our motivations were very different. While I saw this business as a possible boon for my family, Claudia didn't—for her it was more like a hobby. During one of our last conversations, I reminded her that she was already a multimillionaire, and there were different consequences for her if things didn't work. The business had the potential to create the kind of financial freedom for my family that she already had. But she didn't see it that way. I don't know if anything hurt me more than when she wrote that she didn't believe in the business. Unsurprisingly, neither did her husband. Looking back now, I can see that he did not believe that we could turn a few baby blankets into a multimillion-dollar company. If you have a partner, you both must believe in the venture to the same degree.

Finally, it sucks to lose a friend. You lose friends here and there throughout life, true, but we went from being in the trenches together—riding the emotional wave of success after success, challenge after challenge—to never talking again, almost overnight. I've never understood why she did it or how she could have cut me off so coldly from her life. It still hurts, but I suppose money makes people do weird things.

So take my heartache and learn from it. If you can't avoid an equal partnership, then you absolutely must have the uncomfortable, tough conversations up front while everyone is on good terms. Document and legalize the partnership, including what shares everyone gets, how disputes are resolved, and how the business is dissolved should everything go south. Perhaps most important, include in your contract how labor is divided and what roles everyone will be responsible for. There are so many scenarios that you just can't foresee, so the best you can do is enlist the help of a good lawyer and document everything. Because, let me tell you, starting a business is a mad sport of juggling many balls while sprinting. It takes everything you've got to keep going, much less check in with each other and resolve issues. As soon as things go off the rails, anger replaces friendship and optimism. That's when things get really complicated.

aden + anais is an entirely different company from what it was when Claudia left. However, we started aden + anais together and I never want to take that away from her. While I can't say I have fond memories toward the end of our time working together, I feel strongly that it's important to acknowledge her contribution to the business.

About a year after the relationship with Claudia went down

in flames, the *Los Angeles Times* did a piece on the business and me. I couldn't help but smile at the thought of Claudia's husband with his morning coffee, opening the paper to the full-page feature detailing the wild success of a New York start-up called aden + anais.

CHAPTER 8

CHOOSE YOUR
DANCE PARTNER WISELY

Back when I was in my twenties, I dated a guy for six years. He proposed twice, and I said no twice. I was still in my party-girl phase; I didn't think I ever wanted to be married and had no real intention of having kids (said the woman who went on to have four). But when he left me, not long after I had refused him a second time, I was devastated. I spent most of the next year sulking and swearing off men, until my sister and a friend persuaded me to attend the annual Australian Jockey Club (AJC) Ball.

OK, so they didn't so much persuade me as demand that I get my arse off the couch. I didn't feel up to a fancy night out, but I went and bought a gorgeous yellow dress anyway.

I was depressed and heartbroken, but I'd been exercising like a maniac to try and take my mind off the heartache. My social life had suffered, since I just didn't want to go anywhere or see anyone. Work, university, exercise, and my couch were all I could handle. I'd also been on the breakup diet (read: I was barely eating). And as I was getting ready that evening, I thought to myself, *this is the best I'm ever gonna look*. Really. If I couldn't meet anyone tonight, well, I figured that was pretty much it for me, romantically speaking. I took one final look at myself in the mirror, shrugged my shoulders, and left for the ball. Of course, no one so much as looked at me that night—let alone asked me to dance. I was crushed. I cried like a crazy person in the cab with my flatmate Danielle on the way home: "I'm twenty-eight and I'm all washed up!" I sobbed. Danielle tried to snap me out of it, but I was a total wreck.

Two weeks later I dragged myself to a going-away party for a couple of friends who were moving to London. (Not surprisingly, I didn't want to go to that event either.) As I was standing at the end of the driveway waiting for a friend of mine to park his car, a cab pulled up, and out walked a really handsome guy. I had never seen him before, but he walked straight up to me and extended his hand, saying, "You're the beautiful girl in the yellow dress." I was confused at first, but quickly realized he must have been at the AJC Ball, too. On our first official date—two weeks later—I asked why he hadn't introduced himself then. He explained that he had been on a date with a woman from work, and that it would have been disrespectful to her had he approached me. I looked at him for a moment and thought, "Oh, you're one of the good ones, aren't you?" A month later, I knew this was the man I wanted to marry.

In 1996, after a year together, Markos was offered a job in New York City. He told me that if I moved with him, he'd take the job. I had been to New York before on holiday—as soon as my cab pulled into Manhattan, the city was in my blood. Its pace and energy attracted me like a magnet. So even though I was working at Pfizer and in an MBA program in Australia, I dropped everything. It was a huge risk—I didn't have a work visa. But our trip to New York City was only supposed to be a two-year adventure, so I figured I'd volunteer full time, maybe even learn Spanish. (Markos was raised in Australia from the age of six, but he was born in Santiago, Chile, and is fluent in Spanish.)

But instead of becoming a New Yorker overnight and hustling my way through the city, I turned inward and never left the apartment. I had no job because I had no work visa, no family, no friends. In Australia, I had been going a million miles an hour, working a stressful job and going to school. I was so busy that Markos and I would schedule our dates at midnight at an all-night café in Sydney; it was the only time we could find to see each other. In New York, I was suddenly aimless. It was such a 180-degree turn in circumstances that I spiraled into a depression (and consequently learned that I am not the sort of person who can ever be idle). I started watching Rosie O'Donnell's talk show every morning, but my depression got bad enough that I resorted to taping it—I couldn't bring my sad, lazy self to get up by 10:00 a.m. when it aired. It was Markos who snapped me out of it. After a few months, he gave me some tough love. He told me I wasn't the woman he had brought to America. "Whatever this thing you're doing is, it needs to stop," he said. "Get up. Get dressed. And get a job." And so I found one, working at the Australian consulate doing data entry (no visa required!). Soon after, Claudia connected me with a gig at the Institute for International Research, which sponsored my immigration papers. A year later I landed at The Economist.

Finally, after four years together, Markos asked me to marry him. I was established at The Economist, but I was kind of marking time about getting married; I figured if he didn't put a ring on my finger soon, I was going home, because back then I had never intended to stay in New York City forever.

Now, I'm not a religious person, but being the Latino man that he is, Markos insisted that we get married in a church. I told him that if he could find a church that will marry *me*, God bless them. I still laugh when I think of our wedding. I wore a dress so fitted you could see the line of my undies underneath it. I had zero interest in walking down the aisle with VPL (visible panty lines), so I took them off. And there I was, standing at the door to this beautiful church in Sydney, on my dad's arm, where Nicole Kidman and Keith Urban were married six years later, thinking, I'm about to walk down the aisle wearing no knickers. I'm probably about to be struck by lightning.

But undies antics aside, marrying Markos was the best decision I ever made. He is the love of my life, and an incredibly supportive partner. He is an exceptional father to our four daughters. He is, however, just like me, far from perfect.

By late 2008, eight years into our marriage, the stress of the business—not to mention the breakup with Claudia, the bout with melanoma, and three babies all under the age of five—had taken its toll. I had run myself down. Between my girls, the company, my full-time job at The Economist, and my habit of going days without sleeping more than four hours a night, I had nothing left for my husband. With everything on my plate, I saw him as just one more "thing" to take care of. Though once unimaginable, we started talking about whether our marriage was really working, and maybe even going our separate ways.

It wasn't for lack of trying to work things out. Our shrink told us that we were insane for discussing a divorce; we were under so much pressure with three kids, a business, and jobs. Not to mention that there were friends dropping out of my life like flies, which is a natural result of starting a business while working full time and managing a family. With little time for all but the closest and most patient friends, my support network was withering away. It was no wonder we were struggling.

Add to that the fact that Markos is an academic with two MBAs and an undergraduate degree in electronic engineering, while I was the drunk girl at school who surprisingly became the CEO of a fast-growth, global, multimillion-dollar company. For a Latino man raised by a stereotypically macho father, this must have been difficult.

It may come as no surprise that Markos's father and I don't get along. His dad is traditional and once told Markos never to marry a woman who makes more money than him. He believes a woman's place is in the home. He didn't even want to meet me because I wasn't Chilean, and from what I understand, he wasn't that kind to Markos or his mother (whom we both adore) growing up.

You might be wondering how Markos turned out so differently. He has some of that stereotypical Latin arrogance, yet he chose to marry a very strong woman. I've always joked with him that if he was married to a weaker person, he would run right over her. I'm a hard woman to handle but Markos is up to the task of matching me in our relationship. He allows me to be my demanding, neurotic, controlling self—up to a point. Once I overstep, he puts me right back in my place. And thank God he does, because I could never be with a man whom I could walk all over, either. I remember reading somewhere once that "the key to longevity in a marriage is that both of you never fall out of love at the same time," and I couldn't agree more. There are times where I think I can't stand him and I can't do it anymore, and there are other times where I look at him and can't fathom not having him by my side. The truth is it's hard to be married; it's even harder when you throw four kids, two careers, and two dogs into the mix. We've bitten off a very big chunk of life, and along with that comes a whole lot of pressure mixed in with enough joy to keep you going.

Becoming an entrepreneur didn't change that or make it worse—it was just different. While I was at The Economist, I may not have had as much pressure but I wasn't fulfilled. I was discouraged over the lack of progress I was making because no one had faith that I could do more than what I was being asked to do. At times Markos bore the brunt of that frustration. When I became an entrepreneur, I found fulfillment, but I was giving it my all and losing focus on my marriage and myself in the process.

Ultimately, it was Markos who wanted to shelve the divorce talk. We came to the agreement that we might have to be ships in the night for the next ten years (and we agreed to try to find a way to squeeze in a new version of those midnight dates at an all-night café) and trust that we'd come out the other end of it. Which is pretty amazing, because I probably would have left me. I was a fucking basket case. I was only sleeping a few hours every night. My hair was falling out. I was exhausted and cranky and emotional . . . and definitely a little dirty. I may have even thrown a few coffee mugs in the direction of Markos's head. I just wasn't coping with life very well.

To be clear, Markos and I rarely fought about the business—I can remember just two arguments in the history of aden + anais. Instead, the tension in our relationship was a direct result of the weight of responsibility we'd taken on: Markos's full-time job, my work with aden + anais, four children, and two dogs. The pressure felt enormous. My frustration was made worse by my preference for separating work from family. I felt I couldn't talk to Markos about anything going on with the company because I didn't want it in my home, which in turn frustrated Markos. Even with all of this, we were keenly aware that we were lucky we didn't have the financial pressure that many couples experience. When I think about the millions out there who do, it blows my mind that they manage to stay together at all.

And yet, despite any turbulence we had, the only reason I was able to do what I did is because I married this man. Though it's perhaps cliché to say so, Markos is without a doubt my number one supporter. When I'm racked with guilt over some aspect of being a working mum, it's Markos who swears up and down that I'm a wonderful role model. He shares most of the work at home and picks up the slack when I'm traveling, and I do the same when he travels. He does this not only because he believes in me and the business, but also because he believes that active parenting is his job, too. Like most working parents, though, we had to figure out how to strike a true fifty-fifty partnership. (Remember our discussion back in chapter 5?)

Unfortunately, men like Markos aren't the majority. Think of the time when the ice-cream server asked Markos where the girls' mother was. That was a stranger, and it's more common than you think. But the shit Markos gets from friends is far worse.

Markos's friends tend to be what I call banker wankers— ironically some of the very same people who invested in aden + anais with their significant others. Years back, we were on a ski trip with a few of these bankers and their partners. We were all talking about one of the top football players in Australia; he had been caught banging one of his teammate's wives, and it was a huge controversy. Interestingly enough, most of the guys took the stance that he should be fired from the team for that. I, of course, had a different opinion.

"Why should he be fired?" I asked. "She consented to it, and that was her choice. Yes, he's a fucking arsehole for sleeping with his mate's wife, but that has nothing to do with his ability or right to play football. Being an arsehole and a cheater is very separate from being the captain of the team."

As usual, my comments were met with silence. The guys seemed annoyed that I had an opinion that differed from theirs, much less an opinion at all.

The boys all decided to go have a cigar and left the room. Markos mentioned later that they told him that he "needed to have a word" with me. I guess they thought that a woman should've felt the footballer's behavior was disgraceful, which I did, but I am very pragmatic and I truly thought it had nothing to do with him captaining the team. Markos's response? "You've got to be kidding. If you disagree with her, you can go talk to her yourself."

Instead of getting credit for being someone who goes against the norm of social expectations and supports his partner the way he does, Markos is often viewed as a pushover, a man controlled by an "alpha female," a name I have been called more than once. But the fact of the matter is that Markos is so fundamentally confident in himself that none of it fazes him. It's a testament to his strength of character that he can let it all roll off his back. I realize that many women are not getting the support they need to excel, and that the men who do choose to be an equal partner often don't get the credit they deserve for doing so and face ridicule instead.

People believe you should get on the same page about religion and finances, where to live, and the number of kids you each want with your potential spouse/partner before walking down the aisle. But your career should also be on this list. Because here's the thing: I didn't marry a guy like Markos by accident. I wasn't surprised when he said, "Just let me know how to help you and I will" (even though it took what felt like forever and a day to ask him for that help, not to mention the fact he needed me to ask at all). I knew when we got married that it really was going to be a partnership.

I truly believe that if you want your business to succeed and you're involved with someone, your partner must be the kind of person who can handle the long hours you will work, the weekends and late nights you will spend on the business, the stress you will experience, and the financial risk you will take on. Without their support, it will be infinitely harder, if not impossible, to accomplish your goals.

If you want your career to be important—which means that your spouse/partner is going to have to do his or her fair share of the work around the house and with the kids—then you need to make sure you have a partner who feels it is as important as you do. While women are fighting for equality in the world, we're assuming our partners are right there fighting alongside us—and that isn't always the case. As we know, the more you have to do at home, the harder it is for you to forge ahead at the office or in your business. I know, I lived it. I nearly lost my mind going it alone. I know it should be obvious, but you really do have only so many hours in the day; you can't accomplish everything by yourself. As Markos likes to remind me when I'm feeling down about myself, doing it the way we have figured out is a great model for our girls as they get older.

Despite our initial uneven work distribution in the home, Markos has lifted me up, every time I needed it. When I was freaking out over the breakup with Claudia, Markos knew me well enough to know that I would never forgive myself if I let the business go, and that fighting to keep it was the path I should take. In fact, he was the only one of my close friends and family who truly understood and encouraged me during this time. While my friends were begging me to give it up, he was the one telling me to fight for what I believed in. I'm sure he had an OMG moment or three, but I always knew he would be behind whatever direction I chose.

It wasn't until Claudia exited the business that Markos started to take a more active role in the company, and even then he understood that it was temporary. That wasn't for my lack of (ill-advised) trying. I once suggested that he work at aden + anais full time. We were discussing going on holiday, but it was difficult to plan because he didn't have the available time off to do it. Suddenly I heard myself saying, "Why don't you just come work at aden + anais and we'll figure it out? Then we'll never have to worry about you having the vacation time again."

"Are you joking?" he said without hesitation. "You're the CEO of this home. You're not going to be the CEO in my office, as well. You can't be the CEO on both sides of my life because I can only handle you in one." Thank God his common sense reigned on this occasion.

Markos has always stepped up when I've needed him most, but he's never given up his own career, never lost his professional identity, never had to deal with his wife being the boss or having an office power struggle spilling over into our home. I do know people who've managed to make working together work, but for Markos and me, I'm certain it would've been a disaster.

Despite the fact that we worked together briefly (which I'll discuss in the next chapter), we have a silent agreement that we rarely talk about work when we're at home. By the time I walk through the doors at the end of a long day, the last thing I want to talk to my husband about is business. If something happens and I need his advice or input, sure, but other than that, I need the separation. And so does he. We rarely talk about his work, either. Every couple operates differently, but these boundaries work for us.

CHAPTER 9

LEAD YOUR TEAM

Back in grade school I was terrible at math, and I'm not sure I even passed it in high school. The one subject I struggled with most when I was going for my MBA was accounting. I am fairly sure the only reason my professor passed me was so he didn't have to see me in his class again. I drove him to distraction because I just didn't get it (and a part of me didn't want to get it). While I could work out 18 percent of 368 in my head, I could never put together a P&L (profit and loss statement) or a balance sheet, and I could never understand T accounts (those double-entry accounting methods that look like the letter T). Markos, on the other hand, can look at a quadratic equation and solve it instantly. It blows my mind just thinking about it. We could not be more different when it comes to our mathematical abilities.

So, despite the fact that I've just told you not to go into business with an equal partner or with your spouse, I roped Markos into helping me—temporarily, and not in an official capacity as an aden + anais employee. After Claudia, who had covered finances (though not so well, as previously discussed), was no longer around I couldn't handle the books all on my own; I needed help. It was early 2009, and Markos was in between jobs. Since he knew far more about the financial side of things than I did, he came on for a month as my unofficial controller to help me straighten things out.

While I was happy to have Markos at the helm of our financial ship, we had a new problem: Everything was in our apartment. The dining room table had become our office, and every closet in the house was stuffed with inventory and marketing materials.

With three kids at the time and a small New York apartment, we had no room to spare. And we had a large demand for our product and a growing pile of work, but not enough hands. We needed help, and we needed space. Previously, Claudia and I had outsourced everything that we couldn't handle ourselves. Like our nonexistent marketing budget, we had no money to hire employees, bar one jack-of-all-trades who helped us out for about six months prior to our breakup. But with aden + anais making a consistent profit and growing larger by the day, it was time to bring on help. I hired our first full-time employee in New York, Andrea "Ang" Veiga, ten months prior to leaving The Economist.

It was David who came through with the recommendation. He could see that the stress of managing the growing company was taking a toll, so he suggested Ang, who has been his best friend since high school. Entrepreneurs often hire people from within their friend pool for better or worse since you need people ASAP who can run with whatever task they're given. Ang had been miserable in her previous job at a real estate company and David knew her to be smart, capable, and incredibly hard-working. The exact skills you want to have in your first employees at a start-up.

Ang was everything the company needed. At her request for a job title, I quickly dubbed her "Queen of the World." True to her moniker, she literally did everything. She worked wherever she was needed, in finance, production, sales, customer service, compliance, and when we asked her to step in to these different roles, she was more than ready and willing to take on everything we threw at her. Ang was the heart and soul of aden + anais for a very long time. When she finally left in August 2016, she was the head of new product development and managed our relationship with the manufacturers.

David wanted to help in more ways than one. Flashback to that ridiculous trip to L.A., which hadn't been a total disaster after all, since it was where David got bitten by the entrepreneurial bug. Not long after the trip, he pulled me aside and said: "If you ever leave The Economist to do this full time, please take me with you. I believe in what you're doing, I think you're going to be a huge success, and I really want to be a part of it." David is passionate. He has an incredible work ethic. He is also extremely smart. He was the first person besides Markos to really believe in me and what I was doing, and he started to pitch in, as the chief of operations, to help aden + anais grow.

We were all working hard to keep up with demand, so I can't tell you how sweet it was for us to reach a milestone together that made it all worth it: We hit $1 million in revenue in May 2009. It wasn't just a big number; it was *the* number I had set for myself when I started the company. It was the number that meant I would finally allow myself to quit my day job at The Economist.

It felt amazing!

Now, not only was I ready to leave, but David was ready to leave with me.

I remember the day I walked in and gave Jack my letter of resignation. He glanced at it and asked, "What's this?"

"Well, I'm leaving," I said.

"Are you going to another publisher?" he asked.

"No, I'm not. I'm going to try something on my own."

He looked at me dumbfounded. "What?"

"Well I'm not really ready to talk about it," I said, "but you have my word that I'm not going to a competitor."

He paused a moment and studied me. "What are you and David up to?" David had left two weeks earlier.

"Oh, nothing. You know . . . it was a timing thing."

By the time David and I exited, the two of us alone had grown that division from zero to just under $2 million in revenue over the course of three years. We made sure we left The Economist above budget with a very strong pipeline; I never wanted anyone to say that aden + anais was successful at its expense. Less than a year after we left, the division collapsed. They tried to hire four people to replace David and me but had little success with any of them. The Economist eventually sold that part of the company, which I didn't take any joy in hearing.

Well, maybe a little.

I was finally free from the constraints of carrying two jobs, but I had to take a salary cut. I was able to pay myself a mid-five-figure salary—the first money I'd ever personally taken out of the business—although that amounted to a big reduction in income from what I had been earning at The Economist. David also took a sizeable cut in his salary when he came on as COO, for no other reason than that he believed in the business and where he thought we could take it.

Our shitty little sublet office, a tiny windowless room in our DUMBO neighborhood in Brooklyn, where Ang had been working for ten months, wasn't big enough for all of us. So David and I continued to work from home for the first few months until we were able to find a bigger office that would fit all three of us, which allowed Ang and Markos to use the space when they needed to. Our landlords were running a hip-hop promotional company in the next room, and there was a lot of tough-guy street talk flying around. While Ang was trying to sell baby blankets to a boutique owner from, say, Albuquerque or Des Moines, invariably some profanity-laced sales pitch would ring out in the background: Yo! What's good, motherfucker? Though Markos found out several weeks later, when one of the guys popped his head in and asked if he'd like an herbal tea, that their hardcore hip-hop routine was somewhat of an act, or at least only a small part of who they were. They knew what they had to do to get the job done. To this day, that story still makes me laugh.

As for me, I spent the majority of the time trying to find money to keep the business going. While I had managed to gather enough to buy out Claudia, it was still a challenge to keep the cash flow positive. There were many times when David, Ang, and I would sit down at two in the morning and go through what we needed for inventory, only to realize *Oh shit, we can only afford half of that.* Luckily, I've never been in a situation where I couldn't pay someone's salary, but it was touch-and-go a few times before we eventually brought in private equity money. Markos knew that it was OK to not pay an invoice on the day it was due, which I didn't understand. I just thought that if you got a bill, you paid it. Working capital, or lack thereof, quite honestly remained one of the biggest pain points for the business right up until the time I left it.

At first, we continued to outsource everything we couldn't adequately do ourselves: accounting, IT, all the key functions. But when you're a small enterprise, you're just a blip on your service provider's radar. The attention you get is determined by the amount you can pay them, and when you're a start-up, that's not very much. When you need something, you pick up the phone, tell them you need something, and then wait in the queue. It's not an efficient way to run a business, as you can imagine. As soon as I could, I brought those roles in house. If I had to do it again, I would have hired people to fill those positions much sooner, and the first person I would have hired would have been a finance person. But that's specific for me— your first hire should be determined by your personal skill set (and what's missing). Obviously, the financial side of the business is not my strength, despite being named as the CFO at one point (cue the eye roll).

It was becoming very clear that there was no way that Ang, David, and I would be able to sustain this type of growth and give aden + anais what it needed to succeed, even full time, whether Markos pitched in or not. It was time to expand and start hiring more people.

After Ang and David, the next hires at aden + anais were

almost exclusively friends and/or ex-Economist employees: my first salespeople, my first in-house designer, my CFO. This is pretty common—we didn't advertise for these positions, we searched our networks for people with ability and a good work ethic. We needed talented people and fast, which left no time for formal hiring processes. While this may seem like a natural way to fill roles, it can lead to trouble if you're not paying attention. We made sure to look for people from diverse backgrounds with complementary skill sets when we hired from our network.

By the time we were looking for employee number nine, though, we were ready to advertise for the position. In came something like a hundred résumés, which David pored over for the next two or three days. Finally, late one night—we'd all been sitting around drinking wine and working—he leaped out of his chair and started waving a résumé around, shouting, "This is it! This is our person! I've got him!"

I couldn't imagine what had gotten David so excited—a Harvard MBA who was prepared to work for forty grand? Who was this amazing, highly qualified candidate?

It was a young guy named Brian James ("BJ") Matthew, whom David wanted to hire for no reason other than that his initials stood for blowjob. Obviously, he had work accomplishments outside of this fact, but his initials absolutely got him the interview, and I can happily report that Beej went on to become our vice president of operations up until 2017. He is now a senior manager at Amazon in Seattle.

We at aden + anais clearly took ourselves very, very seriously.

At the end of 2009, we had eleven employees who were working remotely. We had a real need for an office, so we rented a bigger office space in the same building. I remember going to look at the space with my cautious engineer husband, who said, "Are you out of your mind? You don't need this much space!" But within a year we grew out of it and relocated once again.

When I started hiring people, I looked primarily for five traits: the willingness to work hard, intelligence, humility, kindness, and a sense of humor. People with those traits can accomplish anything. I'm a hard worker, reasonably intelligent, I love to laugh, and I treat people well, and that's how I was able to build aden + anais. Whether job candidates came from within our networks or responded to an advertisement, I asked questions to discern if they had those traits, and if they were willing and able to teach themselves and learn. Were they willing to humble themselves enough to admit what they don't know and learn something new, or more important, take out the rubbish?

Because we had very limited resources, it was important that we hired people who were nimble and could fill many different roles. Our first hires wore ten hats, just like I did. I was both CEO and the woman who took out the rubbish and washed the dishes in the office kitchen, so I expected our employees to be able to pick up any job, no matter how lowly it might have felt. For that reason we let them choose their own titles. Aside from the fact that their roles were always shifting and titles felt temporary, I wanted a democratic culture where everyone was treated with the same respect regardless of their duties. Letting them choose their own titles helped create a culture that was a far cry from the hierarchical world of business that I had worked so hard to leave behind. Years later, this requirement changed. We started to hire people who had experience in specific roles that are typical within a company that produces consumer goods, like supply chain analyst and financial controller. In the early days, though, it was all hands on deck when you were needed.

It was also important that whoever we hired would bond with the team. If I couldn't imagine sharing a meal with them, they weren't the right fit. Of course, they needed to have the skills necessary to help our business succeed, but we were such a small entity that personality was just as important as the skills and work ethic someone brought to the table. In interviews, I would ask them about their families, what they liked to do for fun, what makes them laugh. You can learn a lot about a person by asking them about what they find funny. I also looked for people who had worked in retail or fast food while they were at school. That might seem unusual, but I've always thought that if you are willing and proactive enough to work in retail or restaurants while studying, that speaks volumes about your work ethic and what you're prepared to do to make a living.

The success or failure of a business comes down to the people in it. Look for employees who will work well with your team. Because of the nature of start-ups, you're going to be spending a lot of time with them. I'm a big believer in the idea that everyone in an office should get along, and everyone should enjoy walking through the door when they come to work every day. If it becomes about a paycheck, then you're in the wrong job.

While it was a thrill to hire our first employees, the problems we faced then were the same we faced when the company was doing $100 million in revenue: It's a challenge to find fabulous people. What I knew then (and definitely know now) is that the people you hire are *everything* to your business. If you put the wrong person in the chair, you are fucked. You put the right person in the chair, and your business thrives. By far, the worst mistakes you can make are bad hires.

I learned that lesson the hard way when I hired our new head of marketing in 2015. (I'm jumping ahead here, but stay with me.) Let's call him Sam. Sam came across as a humble, hard-working, intelligent, team-player kind of guy. He came with incredible references from Fortune 500 companies and seemed like the perfect fit for the team. We were excited to have him come on board, and he seemed excited to be working with us.

The first sign of trouble came when Sam organized a team outing shortly after he started. We were visiting a few of our boutiques and big-box stores in New York and New Jersey to see what our brand looked like on the shelves. Sam had organized the trip and was adamant that the head of sales, the head of marketing, the head of customer service, a few other members of management, and I all go together with him. Just a few hours before the outing was scheduled, Sam emailed us that he personally had a unique opportunity to be on a photo shoot for the headphones brand Beats. It had nothing to do with aden + anais; it just happened to be filming in Brooklyn, so it was convenient for him. "I just think that my time would be better served doing that than being with the team," he wrote.

I was pissed off. *How could that possibly be a better use of his time?* I thought. I emailed him back and told him that I thought he was making a very bad call, that this would not sit well with the rest of the team if he blew this off. He went to the photo shoot anyway. In retrospect, I should have fired him the next day, but I didn't because I stupidly thought that his experience was worth more to the business than this glaringly obvious lack of dedication to the team. In other words, I thought I needed him to succeed. I was so wrong.

It wasn't just that Sam blew off a team outing for a photo shoot. He came from a completely different work environment, with established systems and processes and lots of support staff. In a start-up, employees have to be prepared to work things out for themselves. There are no standard operating procedures to turn to; they have to be prepared to create them if they're needed. In his job interview, I had asked Sam if he was prepared to "roll up his sleeves" and work. Like everyone else, he said he was, but his work ethic wasn't suited for it.

Sam was one of those who said he could roll with the punches, but it turned out that he wasn't willing to do the hard work it took to move forward. Instead, he tried to run the marketing department the way he'd run it at a Fortune 500 company with a team of thirty, which just didn't work for us. That approach never does at a start-up, or even a fast-paced $60-million business.

In the end, it was clear that in contrast to the seemingly humble person I thought he was, Sam was actually the most Machiavellian, egotistical person we'd ever hired. He acted as if he was superior to everyone else and belittled the other employees. He used his credentials and his intellect as a way to establish superiority over the staff. Sam came into a democratic culture where everyone was treated equally and wanted to make it hierarchical. I knew it was bad, but I worried that we needed his experience. I kept him on because he was a marketing guru of sorts, and I felt he could take our branding and marketing to the next level. My own confidence waivered, and I thought I couldn't do it without him, which I know is in no small part due to his Ivy League education and his stellar corporate career, and my lack thereof. So, despite knowing two months in that he was a bad hire, I let him stay for ten—and in the entrepreneurial world, you just don't have that type of runway for a bad hire. In the short time he was with the business he had a very negative impact on the culture of aden + anais.

Hiring a good team and creating a healthy, enjoyable culture is hard work. And perhaps what I found even more challenging was learning to delegate. It was hard for me to let go. People had to tell me that I needed to move out of the way and let them do their jobs. I had to remind myself that I hired them because they were capable and I trusted them to do the work. I also had to get comfortable with the fact that they weren't necessarily going to do it the same way I would have done it, but they were getting good results anyway.

EY Winning Women, a group of women entrepreneurs that I've been a member of since 2013, teaches women a key tenet of entrepreneurship: You need to learn to work *on* your business, not *in* it. This means cultivating the ability to step back and look at your business from the bigger picture, to avoid being in the trenches all the time. It took a while for me to learn this lesson. It got to the point where there was no way for me to know what was going on in the day-to-day operation—there was simply too much information for one person to track. I went from knowing all of the minutiae to walking down the street one day saying to myself, "Shit, is that a new aden + anais design?" as a stroller passed by.

The role of a good entrepreneur is to have confidence in

knowing when it's time to step in, or more importantly to step aside and bring someone else in, or even to alter your role within the business. Eventually I got comfortable with the idea that the team was only going to bring me in when a task or a project got too complicated or they didn't want to make a decision without me. In other words, I was the problem-solver. It's still hard for me to watch someone else try to fix our problems when I could just do it myself. I had to teach myself to be OK with that. And the only way it happens is when you trust the people on your team. Time and practice help you get more comfortable with this.

A crucial part of learning to let go is learning to be OK with the mistakes your team will inevitably make. As the team grew, so did the size of our mistakes. In the beginning, any error was nominal—maybe something to laugh about and learn from. But as we grew, the stakes got higher and the fuckups got bigger. Once, one of our employees made a mistake with the routing of some of our goods in another country. They'd been sent to the wrong place, and that little error ended up costing us $100,000. The employee who made the mistake was devastated. I can still remember the look on his face when he came over to my desk to tell me what happened. He just kept saying "I'm so sorry, Raegan." I reminded him that he was human and we all make mistakes. While it was a big number, we were thankfully in a place that it wouldn't put us out of business. I told him it was annoying, but it was all going to be OK. My take was that you can make a mistake once because you're human and it happens to all of us; I think it's ridiculous when people get fired over one misstep. The second mistake means we have an issue. If you make it a third time, you're out of a job. That's the approach I took with all of our employees.

And it wasn't just our employees who screwed up; I made my fair share of mistakes, too. When I did, I made a point to be transparent about them with the whole team. I would stand in front of the entire group during our Monday morning meetings and share every one of my screwups. People were so devastated when they fucked up that I wanted them to see that I did it, too, and that it was not the end of the world.

Throughout all of the mistakes and the shifts in roles, it was up to me to hold the vision. I was always very transparent about what I wanted to accomplish and why. I would share the goal, the time frame, and what I thought we needed to do to get there, and then I would get a consensus from the rest of the team. That was the key—I never stood there and told them what we were doing. They were a part of the goal from the beginning, helping shape the idea and then determine the course we needed to take to accomplish it. Our democratic structure worked well here. While I made the final decisions, I made them based on the input from the team around me, which was always evolving as we grew and learned.

Our culture evolved, too. When we were only eleven people in start-up mode, we were always running hard. What I loved about the early days is that we were all in the trenches together, some days until three in the morning, working side by side to make this company into something great. We celebrated the wins and lamented the losses together and it made us feel like a very tight-knit group. There were late nights figuring out problems over wine. I never stated out loud that we were a booze friendly office, but it was part of the deal (within moderation of course). We also had dogs running around so none of our teammates ever had to worry about their fur-babies sitting home alone. To work that intensely to build a business, you need healthy outlets, and for that reason dogs have always been welcome at aden + anais. Edi, David's cockapoo, who'd spent his days in the office since he was a puppy, thought he was the CEO and sat on my lap during most meetings.

The aden + anais offices have open floor plans—no corner offices, no cubicles. Since I always hated working on my birthday, everyone got his or her birthday off. The sales team knew that if they made their budget in half the month, they can effectively have a two-week vacation. While my lawyers fought against it adamantly, I was equally insistent that we would have a bar in the office. We spend so much of our time at work, why not make it as fun as possible? I trusted the people I worked with not to abuse the freedom they had, and they generally didn't. The bar, the popcorn machine, and the pool table were all designed to bring a little fun to the day and the team closer together.

More than one person visited our offices and remarked that it's not what you would expect from a baby-goods company, that it felt more like a tech start-up. I didn't think much about it when I was creating it. What I did think about was the fact that I'm a mother, and having an interest in baby products is one part of who I am as a person. But there's also the crazy party girl part of me that dances on the bar. Then there's the businesswoman with a vision for her company. Our culture reflected all of the different parts of who I am.

I also wanted my company to be the complete antithesis of

every company I had ever worked for. Because I worked for many arseholes, my vision included a lack of politics, an absence of hierarchy, and a whole lot of fun. As far as I was concerned, the assistants were just as vital as the senior managers. Everyone is at their best when they're being treated as equals, with respect and kindness. I created an atmosphere where everyone had an equal voice, everyone's opinion mattered. The bar, the work-free birthdays were all intentional parts of creating that kind of culture.

For the most part, I ran the company like a democracy, where everyone's opinion mattered. I hired people on gut instinct, I looked at potential over past accomplishments, and I selected people I trusted. When you treat people well, you build loyalty. It's why an employee once told my sister, who also worked for aden + anais for six years, that if I ever killed anyone he would help bury the body. There was a running joke afterward that we would be sure to wrap the dead body in muslin. Very few people left aden + anais, before SPC, my future investors, took control. When those people did leave, many of them called a few months later and asked to come back.

Many entrepreneurs put a lot of time and effort into building their company culture. Ours came along naturally. I didn't think to myself *I have to build an amazing culture*. It happened organically—because I cared so much about everybody in the business, everyone felt they belonged. It came from pulling together a group of people who could work hard and have a good time, and everyone brought the best of themselves to work.

Looking back, I would do it the same way—organically— but as we grew and scaled up, I would have made more of a concerted effort to maintain the amazing culture we built in the early days. It gets harder to maintain culture the bigger a company gets. aden + anais had over 120 employees and each one of them brought their own beliefs, attitudes, and insecurities to the job. There were days where it seemed like an episode from *Game of Thrones*, with strong personalities vying for power at the expense of others. It kept me up at night. But that's a story for another chapter, which we'll get to soon enough.

From the beginning, I built a culture that placed value on emotion—I made sure that everyone felt comfortable expressing themselves at work. I wanted aden + anais to be a place where everyone felt free to be themselves, to be as expressive and emotive as they wanted to be. I came from a business culture where emotions and strong opinions were unwelcome, especially if you were a woman, and I wanted the opposite of that. I wanted to be able to show that contrary to the misconception that women are too emotional to affectively manage a business, it's actually OK to have emotions and still run one successfully.

By now, I don't think I need to belabor the point that the perceptions about women in business do far more harm than anything else. Women are encouraged to be more like men in business—that is, less emotional, less reactive, less feminine. I couldn't disagree with this sentiment more. My emotionality is what makes me the kind of leader who can connect with people. I hugged employees, I cried in meetings. They've seen me get angry and upset. I went out of my way to show them that I care. Throughout the history of aden + anais, I've been very much engaged on a personal level with the people who work for the company. And I know quite a few male CEOs who have displayed the same level of emotion. There is no shame in showing how you feel at work—we're human. How can we not?

In contrast, I recently met with two male entrepreneurs who own a manufacturing company with revenue of over $200 million. They were initially making contact to see about buying a+a. During a visit to our offices, they commented on the fact that the environment felt very different compared to theirs. I explained to them that I am very close to most of the people I work with. They responded by telling me they don't speak to most of their employees. "We don't know them, we have our senior management team handle them. We don't even acknowledge them," they said. When I asked why, they told me it was too hard—it was better not to get emotionally involved with employees because of what might have to be done in a business setting. This approach might have worked for them, but it most definitely isn't the way I would run a company. They have a successful business, but I wonder if it could have been twice as successful if they had created a warmer working environment.

This leads me to believe that it's not about being less sensitive in business. It's actually about having the ability to be adaptive. While I care a lot about my employees, I've also fired my friends, both old and new, from my company. I've always been able to do what's right for the business, because I've always made it clear up front to the people I hire that my job is to make sure the company is operating as well as it can. If that means firing a close friend, then I will do it, but I will do it with grace and as much kindness as I can.

I have never allowed my emotions to get in the way of moving forward. The team who helped me build this, who knows me best, will tell you that they liked the fact that I was always decisive. I always listened to the input of everyone who had a say in the matter, and then I would choose one path forward. I never flip-flopped on decisions once I made them. When you're looking to someone for guidance, you don't want to see a leader who one day says the team will go one way, and the next day says it will go in a completely different direction. One thing I'm certain of: My ability to be decisive is a direct contributor to the success of this business.

That's not to say I haven't struggled with indecision, but when I did, I used action to boost my confidence. When I'm racked with insecurity, flipping back and forth or stalling over a decision was more of a confidence killer than anything else, so I made sure to get input from everyone around me whom I trusted, considered all of the available information, and then made a decision. That didn't guarantee I always made the right decision. I've certainly gotten it wrong on occasion, but the people with whom you work, from vendors to partners to (eventually) employees, much prefer a decisive leader who gets it wrong from time to time than one who fails to make a decision at all. When I do make mistakes, I own them.

I also made a point to be as direct as I could be with my team. I think it helps avoid confusion and provide the most effective leadership. While I'm direct, I'm careful not to be hurtful; I just tell it like it is.

The flipside of believing that emotion is bad for business is that those of us who are decisive and opinionated are labeled as bitchy or abrasive. Because women are often expected to be gentle, more expressive, and more socially oriented than men, we typically come under fire when we display characteristics that go against that social expectation. When we violate it, we are less likely to be liked by our peers or subordinates. Ironically, though, this same directness and toughness in men is lauded and viewed as exhibiting confidence, being a valuable team player, and showing leadership potential.

It might not come as a surprise to you by now that telling it like it is comes naturally to me. This hurt my career when I still worked for The Economist Group but helped me build my business when I left to focus on aden + anais. Later, my directness would come to be a problem again, but that's a story for another chapter. Though it hurts to be labeled that way, I had to make peace with the fact that when you're decisive or opinionated, a lot of people are going to think you're a bitch. You can't change that perception, and it's better to be thought of as a bitch than to be inauthentic just to make someone else feel better. This also takes a certain comfort level with yourself. I know that I'm a respectful and kind person, and if people equate honesty with bitchiness . . . well, it's not really my problem, is it? This hasn't changed over the course of my career, either. I'm the same blunt Raegan now that I was when I worked for Pfizer, for example. My personality and behavior have been consistent across the board, which is why I believe I didn't make it that far in the corporate world. I've never been anything but direct, so I have a hard time coming up with advice to someone who might have trouble expressing themselves. I would suggest that you spend more time around women whom you know to be strong and opinionated and teach yourself that way. If you're already decisive, it's just about getting comfortable with the labels. I know who I am in my heart, and if someone wants to label me a ball breaker, I'm all good with it. All I can do is remain consistent in how I behave and true to myself. Contrary to popular belief, directness isn't in conflict with being a team player; it's actually a part of it. When you can be direct with your teammates and tell them what you truly think, you can all reach a better place more quickly.

In fact, hedge fund investor Ray Dalio used a similar policy to foster the unique culture of his company. Dalio is the founder of Bridgewater Associates, a company that changed the investment industry with his concept of "radical transparency." Bridgewater Associates was eventually named by *Fortune* magazine as the fifth most important private company in the United States. In his book, *Principles*, which is part autobiography and part detailed description of Dalio's methodology for making decisions, he preaches his philosophy of "radical transparency" and "radical truth":

> Learning to be transparent is . . . initially awkward, the more you do it, the more comfortable you will be with it . . . Imagine how many fewer misunderstandings we would have and how much more efficient the world would be and how much closer we all would be to knowing what's true— if instead of hiding what they think, people shared it openly. . . I've learned firsthand how powerful this . . . is in improving my decision making and my relationships.

I'm a little more blunt with my terminology than Dalio: When you all pussyfoot around the truth and fail to say what you mean, your team will get lost. Teams only work if everyone at the table is unafraid to say what they think, and if the person at the head of the table is willing to listen. If you're at the head of the table, creating this kind of culture is up to you. A positive corporate culture, where it is made clear that you care about your employees, is vital to the health of your business, and there are challenges to maintaining such a culture in the face of exponential growth. Managing competing personalities, dealing with the personal stuff, is absolutely the hardest part of scaling an entrepreneurial business. If you're able to treat your people with kindness and respect, you'll get the best out of them. In fact, being an emotive leader is what led to building this wonderful company. The people who worked with me, and showed the company and me kindness and respect, knew that I would do anything for them because I always made a point to be human with them, first and foremost. That's not something you can fake. I'll never forget the time that Brian, one of our IT support people, came up to me when we were hanging out at our bar on a Friday afternoon. He said, "Raegs, I've never worked at any place like this. The fact that you even talk to me as the CEO is one thing. But the fact that you'll come up and give me a hug when something is wrong. You just have no idea how much that means."

It meant a lot to me, too. The relationships I made while building the company helped me to grow not only as a leader but also on a personal level. As we grew, so did I. And while our little aden + anais family was growing, waves of emotion and all, so were our revenues. I believe the fabulous culture we created directly contributed to the financial success of the business. We were a group of people who all very much believed in what we were doing and were extremely passionate about it. My team encouraged me to grow as much as I encouraged them. Everyone was marching in unison toward the same goal.

In May 2009, we had three employees, and by the end of the year we were up to eleven. By early 2010, we really started to see the growth, doubling our revenues and headcount. Finally, it was time to find some real money to help us scale.

CHAPTER 10

THINK BIGGER

With the flood of positive media coverage and the quick popularity of our product, it wasn't long before the competition picked up. When we started aden + anais, there were so few swaddling blankets on the market, and none of them were made of muslin. One competitor in particular was selling swaddling blankets, but they used flannel. I didn't know about them when we started the business, but I soon found out once they started sending threatening legal letters.

What a legal headache it was. The first sign of trouble was a nasty Facebook post with language like "a + a does not comply with US safety standards." Hmm, not true, but slightly concerning. Then they started sending unmarked letters to our office threatening to shut us down, charging us with making false marketing claims about our products, and warning that if we continued to sell them, we would be liable. It wasn't hard to tell who had sent the letters since they used the same language as the Facebook post. Next, they upped the ante by sending letters to our biggest customers. The customers' legal teams would call us, asking what these letters were all about. Apparently, the letters called me a liar and an unethical marketer, claiming I was misleading customers. I was also apparently putting babies in danger by "falsely" claiming that the fabric was breathable! The owner of the competitor even threatened to sue retailers if they continued to carry my product. Luckily, as soon as the retailers and I spoke, it became clear this was just a malicious attempt to knock aden + anais down and nothing more—and thankfully, it didn't work. Not one retailer stopped carrying our products. I had built a brand based on honesty and transparency, and it showed.

Even though I had never thought of the company in question as a competitor, the husband and wife who owned it did not feel the same way. They were not happy. In just a few years, we had taken over the US swaddle market, which had a major impact on their business, albeit unintentionally. Prior to aden + anais, this company had the swaddle market basically to themselves (a luxury that is bound to be brief in any industry). However, they had been selling a different product. When they saw what we were doing, they, like so many other baby-goods producers, quickly went into muslin and created copycat products. Although I knew it was inevitable, it still pissed me off to no end.

As the company grew, competitors became more of a concern, especially when new companies would appear on the scene. As we grew bigger, we had more resources to fight the competition, but it was much harder to keep up with the new kids on the block. We used to be a nimble little company that could turn on a dime, but we now had multiple people in decision-making roles and processes that took time and collaboration. We were at risk of becoming a slow-moving business, the kiss of death in my opinion.

Although we had a competitive advantage for a few years, I always knew we didn't have much lead time before the rip-offs would start. And damn did they. I didn't quite fathom how blatant the copycats would be. When we started, I knew it would be an absolute sprint to get the product everywhere quickly. It was our only shot at owning the market. I couldn't protect our product from being imitated: You can't patent a piece of fabric, and I didn't invent muslin. But I had completely revamped muslin swaddling blankets, making them softer and higher-quality, designing them with a unique style in a way that no one else had. To this day, it drives me crazy to see how many direct rip-offs have emerged over the years.

Those who enter our space, draw inspiration from those who are already in it, and try to do something unique, well, that's a different story—more power to them. But I've never understood how a person can sleep at night knowing they copied someone else's ideas and passed them off as their own. When we brought the blankets to market, we spent two years perfecting the softness of the fabric and the design. Ours was an innovative take on something that was plain, boring, and scratchy, and hadn't been changed in years. Our competitors didn't bother with innovation; within six months, they were ripping us off directly with the same designs and the same packaging as ours. The upside was that we were forced to continue innovating. That's the reason we offered every type of design, from pastels and geometrics to bold colors and characters, since selling a design aesthetic that we didn't offer was the only way any competitor could have a serious impact. For a long time, our competition didn't understand how to make muslin the way we did because we had spent years and lots of money developing and perfecting our product. But they were starting to catch up, and if we didn't continue to innovate from a design and product perspective, we would be eaten alive. The pressure was on—we had to keep moving.

Customer service was our next big priority. Longtime customers would call and tell us their kid's blanket had a tear in it. It didn't matter when they bought it; we replaced it, because it was the right thing to do. A customer who cares enough about their twelve-dollar blanket to pick up the phone and call is more than likely a customer for life. Retaining these customers was crucial for us to remain competitive in a pressure-packed marketplace.

But a year or two after going to market, I started to hear grumbling from some of our customers. Although aden + anais was popular with the mummy bloggers, there were enough complaints among readers (and a few writers) that the product was amazing but too expensive for me to take notice. I had tried to keep the price point affordable, but I heard what they were saying. From the very beginning, I wanted all mums to have access to high-quality muslin. I was upset that I hadn't yet made that possible. Especially because it drove me crazy to see mums using crappy synthetic materials for their babies. I was at a rodeo in Colorado (yes, me, the woman who wears five-inch heels almost daily) and saw all these mothers with their babies wrapped in hot, unbreathable fabrics in the dead heat of summer. It bothered me to no end that they obviously didn't know about muslin. Had they been using muslin swaddles, their babies would be much more comfortable. So I began working on a way to bring the costs down and create a more affordable diffusion brand to be carried at big-box retailers.

Originally, I wanted our boutique four-pack to be priced at $39.95, essentially $10 a blanket, but quickly found that we couldn't maintain the quality we wanted or the profit margin we needed to run a successful, sustainable business for less than $42 a pack. Still, it was important to keep our prices as low as possible. I didn't want aden + anais to be unaffordable; I wanted people to think of muslin blankets as being like nappies. In other words, indispensable.

I started looking for a way to decrease our prices. The biggest obstacle was that we had built and grown our brand around our existing retail customer base, specialty boutiques, and that came with a certain feeling of exclusivity. Putting our products into big-box stores without adjusting them in some way would do two things: change the feel of the brand, and piss off our boutique retailers who had the exclusive on aden + anais. A larger company with infrastructure and sales and distribution channels could crush us in muslin production if they wanted to, but no one could emulate or replicate our reputation for design and quality or the cachet of our brand, which the boutiques had helped us build. Expanding our product availability too quickly at the expense of our boutique customers would have turned the entire business into a house of cards. We had to find another way.

The new line had to be high quality and in keeping with our

brand, but different from the main line carried by boutiques at a higher price point. Through lots of trial and error, we were able to develop a prototype that worked. We used less cotton, so the blankets are thinner; they're slightly smaller; and they come in a PEVA pack instead of a gift box, which enabled us to bring down the manufacturing cost of developing the product. I also initially included one plain white blanket in each pack, which brought the costs down further. These small tweaks enabled us to set the price at $34.95 for a pack of four compared to $49.95 in the boutique stores.

When the new line was ready, I reached out to the major mass retailers—Target, Babies"R"Us, and Kohl's—and told them I had a product for them if they were interested. They were. Target was the first major retailer to buy into the new lower-priced line. (Remember that story from chapter 2?) We launched in all the Target stores across the US in 2009.

Soon after Target started selling the diffusion products, other retailers came calling. We eventually made deals with retailers including Meijer and JC Penney, among others. We also started to expand our boutique range, from independent specialty stores to upscale chains, including Nordstrom, Bloomingdale's, and other major international department stores. Then, a major opportunity arose: to work with legendary department store Harrods in London. Our managing director at the time, Samia Kahn, and David, our COO, went to Harrods' headquarters to meet with the buyer. We were all excited about the idea of working with one of the largest, most iconic retail stores in Europe.

But it was not to be. Samia and David called me afterward to report that the buyer hadn't even brought them into the office; they sat on chairs in the lobby just outside the elevator vestibule, because apparently we were not yet worthy of an office meeting. They were Harrods, after all. Not to be deterred, David and Samia pitched them anyway. When the buyer started discussing the numbers and what Harrods expected as margins, David stopped her: "Those numbers don't work . . . we would lose money if we agreed to that." The buyer didn't care. "We're Harrods," she said. "It doesn't matter if you lose money because you should just be happy to be in Harrods." Samia and David told her we were actually a *for*-profit company, so that wasn't going to work for us, and thanked her for her time. Though this wasn't the outcome we had hoped for, we weren't too disappointed—we had other stores that were more than willing to work with us. Besides, Harrods came back a year later after we gained some momentum, and now we are often given our own aden + anais section in the store. Being patient and true to our values certainly paid off.

And speaking of crazy margins, Walmart also expressed interest in selling our merchandise around the same time, in 2012. I resisted for five years straight. I prioritized the long-term success of the business, which occasionally meant turning large revenue-generating opportunities away. Dealing with Walmart meant that you had to have the right infrastructure and the right people in place to be able to make it work. Without those, the sheer magnitude of the demands from Walmart could crush a business. Not to mention their margin requirements on the back of extremely low retail price demands—you can sell millions in product and not make a cent of profit if you don't have the supply chain infrastructure set up correctly to work with them.

You must be able to ship the quantities they need in the specific way they want them shipped. If you go from serving boutique stores to filling orders for Walmart, you must change your supply chain to meet their demands.

If I had worked with Walmart too early, we wouldn't have been able to handle that kind of growth and pressure on the business. We might have done better from a revenue standpoint initially, but that doesn't always translate to an increase in profitability. There is no point in being a hundred-million-dollar business that loses money.

It wasn't the first or last time I'd said no to major retail stores. If you move too fast and your product ends up on every shelf, it's no longer special. If it happens too early for a brand, it's difficult to keep the product aspirational. As I described earlier, we had built our brand in boutiques, and our blankets and designs had a certain kind of cachet. I was initially worried that putting them in every big-box store might have watered down our brand appeal. When we did expand, I made a point of making our products the best in that channel, which helped maintain the feel of aden + anais. Nowadays, you can find aden + anais everywhere, but it took years for us to reach that point, and we did it in a calculated way. Few companies have managed to start as a boutique brand and maintain their prestige as they diversify into mass-market retailers. There are many companies in the baby space that choose to do major licensing deals with the likes of Target or Walmart and shift to focus more on the mass side of their business than on their boutique and specialty areas. Because they no longer have the time to manage the relationships with the boutiques, those relationships start to deteriorate.

Eventually, the licensing agreements with these companies end, and overnight 80 percent of their business dries up. In other words, they rely too heavily on one big customer, and when that one customer decides to end the license with them, their businesses pay a massive price. It's a common occurrence, as the mass channel is where all the volume and most of the revenue comes from. This can bring a branded business to its knees, and it might lead to a fire sale, where it is bought for an incredibly low price by a private equity firm or a larger strategic business or, worse, put out of business completely. It's a fact that the boutique side of a business is labor intensive, costly, and less profitable. While it's easy to look at the big sparkly numbers on the mass-market retail side of the aisle and decide to put all of your energy into that, you can pay a very big price for doing it when you are trying to build a premium brand.

Measured growth was our strategy from the beginning and we didn't waver. Jason Fried of Basecamp (formerly 37signals) agrees. In an interview with *Fast Company*, he described his preference for slow growth over the "slash-and-burn" mentality of the tech world:

> We're about being in business for the long haul and keeping the team together over the long haul. I would never trade a short-term burst for a long-term decline in morale . . . I'm a fan of growing slowly, carefully, methodically, of not getting big just for the sake of getting big. I think that rapid growth is typically a symptom of . . . there's a sickness there. There's a great quote by a guy named Ricardo Semler, author

of the book *Maverick*. He said that only two things grow for the sake of growth: businesses and tumors. We have 35 employees at 37signals. We could have hundreds of employees if we wanted to—our revenues and profits support that—but I think we'd be worse off.

Like Fried, I am not convinced that bigger, in the short-term or as a singular goal, is always better.

While we were working on creating our diffusion lines, we also looked to expand into international markets because the growth potential was exponential. First, David and I visited trade shows all around the world, in Japan, the UK, France, Germany, and Italy. If American parents respond to our product this way, I thought, then why wouldn't English and Japanese parents, for example? When I saw they had the same positive reaction, I started working out ways to distribute the product in those countries. We went about putting in the infrastructure, and most important the people, to take advantage of the growth opportunities internationally.

The easiest way to break into new markets is to work with a distributor, because they have established relationships with retailers in other countries that make it easier to sell the product. They sell it exactly the way it is, but they might represent ten other brands in addition to yours, meaning your product only gets one tenth of their attention. And, you lose control over how the brand interacts with customers. To build a meaningful global brand, there needs to be consistency across the brand in every country where your products are sold. Although it was going to be a lot more work, I thought it would pay off if we did it the hard way—incorporating in the countries in which we saw the biggest opportunity, and setting up our own office and direct distribution model, rather than working with an outside distributor.

We incorporated first in Australia in 2008 and shipped stock to a warehouse. My sister, Paige, handled sales and customer service, and my mum took over the bookkeeping. The Australian business went well; we required very little start-up capital and we didn't have to educate our customers on muslin. It didn't take long for us to get it to a couple of millions of dollars in revenue per year. When I was ready to incorporate in Europe in 2011, my investors were adamantly opposed to the idea. Just as Claudia had, they wanted to go the less capital-draining, less risky, distributor route. But I insisted—I had been to those markets in person and had seen the buyers' reactions to our products at overseas trade shows—and I'm glad I did. Today, aden + anais has offices in the UK and Japan, which contribute about 29 percent to global revenue and continue to grow year after year. Incorporating in these areas set the company up for meaningful (and for the foreseeable future, sustainable) growth.

Our new global reach also led us into some problems. In 2011, Disney US reached out about a potential collaboration. We were so excited—until they came back to us with all these rules and expectations for the product, which didn't work for our margin requirements or fit our brand aesthetic at all. They had many demands and weren't willing to compromise. It felt more like a dictatorship than a collaboration, since I wasn't interested in plopping "It's a small world" on a swaddle and calling it a day. We had worked hard on creating our unique designs, I feared it would look like we were selling out if we allowed Disney to tell us how our blankets should look. We eventually passed on the opportunity, and I was left with a bad taste in my mouth.

Three years later, I was headed to our European office for a routine visit. Samia handled all the scheduling during these trips, telling me where I needed to be and when. I would often show up, asking, "Who are we meeting, and what's on the agenda for today?" I trusted her to keep me on track.

On that particular day, we were meeting with a company to talk about a possible partnership—that's all I knew. I walked into the building where Samia was waiting, and as I took a look around, I realized I'd been tricked. *The company we were meeting with was Disney.* I wasn't happy.

"Are you joking, Sam?"

"Please, *please*, just come and hear them out," she said, "I promise this will be a different experience. I think it's going to be a great thing."

Samia is an interesting woman—one of a kind, really. She's the mother of two beautiful daughters, aged nineteen and twenty-two. She wears tutus and blue glitter nail polish, and she loves unicorns and all things Disney. And she was instrumental in building the aden + anais brand in Europe. "Look, Raegan, if it's good enough for Givenchy, it's good enough for aden + anais," she reasoned. (For context: Givenchy and Disney did a collaboration in 2014.)

This caught my interest. "Fair enough," I said. I was already in the building, so I decided to go in with an open mind.

It turned out that Disney Europe was very different from Disney US. They were willing to work collaboratively and let us put our spin on their traditional characters and designs. The final say was theirs—nothing would have gone to market that Disney didn't love and approve—but they were willing to let us unleash our design team on their characters. They were also willing to negotiate on the royalties. This made all the difference.

"You tricked me," I said to Samia afterward.

"Of course. I knew what I was doing," she said, and smiled. She had met with them before and knew what to expect. I told her she had made the right decision, because I had been closed minded and stubborn. I never would have gone there, so I was very glad she took the initiative. Her cleverness resulted in an amazing deal we wouldn't have had otherwise.

This was a major collaboration and I wanted it to go well. For good luck, I bought myself a Givenchy Disney wallet to send positive energy into the world. It's a great wallet with an abstract design; the image on it is half Bambi and half woman. You have to study it closely to figure out what it is, but the Bambi portion of the image is very clear. When business acquaintances saw it, their expressions told me they were wondering what the hell a fifty-year-old woman was doing with Bambi on her accessories. But I didn't care what they thought. This wallet was my good-luck charm, and I loved the reaction my friends had. When they first saw it, they thought it was fabulous "Damn, is that Givenchy? I love that collaboration!"

Perhaps the wallet actually did send good vibes out into the world, because the collaboration turned out to be fabulous. Our design team did a beautiful job of interpreting Disney. Once they started the process, it was clear to me that the collaboration was going to stay very true to aden + anais and still represent Disney the way they wanted. People went gaga over it, and sure enough, Disney US came back and asked if they could be a part of it, too. aden + anais now works with Disney all over the world, and they have proven to be an amazing partner and collaborator.

Our decision to stay true to the brand has paid off. While it may seem tedious to obsess over every detail, it pays off when your customers notice the quality and the intention behind your brand and product design. When you take the time to get the little things right, you're signaling to your customer that you care deeply.

Although scaling quickly seems to be all the rage in the media, slow and steady growth pays off in the end. While I was always focused on growth, I was committed to keeping it healthy and steady, rather than chasing growth for its own sake. I wanted to be sure that I was able to take advantage of opportunities when they arose, but they had to be the right opportunities—not the kind of chance that could break us if we weren't prepared. As I said, I knew the Walmart relationship would add a level of complexity that we weren't yet ready for. When we had the infrastructure in place, we took them up on their offer to carry our products. Keep your focus on growth, yes, but don't chase every opportunity that comes your way, especially if it means putting your business at risk. I'm sure it's not unusual for would-be entrepreneurs to wonder how the hell they're supposed to get their product into other parts of the world when they haven't even gotten it into their own backyard. But you don't need to focus on going international right away. Start where you are, but never lose sight of the possibility of becoming a global brand as you're growing it at home. And remember that you don't need to wait to exhaust every growth opportunity domestically before doing it.

When you're faced with the opportunity to collaborate, don't let the excitement blind you to what it might cost your brand. No one says no to Disney, right? But it didn't feel right at first, and I knew that it could cost me my brand integrity. Do your research when collaborators come calling, and make sure that it makes complete sense for your brand before you agree to it. You might be getting a lot of exposure, but if it's the wrong kind of collaboration, that exposure might not do you any good.

And finally, when you think you've made the right call but your trusted employees are pointing out another way, open yourself up to the possibility that they might be right. There were plenty of situations where I thought I'd made the right call, and an employee approached me to tell me otherwise. Sometimes they were right, and sometimes they were wrong, but I always listened. Have the humility to listen to the people you've chosen to work with. Encourage them to challenge your thinking. Thank them for their input, and always be prepared to make the decisions one way or the other.

Most people see a big horizon and shrink at the thought of swimming that far. If you can keep your mind open and maintain the idea that you just might make it, you may surprise yourself when you get there.

CHAPTER 11

KNOW WHEN TO SELL

In 2009, three years after we had gone to market, the company continued to grow at an almost alarming pace. And believe it or not, my number one job was still chasing money to keep the lights on. As excited as I was about the rate of scale, it was grueling. I had pretty much exhausted my family, friends, and friends of friends, which was how we had funded the business up to 2009. I would borrow any amount of money, ranging from $20,000 to $250,000, at 10 percent interest. But we got to a point where those small amounts of money were not enough to keep up with our growth. We needed more and more inventory to keep up with demand, and we needed to add people and infrastructure to keep up with the increasing workload. It was time to turn to other sources that would give us a meaningful cash injection so I could stop chasing money and focus on our business strategy and growth.

However, given that I was new to all this, I wasn't sure whether to pursue venture capital or private equity funding.

Venture capital firms tend to focus on start-ups, with rounds of fundraising referred to as Series A, Series B, and Series C. The series correspond to the developmental stage of the business. Series A is for companies in the early development stage. Series B is all about taking businesses to the next level. Series C is for businesses that are more established and need money to scale. We would have been a Series A. Each round of funding creates the potential for getting more money and larger investments in the business. On the other hand, private equity firms tend to work with companies that are bigger and more established, and their initial investments tend to be larger. I educated myself about both and decided that pursuing venture capital funding was the right decision for us, given how long we had been in business and our size at the time.

But I was nervous. I had heard horror stories about people, especially women, trying to raise money for their businesses. My friends in banking warned me not to do it; according to them, venture capitalists and private equity firms were the devil incarnate. My experiences didn't differ from that impression—most investors I'd met I likened to sharks in the water, ready to take a bite out of you. However, at that point it seemed to be the only way to go.

As luck would have it, in 2009, just after Claudia had departed, a venture capital firm approached me as I was beginning my search. We started conversations about their making a minority investment in aden + anais, and I went about pulling together all the documents they would need to complete their due diligence, which, if all looked good, would facilitate their investment. In the meantime, a Chicago-based toy company with an interest in acquiring my business reached out. Since they were offering a pretty hefty sum of money, I decided to take a meeting and visit the offices of the prospective buyers. At this point I told the VC firm that I was looking at selling the business, so I ended discussions with them.

After the requisite round of handshakes and hellos, I sat down at a long conference table, opposite a large group made up entirely of men. They were lovely and gracious hosts, not surprising, since they were trying to acquire my company. They started telling me all about the new products they were developing, the direction in which they wanted to take their company (and mine), and their exciting plans for the future. Then one of the senior-most managers decided it was time to unveil their upcoming product innovations.

"We've got this great new product," he said, looking up and down the table, ensuring that he had everyone's rapt attention. "It's the first"—and here he paused for effect—"truly comfortable breast pump!"

I laughed. Even though this was a serious business meeting, I couldn't help myself.

"And how many of *you* have ever used a breast pump?" I asked.

After several seconds of stony silence, blank stares, and a bit of nervous laughter, I continued. "With all due respect, there is no such thing as a truly comfortable breast pump. As someone who is extremely familiar with using breast pumps, one of my least favorite mum pastimes, I'm fairly sure that 'truly comfortable' and 'breast pump' is an oxymoron. When you've got a machine attached to your boob sucking milk out of it, there's nothing comfortable about it." They laughed and ultimately saw my point.

I remember looking around the table at all these men, considering the ridiculousness of our conversation and thinking: *So it's all just men, then? There isn't a single woman high enough in the company to merit an invite to this meeting? Or to provide input on this "killer idea"? Really?!*

The courtship didn't end right away, though; they offered money, I declined. They offered more money, I declined again. But they kept making higher offers, and eventually I said yes. We began the due diligence process of selling the company, which took about three months and included their digging into our numbers. It was during this time that I started to get cold feet. Right before I was supposed to sign the contract, I decided I couldn't go through with it. I wasn't ready to let go. I knew there was so much more I could do with aden + anais, and I wanted to be the person leading the team and guiding the vision. I called the CEO and told him I'd changed my mind. He was incredibly gracious about it in light of the fact that we had spent months working on gathering all the information required to make the sale. He wished me luck and said that if I ever changed my mind, I knew where to find him. That was the first time the reality that someone else might want to buy the company hit me, something that until then had just been a vague idea in the back of my mind. And it made me certain that I wasn't ready to exit quite yet.

By the time the discussion ended, months had passed, and we were in a bind. We had focused on the sale, not on funding the business—the never-ending paper chase—because if the business had sold, we wouldn't need the capital, as the new owners would have rolled aden + anais into their existing infrastructure. I suddenly had to scramble to find more money to maintain our cash flow. Back I went to the VC firm. In the months since we had last spoken, we had almost doubled our business; we were like a rocket ship that year, 2009. Despite the tremendous growth, they offered the same deal. I was frustrated. Confused, I called them and said, "Listen, just because I have a vagina doesn't mean I don't have a brain. Why would we agree to the same deal despite being double the size? You banker-wankers must think I'm dumb. Can you please go back and sharpen your pencils and come up with a better deal?" Yes, I was so annoyed I actually called them banker-wankers. They laughed and came back with a slightly better deal, but I felt their valuation of the company was still way off. I rejected the offer.

We did, however, end up winning the investor lottery in an unexpected way. Remember Matt—the car guy—and his wife, Paula, who invested early on? He made an introduction that would change the trajectory of aden + anais. At the time, he was working in private placement at Credit Suisse and knew the Seidler brothers, founders of Seidler Equity Partners, a Los Angeles–based private equity firm. He told them aden + anais was growing like crazy and needed funding. The Seidlers usually worked with companies much larger than mine, but they were willing to take a meeting with me anyway. It's funny to think that good old Matty, the naysayer who didn't want to invest at first, was the one who saved the day.

When I met Bob and Matt Seidler and their other founding partner Eric Kutsenda, I knew instantly that they were exceptional people. They were kind, reasonable, whip smart, generous, and respectful. They were the complete antithesis of anyone in private equity I had met before, and to this day, with the exception of one or two others, they still are. They cured me of my fear of private equity, investing in aden + anais with a minority ownership in the business, while I remained the majority shareholder. Meanwhile, two of my three original investors—the friends who had given me the $490,000 to buy Claudia out— were ready to exit. Their respective investments of $150,000 had doubled their money in eighteen months. Paula and Matt maintained their equity stake, making them the only remaining initial investors. Now it was just them and the Seidlers.

Over three years of working with the Seidlers, they became like brothers to me. They helped me fully understand that a company bringing in $55 million in revenue must operate differently than a company bringing in $15 million, since we were growing so quickly. They taught me how to run a healthy business. They helped me develop as a leader. They explained the importance of watching the bottom line number as much as the top line. Their guidance was instrumental in helping me understand the financial side of the business, and ultimately, I give them credit for making me a better businessperson in general. They were absolutely my partners from the first day they entered the business and remain my trusted advisers to this day.

It also didn't hurt that they understood my sense of humor. One day, about two years into our partnership, they asked if I was going to provide a deck for our upcoming board meeting. I responded with an email saying that I had decided to forgo the deck for this board meeting, and that we would be presenting the quarterly results and business strategy through interpretative dance. They responded by asking if David would be wearing a leotard for the presentation. I wouldn't have been comfortable making jokes had I not felt we had mutual respect and an understanding of how we both operated within a business culture. They were comfortable enough to truly allow me to be who I am, which made the working relationship that much stronger and our partnership that much more productive.

The Seidlers and I have a personal affinity for one another, which enabled us to establish a relationship open to teaching and mentoring. Before I met the Seidlers, I used to think of a mentor as someone who focuses on you, teaches you, champions you, and encourages you to push beyond your limits. However, I've learned that that's a rather high expectation of a mentor, and those who have been guides and advisers for me were really just people whom I connected with, whom I trusted, and who had been where I wanted to go. Most of all, they were interested in seeing me succeed and were willing to give me the occasional pointer when I needed it. The Seidlers were all of those things.

Lack of a support network—that is, industry contacts, influential clients, advisers, and prominent women role models— are regularly listed as yet another gender-specific hurdle facing women entrepreneurs. A 2010 survey of more than four thousand "high-potential" workers across Asia, Canada, Europe, and the United States found that women actually received an almost equal amount of mentoring as men. However, they weren't seeing as many concrete benefits from said mentoring because men's mentors were higher status within the organization than women's, which allowed promotions and opportunities that women weren't privy to.

I don't regret not having a mentor during my corporate career. After all, if someone in the corporate world had been advocating for me, I might have thought *You know what? This is good enough,* and never have found the fire in my belly to go and do something on my own. I might not have pushed myself. Entrepreneurs, by their very nature, are striving to do things that most people haven't done before; advisers and mentors—though lovely if you've got them—aren't a substitute for passion, curiosity, clarity of intent, work ethic, or confidence and vision.

What this says to me is that women need to not only look for mentors, but they need to look for mentors who have the experience, the knowledge, and perhaps even the clout to help them get where they want to go. This might seem obvious, but women tend to turn to their friends and family to talk out our problems and figure out a solution. While emotionally cathartic, turning to friends who have no experience building a business can be misleading, maybe even dangerous if you act on misguided advice. Not all advice is relevant or even helpful, not even that of a mentor. You have to be able to discern whom to trust and what to trust about the advice they give. I can't tell you how many clients and storeowners tossed off comments about how we might change our design aesthetic or marketing strategy. These kinds of detours are exactly the type of things that can knock you off track and slow you down. I didn't want to be influenced by people who weren't as invested in the business and brand as I was.

Nobody cared more about the direction of aden + anais than I did, so I learned to rely on my instincts and what I knew. And that matters. Otherwise, you become a watered-down version of yourself—and what good does that do anyone? I knew immediately that Bob, Matt, and Eric stood out from anyone else I had met in the investor world, not just because they had the experience to back up their advice, but because they are quality people. I also knew I needed to improve my understanding of finance, especially to run a larger company. Their experience combined with my self-awareness and drive made for a successful relationship.

Furthermore, there is no one person who will be "the one" to take you from budding entrepreneur to millionaire. It's a starry-eyed fantasy to think that one person will do that for you. A huge proponent of success is surrounding yourself with multiple people who know more than you, who have overcome different challenges to create a successful business. One person is not the answer. You need to surround yourself with a lot of experienced and knowledgeable individuals to be successful, whether they work for you full time or just make themselves available to offer direction and advice as you need it.

Now when I'm approached by other entrepreneurs asking for mentorship, I have to smile at the irony. By default I want to lift people up and encourage them, but I'm always careful to tell them that I am only one person. While I am more than happy to share my experiences and relevant advice, I want them to know that they should seek guidance from a variety of viewpoints.

The Seidlers took responsibility for teaching me, for lifting me up to the next level. They had experience in areas that I didn't and they were kind enough to share it with me. From day one, it was clear they were investing in the people, including me. They may not have thought of themselves as mentors by definition, but they wanted to see me succeed and they guided me with the information I needed to do so.

They were supportive even when they disagreed with me. For example, the Seidlers (along with everyone previously mentioned) were not excited about aden + anais expanding into Europe. They were against the time and resources it would take to get the office and distribution up and running. I argued hard for it, determined it was right for the business because I had actually visited these markets in person and had seen the interest in the products firsthand. I also felt strongly that this was the only way to protect the consistency of the brand globally. In the end, they told me they trusted me to give it a try with the caveat that we would reassess in a year. Within a year, it was a thriving business, contributing higher profit margins than the US office.

This went far in solidifying my trust in our relationship, so much so that when the Seidlers brought up the idea of selling the business after three years of working together, I was open-minded.

"Look, we believe in the business, we know you're going to continue to grow and scale," Bob said to me after one of our very informal board meetings. "But we've seen a lot of unexpected things happen to other companies . . . factories burning down, terrorist attacks. Then suddenly everything falls out from underneath you."

Matt chimed in. "You and Markos have so much equity tied up in this. We think you should sell. Take some chips off the table and mitigate your family's financial risk of not seeing a great monetary return for all the years of your blood, sweat, and tears. Then, you can reinvest in the new entity with an amount you feel comfortable with."

I had never considered this. I was under the naive assumption that once you sold, it was over, not realizing you could invest back into your business with a meaningful stake after selling. I also hadn't considered the risk to my family's money. At this point, the company was valued in the tens of millions, so on paper I was a multimillionaire, but in reality, I was just a salaried employee like everyone else. I could have taken out more money as an owner's distribution, but I chose not to, leaving the money in so I could grow the business. If anything happened to the company, all the wealth I had amassed on paper from building the business would vanish along with it. I wasn't leveraged at this point, and I wasn't in a tough spot for money by any means. However, I had built a successful business and wasn't realizing any of the monetary value from it outside of my salary.

When we first started working together, I had the majority share of the business and was only selling a piece of it. Bringing in private equity was simply about getting capital to grow. I was still so emotionally attached to the business that I knew I had to continue to be a part of it, specifically to lead it. Some entrepreneurs don't ever want to leave their business, while others count down the days till they can sell it.

Now, though, on the suggestion of the Seidlers, I was ready

to mitigate the risk of keeping so much of my family's money in the game. If we sold the company, my family would be financially set up—we could ensure the girls' schooling was paid for through college and own our apartment, at the very least. Then I could buy back in to aden + anais and still have a meaningful share of the company.

The Seidlers' suggestion got the ball rolling, and we hired an investment bank to get started on the process. Obviously, the market dictates much of a decision to sell. The timing has to be right; it's better to sell in a seller's market than to try and get the best price for the company in a buyer's market. Everything has to be aligned as far as finances go; you need to be able to demonstrate that the business is profitable and growing. Surprisingly, this is a gray area—many companies are considered successful but are not actually profitable according to the numbers on the books. For a consumer-goods company, demonstrating profitability is the standard catalyst to commanding the right kind of price for the sale. If the numbers aren't where they need to be, the value of the company won't be realized. Thankfully in 2013 it was a seller's market—there were already several transactions that calendar year that had commanded high prices for the sale of companies. We put together an overview of the business and its financials, or what is commonly referred to as a CIM (confidential internal memorandum), and sent them out to potential buyers. At that time, I avoided strategic firms and focused only on private equity. A strategic firm is a company that already has the infrastructure in place to run a business they acquire—think Unilever, L'Oreal, Coca-Cola. There was a high probability that a strategic firm would have preferred that I had no more involvement in the company after the sale, and there was a chance that they might also fire the entire aden + anais management team to bring in their own people to run aden + anais. Private equity buyers, on the other hand, are not operators—they invest in the people and their vision as much as they do the brand and product, as they don't have the existing infrastructure in place to run a business, or so I thought.

Most companies are evaluated using the standard EBITDA (earnings before interest, taxes, depreciation, and amortization) multiples, a ratio that measures a company's return on investment. Investors use EBITDA because it normalizes any differences in accounting that might make one company look better than another, which makes it easier to compare the growth and opportunity investment of one company compared to others. Depending on the market, those multiples can range from three to more than twenty times the EBITDA of a company. When we went to market with aden + anais, we were looking for a multiple of eight to more than ten times a conservative estimate.

I purposefully wanted to value aden + anais conservatively, to the frustration of our hired investment bank (they want you to get as much money as possible, of course, because their commissions are tied to that). In my mind, however, the reasoning was straightforward and simple: Companies are partly valued based on forward projections. Because I wasn't exiting fully, I wanted to set up a good working relationship; if I didn't hit those numbers, I knew my new investors would be on me like white on rice. So I gave them a number I believed we could hit in our sleep. I wanted to ensure happy investors, and I wanted to avoid putting top-down pressure on my team. The extra millions I was potentially leaving on the table weren't worth the additional pressure and stress going forward. Within a short amount of time, thirty-five potential buyers responded with interest, which was a lot. We whittled those down to nine and met them face-to-face. In our meetings, I was looking for people who truly understood the brand, who bought into the management team and my vision. I didn't want anyone to come in and move the existing team out. It was also important to me that the investors we chose were good people.

By the end of our two-week sprint of meetings, I was exhausted but hopeful. Out of the nine we met, two rose to the top. One of them was SPC, Swander Pace Capital, a private equity firm that specialized in consumer products. While they weren't the highest offer we received, I felt they understood the brand and wanted to work with our existing team and me. I felt they got it. And I'd be lying if I didn't acknowledge the fact that out of all nine of the investment firms we met with, SPC was the only one with a woman, who was also a mother, on their team.

So we entered into talks with SPC. For the next five months, things went smoothly. And then, as we were nearing the end of the process, there was a moment that set off my alarms. The head of the SPC team—let's call him "Chris"—and I were in the lounge at the aden + anais offices, discussing some final details of the deal before signing the contract. I had asked if there was any chance they would ever consider a minority investment in any company in which they invested, out of sheer curiosity, because they usually preferred to have the majority of shares. He instantly responded and said, "No, I have to have control."

The hairs on the back of my neck went up. *Oh, shit, this isn't good*, I thought. He didn't say, "No, we prefer to do deals with a majority share," which they had. He was saying he needed *control,* and it wasn't just what he said, but how he said it. I suddenly had doubts about whether SPC was the right partner.

Before the process started, friends and colleagues warned me of "deal fatigue." I remember saying "Deal fatigue? What the hell is deal fatigue? That sounds ridiculous." There I was, not sure whether these were the right investors, but I was already exhausted. In the scheme of business sales, this was an extremely fast one, lasting only five months. The normal time frame for a sale is closer to a year. But going through the process of selling a business is grueling, no matter how much time it takes. You're running your company at the same time that you're preparing it for sale. You're grilled about it by every investor that you choose to meet with and subjected to death-by-meetings. We were running back-to-back, four-hour meetings over a period of two weeks, during which we were expected to pitch the sale enthusiastically to every suitor. My poor CFO, Ciara, and COO, David, were in even worse shape than me—they had to deal with the lion's share of the work, preparing all of the documents and making them available to any interested party.

When I had the conversation with Chris that made my hair stand on end, we were two days out from closing the deal. I briefly considered going back to our second-choice buyer, but we would have had to start the process over again and they wanted to do much more due diligence, like flying to the factories and warehouses in China. This might sound like a short-term decision that cost me in the long term, and you would be right. But here we were; my team and I were nearly broken from exhaustion, and I knew we couldn't hold on much longer, much less switch tracks and repeat the process with a different investor. So we stuck it out with SPC and went on with the transaction, and I brushed Chris's comment off and chalked up my worries to anxiety and deal fatigue.

I remember the day we finally closed the deal. It was right before Christmas—December 23, 2013. The entire team was sitting around the conference table for the closing call. Everyone acknowledged the deal was done, and the moment the call ended, Ciara and I burst into tears. Tears of exhaustion, joy, and sheer gratitude for the fact that it was over.

In the end, we sold the company for many tens of millions. (Sorry, I can't share the number on the advice of my attorneys.) I thought the price was fair for what aden + anais was at the time, and I was happy with the outcome. Despite the large amount of money, I didn't feel the triumph of the sale as you would expect—I was too tired by that point to feel much at all, other than relief. I bought back in at a 23 percent share and maintained my position as CEO. My little company had just netted my family and me tens of millions of dollars, not to mention the financial freedom I had dreamed of when I started this company in the first place. Paula and Matt exited the business, too: After five years, their original $200,000 investment had earned them many millions also. Matt is very happy he did not buy those cars.

I stayed and celebrated with the team for a while. While the employees hadn't owned any shares of the company, I took about two million of my share and divided it among the key players in the business—those who had helped me build the company, who had been in the trenches with me so long that they deserved a chunk of the change. (Once SPC came in, we created an options pool with 10 percent of the shares of the company that key employees could choose to opt into.) I eventually wandered back to my desk and called Markos.

"It's done," I said.

"I'm so proud of you," he said. It meant a lot to hear that from him—he knew better than anyone else how hard I had worked to make this happen. Nobody understood on the level that he did what went into building this business from scratch, since he was the only person who had been by my side since day one. Markos saw every single ugly breakdown, every moment of fear, every bit of doubt; he had seen the warts as well as the beautiful parts and stood by me through all of it.

Later that night I was in a cab on my way to dinner in Manhattan after the money hit my account. Seeing the number on my cell phone, knowing that it was in our bank account, that was a true "holy shit" moment. I rang the Seidlers and thanked them for everything—their support, their kindness, their generosity, and their tutelage. I burst into tears on that call, too (I know, a very "girly" thing to do). Because of their guidance, my family—even my extended family—never had to worry about money again.

Although I knew I never had to worry about it again, I'm not one for spending money extravagantly. But there was one extravagant moment right after the sale. David bought tickets to see Prince at the Mohegan Sun for himself, me, Paula, Matt,

and Ang. If you're not familiar with it, the Mohegan Sun is a casino in Connecticut and it's a hike from New York City. As excited as we all were, no one was thrilled to make the three-hour
drive to see the concert, which, as it turned out, was scheduled
for five days after the close of the sale. As I was working out the
logistics of the drive, I thought, "Fuck it, these are all the people
who helped me build this from scratch and believed in me," so I
decided to do something fun.

Long story short, I rented a helicopter to take us to the concert, and I kept it a surprise. When we all piled in the limo I
had rented for the occasion, the driver started driving in the
wrong direction—toward the helipad, of course, but my friends
didn't know that. Plus, being New Yorkers, they were already
pissed off about the three-hour drive they thought they were
about to endure, so they were loudly critical of the poor guy and
his choice of route. The driver stayed his course, and everyone
was happily surprised when we got to the helicopter—it took us
only forty minutes to get there. Despite being scared shitless of
helicopters, I spent the $10,000 for the trip up and back to make
the event memorable and to celebrate everyone's contribution to
the success of the business.

Truthfully, I got more out of sharing the money with other
people, particularly with my friends Paula and Matt, who had
believed in me in my moment of crisis and had no clue that the
company would be worth millions just four years later. The sale
of the business meant life-changing money for them, too. The
employees with whom I shared the proceeds were truly surprised
and grateful for the money, despite the fact that they deserved

it. That's where the real joy came from—being able to share the financial gain with the people who had helped me the most.

I could never have imagined that this would happen. I was never in this for the money alone, but the money represented the culmination of all the blood, sweat, and tears that went into this business. All my hard work had paid off.

CHAPTER 12

TRUST YOUR INTUITION

In June 2014, I won an EY Entrepreneur of the Year award for the New York region. aden + anais had just crossed the line to $55 million in revenue. I was one of only two women, out of nearly forty finalists. When I was nominated, I was dead set against wearing a black dress. I refused to blend in with the rest of the finalists, who were virtually all men, on the stage. I chose a blood red dress by Roland Mouret that accentuated my curves and stood out against the sea of black suits—no one could miss the fact that I was a woman.

Lisa Schiffman, a longtime marketing professional at EY, felt the same frustration that I did—she knew women were creating great companies but she wasn't seeing them get the same opportunities or recognition as their male counterparts. Determined to redefine the status quo, she founded the EY Entrepreneurial Winning Women program in 2008 to help level the playing field for women founders. Winning Women focuses on "the missing middle," supporting women entrepreneurs who are leading existing profitable companies across the world to achieve their full potential and scale. I've been a member since 2013, the year I was named as a Winning Woman.

While I'm proud of the awards I've won, I don't want you to have the impression that I've risen to success and haven't faced any challenges since. Remember that bit of women's intuition I had about the SPC partner, Chris? One of my deepest regrets is that I didn't listen to it.

By 2016, it had been three years since we sold the business; aden + anais had grown top-line revenue by 45 percent and developed several new products. We had also launched a skincare line and begun the development of a disposable-diaper line that launched in 2018. In December 2016, aden + anais acquired a company called Halo, which sells sleeping bags and swaddles, and more recently, bassinets. I'm immensely proud of the growth, but it wouldn't be the full story if I stopped there. While our revenues continued growing, our culture—the culture I worked so hard to build—fell apart.

Three months after the sale, the first (or should I say second) glimmer of trouble with Chris surfaced. I had made the decision to fire our head of sales because it was clear that we needed someone with a different skill set as the company entered the next stage of growth, and I didn't tell Chris before I did it. Because I'd made all the hiring and firing decisions with my team in the past, and I was the CEO, I thought this was just another day at the office. Besides, the Seidlers had never needed to know about these decisions in advance. The first time I made a truly big decision after they came on, I felt I had to tell them, but they said, "Well, you run the company. Unless you want to spend a million dollars on a private jet, you do what's right for your business." I assumed SPC would feel the same.

I assumed wrong. Chris was furious.

"How dare you," he said. "You're not allowed to make decisions like that without consulting us." What he was saying pissed me off, but it was the condescending tone that really put me over the edge.

"You don't know the business yet, you don't know the person I fired . . . what value could you possibly add to this difficult decision?" I asked.

"That's not the way this is going to work, Raegan."

After that, I couldn't make one decision without intense scrutiny. For example, I needed to hire key people quickly, but SPC was now holding the purse strings. And they wanted me to pay new hires well under what I knew it would take to get great, experienced people in the New York market. Meanwhile, they hired a string of useless consultants for hundreds of thousands of dollars. Even when we were a $55-million company, we were always frugal. My CFO and I shared a room at conferences to save money; we were careful about spending and would only do so where it mattered most—like hiring talent. After about a month, I sat down with Chris and told him that it wasn't going to work if we continued like this. "Every time I'm on a call with you, I'm treated like a petulant schoolgirl and I don't deserve that," I explained as patiently as I could. "You paid millions of dollars for a business that I built from scratch. Is all my experience negated now that you're the boss? Do you not acknowledge that I accomplished something pretty great? You've never built or run a business before in your life, but you know better than I do in every single situation?" Not surprisingly, he did what most men do in that situation—he apologized. We ended the meeting on an agreeable note (and with a hug if my memory serves me correctly), but Chris continued to question most if not all of my decisions. It was becoming clear that my usually sound judgment of character had failed me this time around. It was also clear that the Seidlers (my guardian angels) and SPC (the devil incarnate) couldn't have been more different. I had expected my relationship with SPC to look somewhat like the one I had with the Seidlers: respectful, inclusive, transparent. I had thought SPC invested in the business knowing that my management team and I were going to continue running it the way we saw fit, but instead they were trying to run it from afar, making decisions purely on quarterly numbers they saw on a spreadsheet—which doesn't work. In an unusual move, the Seidlers had agreed to stay on as a very small minority investor when I sold the business to SPC. Part of the deal with SPC was that I would retain two board seats—one for me, and one seat for me to fill with the person of my choice. Initially, Matt Seidler held my other board seat. That was until we acquired Halo. SPC gave the former CEO of Halo a board seat, but then also suggested that Matt should be removed from one of my two allotted seats because, according to them, he wasn't an actively contributing board member. Matt didn't want me to protest, saying that it wasn't worth fighting to keep him on. But I felt it was, because SPC didn't like having someone on the board who was able to call them on their bullshit, and I was worried they were trying to diminish my influence overall.

With Matt off the board, I had a seat to fill, so I set about finding someone else of the Seidlers' caliber to come to the table. For over a year, I put forward several people as potential board members. SPC rejected all of them under the guise that the seat had to be filled by someone "with more relevant experience." For example, one potential board member I recommended was the former president of a $1.5-billion cosmetic brand. She currently sits on the boards of three publicly traded multinational organizations. She clearly isn't a lightweight as far as experience goes. I didn't know her personally—I found her through a headhunter and quickly set up a lunch with her, where I learned how amazing and qualified she was. I thought she would make the perfect addition to the board. It took SPC, who wanted to interview all my potential candidates, two months to even agree to have a call with her. She called me the next day to report that it was "the weirdest and most disrespectful call I've ever had." She told me that the whole way through she was thinking, "I hope Raegan has a good lawyer and an exit plan." She could tell they were undermining me "up, down, left, and right." The final blow came toward the end of the conversation. They said to her "You realize if you come on board you'll always be Raegan's board member." "Well, it's Raegan's board seat to fill," she said. She was certain that they were trying to marginalize my involvement with aden + anais. And of course, she was not approved to be on the board, and when I wrote this, the seat was still vacant.

From hiring to the board seat, I was fighting on all fronts—both at home and abroad. SPC thought we should shut down our international offices and move to a distributor model rather than the direct business model we already had up and running. I'd already had this argument many times over the course of building aden + anais, and I was frustrated to be having it again, especially since our direct business model had been working. We argued hard over whether to shut down the Australian, Japanese, and European offices, despite the fact that the international businesses had grown year over year since the day they opened. Didn't seem like a part of the business you'd want to shut down to me.

At every board meeting, I said, "Don't do this, we are not a distributor business. If we switch, we'll have to charge so much more for our products, because the distributor will have to put their margin on it to make money. We're already established in these countries at a retail price point. No one is going to pay more for a product they've already been paying $50 for. They're not going to be OK paying $70 for it all of a sudden." It seemed like common sense to me, but they were relentless, like a dog with a bone. They wanted to be done with the overhead costs of having offices, staff, and warehouses in international markets.

I ended up sacrificing Australia for the sake of keeping Europe and Japan open, but I wasn't happy about it. The revenue was only a couple of million because Australia is such a small market, but I knew that turning it into a distributor model would be a disaster. We shut down our office, let go of our four employees there, and started to work with a distributor. Sure enough, a year later, we had lost substantial revenue and market share in Australia. I reluctantly allowed our Australian business to fail to prove a point to the investors—in the hope that watching the results of that decision would make them leave Europe and Japan alone—because I knew it would cost us millions of dollars and ultimately kill the brand in those regions if we went to a distributor model. As I write this, the business in Europe is still a direct model, and so is Japan.

One would think this would be like an elephant in the room, but they refused to acknowledge it. Their focus was entirely on the money—that is, they preferred to ruthlessly cut costs, no matter how negatively it impacted the brand or our staff. This might seem contradictory, but their focus was cutting costs no matter what. In my view, the only way they knew how to make a business profitable was to slash costs, no matter the ultimate expense to the brand or the people within the company. It was almost like cutting your nose off to spite your face. In the case of aden + anais, if you go from a direct model to a distributor model, you might save on the infrastructure costs but you lose out on sales because of the resulting higher retail price of the product and the lack of focus on the brand. Prices go up because the distributor has to add their margin, and if a product already exists in the market at one price point and then goes to a higher price point, sales will decline. It might be cleaner and less cumbersome, but it isn't viable once a market has had a set retail price, as in Europe and Japan, since we had been actively selling in those markets for years.

This is an example of why I was constantly at odds with SPC. It's clear to me that they are penny wise and pound foolish, making decisions from a purely numbers standpoint from afar. This was obvious from their insistence that we move the international business to a distributor model without ever having visited our international markets to understand how consumers interacted with the brand and products there. In theory, stripping out all of the overhead and creating a distributorship could have been more profitable, but this didn't account for the intangibles that ultimately drove down sales.

In November 2016, three years after they took over and just one month before we acquired Halo, Chris and the other lead partner—let's call her "Laurie"—called me to deliver some news.

I had actually flagged Halo as an acquisition opportunity back in 2012 when the Seidlers were still our investors. They were a really strong brand, known and respected for their focus on products that promoted safe sleep for babies. At the time, I felt it was a complementary company that would help scale our business without having to start a new product line from scratch. However, when it came on the market years later, SPC was far more excited about the prospect of buying it than I was. I didn't think it was the right time to acquire a business and I didn't want the unnecessary pressure on us, given the supply chain and operational issues we were dealing with at the time. But SPC was very gung ho on the idea, regardless of me and the entire management team being against the acquisition.

Anyway, back to the phone call. They wanted to tell me that I would be moved out of the CEO position (despite having led the company through tremendous growth). I was crushed. Worse yet, I still had many millions invested in the company and I no longer had a say in how the business was going to be run. When I asked to have the money back, so I could move on and start a business that I could control, they said no. Given their lack of confidence in my ability, I am not really sure why they wouldn't agree to buy me out. In hindsight, I wish I had pushed harder on that.

SPC didn't think I was capable of running the combined entity now that we were purchasing Halo. Their exact words: "We want to bring on a superstar CEO." They wouldn't give me a title or define my new role—they told me to wait and see what title the new CEO would want me to have. It would be up to them to decide what role I would play in the company going forward, or if I had a role at all.

With the purchase of Halo, my shares were diluted, whereas SPC increased their percentage of ownership and earned a very sizable transaction fee. We took on a whole lot of debt to buy Halo, something that is commonplace in the PE world.

And then, to make matters worse, SPC hired a COO who brought the company to its knees in five months. He was a friend of a friend of Laurie's. One of the first things he did when he took the position was to forgo the months of research we had done on a new warehouse facility in favor of a warehouse from his personal Rolodex. That one little move tripled our fulfillment costs, due to the contract he negotiated with his "contact." Around the same time, our primary supplier dumped us with no notice and started working with a competitor. Because of the production and warehouse issues, we suddenly had bigger problems than we had before the new COO came on board.

It was the perfect storm, but SPC was uninterested in hearing how the COO was affecting the business—from me, at least. I had to appeal to a male board member for help, which felt a bit ridiculous. When the male board member went to bat for me and told them the COO was a train wreck, they finally fired him.

Perhaps even more frustrating was the fact that it took them nine months from that phone call to find their "superstar" CEO, while I sat on the sidelines. I was a dead man walking. I had to keep up the CEO "act" for the sake of the morale of the rest of the aden + anais team—an extremely difficult task given that I didn't have any real authority to do anything—by this point I felt like I had to ask SPC for permission to blow my nose. I was still involved in branding decisions, and technically the "face" of aden + anais, but I had hardly any say in how things were run. Employees still considered me the CEO because it appeared as though I was, but I felt ridiculous and just wanted someone to give me a specific, useful role.

When they finally found their new superstar CEO, I advised them not to hire him. Nothing in his résumé made me believe he was the right person for the job, despite the fact that he appeared to be a very nice man.

I will never forget the Friday before he started, before things really went to shit. The usual Friday late afternoon at the office meant that everyone was relaxing together at the bar—the booze was free, and they would rather stay and talk with one another than go out. For some reason, this Friday was different. I looked up and suddenly realized the office was empty at 7 p.m. I was alone. As I made the rounds turning off lights and closing down the office for the weekend, the stillness of the place struck me. In that quiet moment, I had the first and only emotional reaction since the turmoil within the company began. I was filled with sadness, but also pride. I had never stopped to give myself a pat on the back and say, "Well, fuck. This started at my kitchen table ten years ago, and now it's a $100-million global brand." There had been so much going on that I had never taken a second to be proud of this huge achievement. I looked around at what we had built, what I created. Now someone else was going to run it.

Just then, Markos called to ask what time I was coming home. I promptly burst into tears. "It's just hit me that this is my last day as CEO. When I walk through those doors on Monday I won't be leading this business ever again." "I'm coming to get you," he said. He and the girls drove four blocks to pick me up, and the girls told me they were sorry I "didn't have my job anymore," which was surprisingly cute. Amelie wrote me a card that said, "I'm sorry you are sad mummy. I think you are very kind to give that man your job." That night, I was a bit of a mess, but I decided that I would give myself until the following morning to wallow. The next day, I would wake up, shake it off, and move forward. And that's exactly what I did. I knew I needed to grieve, but I also knew I didn't want that feeling to get ahold of me. Despite my disappointment in the decision, I was ready to make it work with the CEO, especially because my money was still tied up in the business. I didn't want to walk away from aden + anais not knowing what would happen to the investment and the brand that I built and love.

The new CEO they brought in lasted only five weeks. After that, they hired a friend of one of the founding partners of SPC—a former mortgage salesman who has never run a company in his life. The real insult? They paid him almost twice what they paid me to do the job. He's still there as of the writing of this book, which is beyond confusing to me.

When SPC first came in, Chris had asked Bob Seidler if he had any tips for moving the business forward. Bob had said, "Absolutely do not destroy that culture. Of every business I've seen in my entire career, I've never seen a culture as strong as this one." Sadly, SPC simply didn't understand the value of our culture to the bottom line. Nothing hurt worse than watching it be destroyed.

The beginning of the end came after the COO and the first CEO to replace me came on. The pressure SPC was placing on the business was so intense that it filtered down through the management team. The investors were making the decisions, but the mistakes (like the expensive move to a different warehouse) fell to my staff to fix. To make matters worse, my team kept looking to me to do something about it, but my hands were tied. I tried my best to protect everyone from it, but there was only so much I could do.

Our management team had it the worst; they would agree with one another and cooperate in meetings, but as soon as they were no longer face-to-face, the backstabbing and finger pointing began. These were people who used to work well together. Now, they were turning on each other out of fear. I had to sit them down and tell them that the infighting was not OK. And the rest of our employees were feeling the pressure, too. How could they look to us for leadership and guidance if everyone was at each other's throat? I reminded them that I had built this business to be the opposite of every hierarchical, politically driven office I've ever worked in. But it wasn't like that anymore. It was soul-destroying. Miracle of miracles, they understood what I was trying to say. The team tried to work out their issues. Some of them left, and some new people changed the dynamic. From this experience, I learned that it's not enough to have key people with depth of experience in important positions—you also need to screen for tolerance to stress and pressure. As soon as the shit hit the fan, it was telling to see who was able to stand under pressure and who wasn't.

To add insult to injury, SPC decided to shut down the bar in an effort to get everything "back on track." In aden + anais's history, we had never had an issue with the bar, until one of the people whom SPC hired took advantage of it. SPC saw the bar as a symbol of excess and drunkenness, instead of a place where employees connected at the end of a long day. I told them that it would be another morale destroyer for the team in an already cracked culture, but they were adamant. We were removing the bar, and our culture was falling apart one piece at a time. From a leadership perspective, it takes a certain skill set to get everyone back on the same page. I was no longer in a position to fill key roles, and I was no longer in a leadership position to get everyone on the same page emotionally, either. Not to mention the fact that I was going through my own emotional turmoil, too. So there was no one standing at the helm encouraging people to come together and to fix this as a team.

The people who worked for me didn't understand the decisions the investors were making and were frustrated. They constantly told me that I should be the person leading, and I had to remind them that the ship had sailed, and we had to make peace with the new way forward. As in every situation, the stress and the dysfunctional relationship between the investors and me had a trickle-down effect. The management team felt the stress first, but it wasn't long before the turmoil had permeated the entire business and we started to lose key people. Both long-term and short-term employees left because they were devastated at the changes taking place in their work environment. The company they knew and loved was changing fast and hard. A fractured culture has an enormous and negative impact on the success of a business. The reason we accomplished so much in a short amount of time early on is because we had such an incredible culture; everyone was in it together. After the changes in leadership, we had people who focused only on doing what was right for them. We had a whole lot of beaten-down people walking around, and it's no surprise that we didn't get the same performance. The people and their positivity are what determine the success or failure of a business.

The tension in my relationship with the investors was at an all-time high. Despite the fact that I was no longer the CEO, it's not in my nature to keep quiet, especially because I was (and still am as of the writing of this book) the single largest individual shareholder in the company. I felt they were making too many bad decisions about the business and the people they were bringing in to run it. And in the end, that was probably what did me in.

CHAPTER 13

EXIT WITH GRACE

At the beginning of 2018, after four full years of working with SPC, I retained counsel on the advice of some friends in the industry. "They're ignoring you, and the only way to get them to stop ignoring you is to get counsel," they told me. While I was no longer in a leadership position, I was still a minority investor and millions of dollars of my family's money was wrapped up in the business. It was impossible to keep quiet while they made decisions that I felt jeopardized not only the future of aden + anais, but my family's money, too.

The tension grew worse when the investors appointed the next CEO, a former mortgage salesman. He just couldn't work with me, despite talking a good game to SPC. It was clear that this was another man who needed complete control, and he was not comfortable having the founder and former CEO looking over his shoulder. He began to block most decisions I made. In meetings with others, he would agree with my choice of direction, but then he would go behind my back and tell the staff not to carry out what I had asked them to do. What he didn't realize is that the team was still fiercely loyal to me, and they all immediately told me what he'd said.

Of course, I confronted him about it. "The deal was that we stay in our own lanes, but you keep telling me what to do in my lane," I said. "I have a lot of experience in this business—I built the brand and have forgotten more than you could possibly learn in a few short months, so what are you doing?" That went over like a lead balloon. He grew aggressive and the conversation ended badly.

By March of 2018, my relationship with the investors felt like a train wreck. I asked for a meeting so we could talk about our relationship and how to move forward together. Up to that point, the investors had been working hard to avoid me for months; during one visit to our Brooklyn office, they came and went through the back door to avoid interacting with me. I was frustrated—my work at aden + anais felt irrelevant, and my responsibilities were increasingly unclear. I wanted to be back in a position where I could focus on the front-facing, brand-building portion of the business. Given that I had sold the product and fostered the relationship with most of our customers, I wanted to be in a position where I could continue to work with them.

We met on March 14, 2018. One of my attorneys opened the discussion.

"This relationship has become rather estranged. Raegan's goal is not to antagonize but to try to find a way forward, where everyone can agree on who is doing what, and really allow that to happen because it hasn't been the case up until now. Raegan still cares deeply about the business and the brand—it has her

daughter's name on the door. We're not here to rehash griev-
ances, only to find a way forward."

In response, Chris said, "This is going to be a very short
meeting, because effective immediately, we've decided to termi-
nate Raegan." He then slid a termination agreement across the
table.

It felt like all of the air had been sucked out of the room. But
I'm proud of my reaction. Despite the impulse to jump across the
table and strangle him, or burst into tears, I kept it together and
kept a small smile on my face, looking Chris directly in his eyes.

The investors were offering one year's salary in severance pay
and the chance to act as a consultant at the rate of $1,500 per
day. In their mind, I could still be the face of the brand. Their
terms came with some clauses: They wanted a five-year non-
disparagement agreement and a noncompete clause. It seemed
they thought that $300,000 pre-tax could buy me off for an-
other five years.

We requested a few moments to ourselves. We were dumbfounded and my lawyers hadn't seen this coming. When we
went back into the meeting, we explained that I needed some
time to think it all through, and we would be back in touch in
the next couple of weeks. But I did have one question. "Have
you thought about the messaging of all of this?" I asked. "You
know, for the staff?"

"Scott is going to address the company," Chris explained.

My attorney laughed. "That's all fine and well, but these
people have worked with her for ten years. I think she deserves
the right to go in and say good-bye."

"Chris, you realize these people probably already know,

right?" I said. "I'm fairly sure you had them cut off my email already. If you've cut it off, you had to tell the IT people to Kdo that. The cat's already out of the bag. The team that is loyal to me is probably already having a nervous breakdown over this. The business is already in turmoil. Isn't it in your best interest to let their friend and founder say thank you and good-bye?"

Chris looked at me as if he hadn't considered all that. He said we'd "work something out."

We weren't ready to sign the termination papers, but I was worried about the money I had reinvested in the company. The millions I had made during the sale in 2013 were now jeopardized by any bad decisions made by the investors and their newly appointed leadership team.

"Would you consider liquidity for Raegan?" my attorney asked.

"Sure, we'd do that, but her money's worth nothing right now; it's got zero value," Chris said.

My attorney didn't waste a second. "Zero value? So, is that what you're reporting to your investors—that the company has zero value?" he shot back.

Chris wasn't prepared for that response. "Well, we'll have to look into that, and I'll get back to you," he said. With that, the meeting concluded. It was only moments later that SPC's attorneys emailed mine and said that I was no longer allowed to go into the aden + anais offices.

I stayed pretty stoic until I left my attorney's offices. I took the elevator down to the lobby and sat on the ledge of the lobby garden as people walked by on their way to and from work, just trying to process what had happened. It took me a moment, but I finally wrote out a quick text to my people, the ones who are closest to me. "Guys, they just fired me."

As for the aden + anais staff, because they'd cut off my account, I couldn't email them to tell them what had happened. We had a group emergency text thread, however, so I sent out a message saying that I had been fired, that I was sorry, and that I wanted to say good-bye to everyone in person. I invited them all to meet me that evening at a bar in DUMBO, and the drinks were on me.

Over the next two and a half hours, I answered the calls of my family and friends and explained what had happened. Markos called immediately, of course. "You know what, Raegs? It's been soul-destroying for you," he said. "It's been frustrating to watch you go through this and I think, in the end, this will be a good thing—this situation was making you miserable. You're going to go through a grieving process, and then you're going to be OK."

Eventually, I got up from the ledge in the lobby, got a cab, and made my way to the bar in DUMBO where I met the team.

It was hard to see them, but it was also a relief to give hugs and cry with everyone who had worked so hard to make aden + anais successful. For at least a year prior to my termination, I had been pulling away from the people I worked with. I was too scared to be close to them for fear of showing my own inner turmoil, or for fear that the day might come when I would have to watch them get fired by the investors. I was worried that anyone closely associated with me would later become a target, so I put more distance between us. Those people were now relieved to hear why I had pulled away—they had thought it was something they did. It was nice to be able to speak openly about what it had been like for me for the first time.

It was hardest to see Alex, my friend and one-time executive assistant. By the time I left aden + anais, she had stood by me for four years and had helped me manage the business and my life. The investors had removed her as my executive assistant eight months prior when the new CEO came in and she had been supporting the finance and human resources departments, but she was still my very good friend. The moment I saw her, we both burst into tears. It was even harder knowing that she would more than likely be fired soon—which she was, two days later.

The gathering eventually wound down and I headed home at around 11 p.m. Markos was waiting up. While I had somewhat held it all together for everyone else, when I saw Markos, I was able to let myself come undone.

What I really struggled with was how (and what) to tell the girls. I didn't want them to see the uncertainty or the sadness that I felt, and I didn't want them to feel frightened. It took me two days to tell them, but they knew something was up because I was home when they got home from school. Anais was the first to ask what was going on. When I told her I was fired because of the tense relationship with the investors, she said, "Those assholes, Mum. You're going to fight them, aren't you?"

I couldn't help but smile. "Yes, darling, it doesn't end now," I said.

"Does that mean I don't get free aden + anais blankets anymore?" she asked.

"I'm sure I can get you a blanket here and there if you want one," I said.

"Good. We're not paying for them after what they did to you!"

Lourdes and Arin came over to give me a big hug. Lourdes wanted to lift me up and told me that she was proud of me. "Don't let them get you down, because you're amazing," she said. Arin, my little worrier, bit her nails. I gave her a kiss and told her this would be a good thing in the end and that everything would be all right.

Amelie, my youngest, came home later that day from school. When she saw me sitting in the living room, she said "Mummy, you're here again? Can you be here every day after school?"

"You really like that?" I asked.

"Yes! That would be so great if you were here, Mummy!" she said.

"Ok, I'm going to be here most days after school now," I told her.

"Promise?"

"Promise," I said, and we high-fived on it.

It goes without saying that I've learned some very valuable lessons the hard way.

Never sell the controlling interest in your business if you still passionately care about it. It is soul destroying to have to sit and watch people make bad decisions from afar and have zero ability to do anything to stop them. If you sell a majority share of your company, just get out (unless you sell it to Seidler Equity Partners, of course). Don't buy back in a meaningful way, don't tie up your family's resources in a company in which you could potentially no longer have a say. I would like to think that it's possible to do so, but I know too many founders, aside from those who work with the Seidlers as investors, who have been ousted from their companies by PE funds. While the original agreement with SPC was that I would stay in the CEO chair, that changed within three years, and I was forced to stand by and watch while they made decisions that I fundamentally disagreed with and that I believed were damaging the business.

I was lamenting to a friend over the fact that I sold my company to people who have no real understanding of the value of the brand they bought. My friend quickly pointed out that *I* was the twat for selling my hard-won, global boutique brand to a private equity firm whose brand experience was in dog food, cold cuts, and vaginal yeast infection cream. He had a point. But I would be dishonest if I didn't tell you that I think the greatest lesson I've learned is that the struggle for women in business is far from over. There is plenty of research to suggest that when a company gets shaky and a woman is at the helm, the woman is blamed and is often removed, whereas when a company gets shaky while a man is at the helm, it's the circumstances that get the blame, and he is given the support and opportunity to fix the issues. My situation is no different. I didn't pick the wrong warehouse; I didn't make my manufacturer of ten years dump us with no notice; I didn't acquire a company that put us into an overly leveraged situation and put massive unnecessary pressure on an already strained business. In my eleven years at aden + anais, I've made plenty of mistakes, but the two biggest ones were selling aden + anais to SPC and not having the courage to dig my heels in when I felt the decisions they were making were wrong. While I was very vocal about disagreeing with their decisions, I caved far too often and let them move forward, despite knowing that it was the wrong move for the company. I know why I didn't. I was scared for my job, and I knew if I pushed too hard, they would fire me. As soon as I did, that's exactly what happened. So here I am, taking the blame for many of their decisions and circumstances that were out of my control, despite warning them against these very decisions. A lot of what went wrong I got blamed for, and they took the credit for what went well. When I look back at my life, I now understand how difficult it is for a woman to secure capital, how difficult it is for women to get support from their own families and social networks. How difficult it is for women leaders to be given assistance and support when things go off track, rather than blamed. Would it have been a whole different story if I were a man?

At the end of the day, I think it's difficult for most men to yield the ultimate power to a woman. No one of us alone is going to change that; it's the collective that will make the difference. In addition, the real change will come when men stand beside us. Not only do we need women to own their power, but we need the "good guys" out there to loudly shout with us.

As women, we have work to do, too. We perpetuate the notion that "it's just the way it is." We go into situations knowing that we'll be looked down upon as women, expecting it. We have to look deep inside ourselves and realize that we have the ability to lead. There is absolutely no reason at all for any of us to accept that a man should, by default, have all the power, or make more money to do the same job, simply because he is a man.

So you see, I've come full circle. When I was at The Economist, I had men telling me what I was able to do—or not do, as it were. And now, years later, people in a business I built from scratch are treating me the same—but just like I did twelve years ago, I refuse to accept someone else's idea of what I'm capable of. I've seen what success can look like, how well the business I created ran, and I know my potential. I'm questioning, and I'm challenging, and I'm unwilling to just defer to someone else because that's the way they've decided it will be.

I left a corporate job to do my own thing because I wanted the freedom to grow something that wasn't limited by someone else's beliefs about me and about my capabilities. On the surface, I'm right back where I was before: being told by men that I'm not capable. But guess what? Not only do I know I'm damn capable of running a company, but I also know I'm capable of building a company from nothing more than an idea at a kitchen table into the $100-million global business it is today.

When people are constantly trying to tell you that you're not good enough, you're not smart enough, or you don't have a Harvard degree or a penis, it can start to wear on you. There were days I thought about giving up, to be sure. There were plenty of mornings where I lay in bed thinking, "Fuck, what's going to be thrown at me today?" But I was never going to just walk away from the company I built from scratch. I can't lie, though, and say that I didn't feel a sense of relief when SPC fired me, but there was no way I was going to be a quitter.

In my head and my heart, I know what I need to focus on. I'm a huge believer in the law of attraction. I generally believe that if you give good, you get good back. The more I focus on negativity and anger, the more deeply and frequently I experience negative situations. If I focus more on the abundance of wonderful people and opportunities in my life, the more I experience positive situations. The key is to keep the negative experiences from consuming you and to return to your positive, good-hearted center, even if it's no easy task when you're fighting against people who don't believe in you. When I start to get shaky, I look at my accomplishments and all the love that surrounds me and think about all the good I have in my life, which is not always easy to do but has never disappointed me.

Although frustrating as hell at the time, in the end I am grateful to my bosses at The Economist who tried to stifle me. I'm grateful to all of the people in my career who had no faith in what I could accomplish. It just so happens that I'm the kind of person who says "Fuck you, watch me do it" in the face of adversity, so their deterrence and disparagement had the opposite effect: It only encouraged me to prove them wrong.

And you know what? With what I've got up my sleeve now, I'm sure that one day I will be equally grateful to Chris and Laurie and the gang at SPC for inspiring me once again.

CONCLUSION

I never really thought that I wanted to have children, so the irony is not lost on me that not only did I have four daughters, but I also started a baby-product business.

Somewhere around the age of thirty-five, after Markos and I had been married for two years, I realized that I wanted a family around me as I got older. The idea of my husband and me celebrating Christmas without kids and grandkids, just sitting next to the tree, staring at each other, was sort of . . . depressing. Maybe we'd just have one baby?

So, I got pregnant. I was not a particularly great pregnant person—I experienced none of the pregnancy glow, joy, or euphoria that I'd heard and read about. And when I finally had my daughter, I was overcome with the sense that I had made the biggest mistake of my life. When Anais was only a week or two old, I actually said to my husband, "Can we give her back?"

He stared at me blankly. "Give her back . . . to whom?" he asked.

I realize now that I probably had a minor case of postpartum depression, what's sometimes referred to as the "baby blues." I also believed I was ill-equipped for motherhood and that everyone was better at raising children than I was. One day I felt like I wasn't reading enough parenting books, the next day I felt like I was reading too many. Unlike in business, I took advice from everyone who offered it—my family, friends, doctors, nurses, and lactation specialists. I was desperate for guidance but suffering from information overload.

Miraculously, around the time Anais turned seven months, everything changed. The primal urge to protect, the divine sense of purpose, all of it came rushing right in. I loved her more than I thought it was possible to love another human being. The fractured relationship I'd had with my own mother didn't matter so much anymore. It was like Anais healed something in me. She filled a hole in my heart.

After that, I became, as I like to say, addicted to having babies. The feeling I got every time Dr. Scher handed me one of those precious little girls was beyond words.

They came along, one right after the other. Since Anais was born via emergency C-section, Lourdes and the rest of the girls were born the same way, without the emergency part. I believe our personalities are aligned with our star signs, so when I found out the scheduled delivery date for Lourdes, I put my foot down. "No, no, no, she has to be a Libra," I said to Dr. Scher. "I cannot have a Virgo, with me and her big sister being Scorpios, and it's right on the cusp."

"Are you joking?" he asked.

"No, I'm deadly serious, can we please move the date," I said. And we did.

When my third daughter Arin came along, Dr. Scher tried to schedule the date for Halloween. By this point, he was only scheduling C-section births on Tuesdays. "I'm not having a Halloween baby," I told him.

"But Wednesday is my day off!"

"Dr. Scher, I'm a frequent flyer. C'mon. You can change one day."

"Are you really going to make me do this?" he asked.

"Yep, I am." And so we moved the delivery date to November 1.

I tore my uterus during Arin's birth and was advised not to have any more children. So, in classic Raegan fashion, I proceeded to get pregnant again anyway. (As I say, I was addicted.) When I started talking idly about eventual baby number five, however, my poor husband realized he was going to have to stage an intervention. After delivering Amelie, Dr. Scher leaned over the surgical partition. "I just want you to know," he said, while performing my tubal ligation, "I'm triple-knotting these."

Between Arin's and Amelie's births, I had begun to research adoption. My husband and I both wanted more children, and after three little girls, and a torn uterus, we hoped to adopt a boy. I'd just had no idea that my age was going to be a problem within the adoption system. I was forty-one; I wasn't dead! Annoyed, I began to research international adoption and the possibility of going directly to an orphanage.

I am not sure I believe in coincidences. Rather, I think life has a way of revealing new possibilities by drawing you into eye-opening experiences. The decision to embark on adoption research proved life-changing, despite the realization that— according to the rules—I was too old to adopt a newborn baby.

I learned about horrific conditions in far too many orphanages across the developing world. Aside from lack of cleanliness and basic access to medications and drug therapies, babies are sometimes left alone in their cribs for as long as twenty-two hours every day. Babies around the world are left alone without being touched, cuddled, rocked, or held in any way. I learned about infant touch deprivation, which leads to higher levels of the stress hormone cortisol, lower levels of the emotional and social-bonding hormones oxytocin and vasopressin, and even physically smaller brains and developmental delays.

In the early stages of my business, there were two things I allowed myself to dream about: to create a work environment that made people happy, and to get to a point where I could help people in a meaningful way.

I had to do something. I couldn't *not* act. So I rang David in the wee hours of the morning, manic: "We're starting a foundation!"

He sighed, no doubt still half-asleep, resigned. "Of course we are, Raegan, because we don't already have enough to do."

That was the birth of our nonprofit, the Swaddle Love Foundation. The foundation was designed to keep orphanages all over the world properly staffed. We provided funding so these organizations can hire enough women to care for and watch over babies who cry out during the night or need to be soothed during the day. The extra helping hands are there to console infants and toddlers when they need a hug or, with a simple touch, to remind babies that they are not alone. Turns out that running a nonprofit is a complicated and time-consuming undertaking when tied to a for-profit business. Ultimately, after three years and many donations, we shut down our foundation so that we

could focus on helping already-established nonprofit founda-
tions accomplish their missions.

We decided we would be able to do more good by aligning with an already established cause for babies, which is where
(RED) and Hopeland come in.

Though aden + anais has donated to a host of charities since
its inception, my commitment to charitable giving kicked into
high gear after learning about the work that (RED) and Hopeland are doing. I embarked on a now three-year partnership
with The ONE Campaign and (RED), which has become, hands
down, the single proudest accomplishment in my aden + anais
journey to date. The ONE Campaign, whose mission is to end
extreme poverty and preventable diseases especially in Africa,
partners with businesses to sell products via its (PRODUCT)
RED collections. The organization raises awareness and funds
for the AIDS epidemic by engaging with iconic brands and companies to create unique (RED)-branded consumer products. A
percentage of the sales of each product goes to the Global Fund,
which facilitates counseling, testing, and the administration
of medicine to women and their families globally. The Global
Fund's mission is to accelerate the end of AIDS, tuberculosis,
and malaria as epidemics. The aden + anais contribution goes
toward preventing transmission of the HIV virus from positive
mothers to their unborn babies. Contributions from the aden +
anais (RED) collection have helped provide the equivalent of
300,000-plus days of lifesaving medication as well as other services to help HIV-positive mums give birth to HIV-free babies. I
am so grateful to be able to help this incredible cause, in even a
small way. My hope is that aden + anais will be by (RED)'s side

when they announce that we have eliminated mother-to-baby transmission of the HIV virus globally, although I no longer have any say in that.

I've always downplayed the philanthropic side of aden + anais because I never wanted it to feel gratuitous. For example, when the earthquake hit in Haiti, we decided to help. We donated $70,000 worth of children's clothing through Hopeland. Hopeland was founded by Deborra-lee Furness and Nicholas Evans, whose vision is to prevent family separation, reunify children who are separated from their families, and mobilize a movement of families to support children who are growing up outside family care. Around the world, 80 percent of the 25 million orphans worldwide have living parents or other family members but for various reasons are separated from them. Here in the States, Hopeland is focused on tackling the problems in the foster care system, which are only being worsened by the opioid crisis. I am immensely proud to sit on the board of Hopeland, which operates all around the world.

After we'd made the arrangements, I was talking with the head of the foundation who was working to make it all happen. He said, "How do you want me to promote this?"

"Promote it?" I asked.

"Yeah, what do you want me to do? How do you want it to be promoted so you can get credit for the donation?"

"I don't want it to be promoted," I said. "I just want to make sure these babies and kids have some clothing."

He couldn't believe it. In his entire career, he had never had an organization say, "You know, we don't need to make a big deal of this."

There are two schools of thought on this. One, that you help where you can and you don't need to talk about it. And the other, which my old marketing department and PR team happen to agree with: People want to know that an organization has heart. You're not doing any favors for the business by not talking about your efforts to give to the community. It's a balance that's difficult to find—well, for me, anyway.

It might be obvious by now that I have a soft spot for anything having to do with women and children. Helping them fills me up and makes everything worth it. I get more joy out of being able to provide some aid, even if only a small amount, than making a million-dollar sale.

While there have been many high-point moments in my entrepreneurial journey that I truly enjoyed, nothing makes me happier than to have the ability to help other people. Building my business has afforded me the freedom to contribute when I find a cause that touches my heart; instead of feeling bad about it, I am in the position to provide resources and connections, as well as ideas and brainpower. The years of struggle and hard work have been worth it, if only because I know that I can now make even a small difference in other people's lives.

I have no influence on the future of aden + anais, now that I am no longer part of the company. My hope is that SPC eventually finds the right people to run it and to build on the wonderful brand we all worked so hard to create.

However, I can admit that I never had any interest in staying involved if it became a half-billion-dollar business. I much prefer the scrappy world of start-ups, when it's just you and a small team of passionate, hardworking people, striving to build something from nothing with endless possibilities in front of you. And I'm happy to say that I've returned to that world.

About three years ago, in 2015, David came into the office one morning and said "Raegs, I had an epiphany over the weekend and I know what our next business should be." The entrepreneurial bug had bitten David since we had worked on aden + anais together, and he had been trying to come up with new ideas ever since.

"Oh, yeah? What is it?" I asked.

He paused for effect. "Moonshine," he said confidently.

"Are you joking? Isn't that for people who live in the woods, have no teeth, and wear overalls?" I asked. And for all the Southerners out there who are reading this, please know that was my very naïve perception of a drink I know many of you love.

He laughed. "Yeah, that is true, but just bear with me. You know how they say to do what you know and love? Well, we both know and love alcohol, right?"

This time it was my turn to laugh. He had a point, but I was not at all convinced. "Isn't moonshine akin to drinking rocket fuel?"

"Well, yeah, it is now, but if we worked on the recipe we could come up with something better," he said.

"I don't know how to make moonshine, and neither do you. And even if you did, I'm sure what you'd make would be awful," I said jokingly.

"Maybe, but I think there's something here."

"OK, well I think you're a little mental right now, so let's get back to selling more swaddles." We laughed and that was the end of that conversation—until about a week later.

I was showering in the middle of the night (as I tend to do) and I thought about my conversation with David. It suddenly occurred to me that there were similarities between muslin and moonshine. When we started aden + anais, muslin was a cheap material that wasn't pretty or stylish at all. Moonshine is the same—it's considered a basic sort of alcohol, almost low-brow. When I thought of moonshine, I thought of getting very drunk for very cheap on alcohol that burned my throat on the way down. I started to wonder: What if we turned moonshine on its head, just like we did with muslin? What if we created a premium, great-tasting moonshine?

All sorts of ideas bubbled up. What if we found a mixologist who could help us come up with great new, creative moonshine-based drink recipes, like moonshine martinis? What if we could get into five-star bars and restaurants or, better still, Michelin-star restaurants and it became a staple on their cocktail menu?

The next morning, I went to the office and said, "David, I've been thinking about your moonshine idea. I think you might be onto something if we elevate it."

His eyes lit up. "Yes, I think that would be amazing."

"But here's the challenge. Neither of us has a clue about how to make moonshine. And we would not only need to find out how to make it, we would also have to make it the greatest tasting moonshine on the market for this branding idea to work."

"Well, didn't you do that for muslin?" he asked.

"Good point."

"So then you're thinking about it?"

"I'm thinking about it, but right now we've got a lot to do

with aden + anais. I just wanted you to know that I'm starting to see the opportunity—if we can get it right," I said.

About three months later, I visited our soap manufacturer in Memphis, Tennessee; I tried where I could to go to every factory where aden + anais products are made. I was chatting with Scott, the head of operations who was overseeing our production run, and he told me he was a chemical engineer.

"So, wow, a chemical engineer with a passion for soap? How did that happen?" I asked.

He laughed and said, "No, soap is not my passion. Soap is my day job. My passion is moonshine."

I looked around, wondering if there was a hidden camera in the office and I was the victim of a prank. But it was truly a moment where life was slapping me in the face, telling me to pay attention.

"Really? Moonshine? Tell me more," I said.

As it turned out, he'd been tinkering with a recipe for moonshine for over ten years. He believed he had the best one out there. It was smooth and molasses-based, made with spring water, and he used a charcoal filter to remove impurities.

"Why haven't you done anything with this moonshine yourself?" I asked.

"I'm a chemist. I don't know how to market and sell a product or build a brand, and I don't have the money to do it, either," he explained.

"You are not going to believe this, but my friend and I were talking about starting a moonshine company. And selling products and building brands just happens to be what we do."

He gave me his personal contact information and we parted

ways, thinking about the possibilities and agreeing to call each other if and when the timing felt right.

While I did see the opportunity, we had our hands full with the growth of aden + anais and our ever-evolving relationship with our investors. Even though we had a possible moonshine recipe, the idea was set aside for the time being. It wasn't until two years later, in 2018, when David resigned because he would have been fired by the investors anyway, that I pulled out Scott's contact information. I gave it to David and said, "I think it's time to call Scott. Let's get this moonshine thing started."

With that, Saint Luna was born under the January 2018 wolf moon (how appropriate for a moonshine brand). David and I created a business together (with contracts, well-thought-out agreements, and a logical distribution of labor), and Scott is now our master distiller. As I finish writing the final draft of this book, we are getting ready to distill our first batch, which will be given to the distributors for sampling. This time around there will be no arguments about direct distribution or using an intermediary—in America, you have to sell liquor through distributors.

I'm proud of what we've built. Saint Luna is a contradiction to what everybody knows as moonshine. I'm a wuss when it comes to liquor—I'm a wine and champagne girl, and moonshine has never been known for its taste. And yet, our moonshine is so good that I can drink it in its original distilled form at 160 proof over ice, and it doesn't burn. The final product will be distilled down to 100 proof, which is still a higher alcohol content than, say, your average vodka or gin. Our goal is to be on the market with Saint Luna in the first quarter of 2019, and as we did with aden + anais, we won't be waiting to saturate domestic distribution before taking it global. We're already in discussions with distributors in Europe and Asia.

So, while this could be a sad story if viewed through one lens, I see it as a story of triumph. I got knocked down, but I'm not staying down. I simply got back up and I'm doing it all over again—transforming moonshine the way I transformed muslin. From babies to booze, I suppose you could say!

Nowadays, I have the privilege of advising other entrepreneurs on their businesses. I'm often asked for advice, and I generally make time to meet with anyone who reaches out to me. As we come to the end of my story, I'm going to ask you to forgive me a moment and allow me to stand on my soapbox, so I can share some of it with you. As you stand on the precipice of your own leap, here are some of my humble suggestions on how I think you can be sure your net will appear.

First, and perhaps most important, never let money become your guiding star—it doesn't make a good one. Whenever I have an entrepreneur sitting across the table asking me about money, saying their primary motivation for starting their business is to make a lot of money, I instantly know they will fail. People do strange things when money becomes the most important factor in a decision. I have never given money power, and I've always trusted that I would have enough of it. Above all, have the courage to walk away from money if it means your profit could negatively impact someone else . . . hopefully SPC is reading this.

Find people you can trust to help you along the way, but know that you don't need a mentor to make your dreams happen. I surrounded myself with people who were hardworking and smart, most of whom were smarter than me, and most of all, supportive. I took their advice. It didn't take me long to realize I didn't need a single all-encompassing mentor to get where I wanted to go—and neither do you.

Get comfortable with failing. The moment you accept failure as not only a possibility but also a *probability*, you realize you have nothing left to lose, and your fear will melt away.

Get comfortable following your instincts, even though everyone and everything around you might contradict them. The only time I ever had regrets was when I failed to listen to my intuition.

Get comfortable with the idea that you will have to work really fucking hard. Along with attitudes about money, work ethic (or lack thereof) is a huge indicator of someone's success. When would-be entrepreneurs ask me for resources or cheat-sheets—as if they want me to do the work for them—I know they're looking for shortcuts. It's often a sign that they're not willing to put in the effort and time it takes to build a thriving, successful business.

There will be moments when you falter and have doubts about your idea, your capabilities, your smarts. When you do, lean on your accomplishments—we've all got them, even if you have to dig deep to find them as I did in the beginning—to remind yourself of what you've already achieved.

Don't let anyone (including you) keep you from dreaming big. My hope for other women in business is that programs like EY's Entrepreneurial Winning Women will one day no longer be necessary—that first-time female entrepreneurs can walk into a networking event or a private equity firm and no longer be the only woman in the room; that a female business owner can be judged on her mind and her merits instead of her gender. In the meantime, I hope that women aren't discouraged by the prevailing wisdom about the kinds of companies we build or the goals we set for ourselves; that they don't let an opportunity pass by because they aren't "aggressive" or "confident" enough; that they choose to define success on their own terms.

Finally, never lose sight of your inspiration. I wanted to create a business to show myself that I could do it—but even more important, to show my girls what was possible. When things got hard, I always knew that I was setting a good example for my children, and that kept me going through the really tough times.

As for my girls, Anais, the original inspiration for aden + anais—as I write this—is fifteen going on forty; she is the definition of an old soul, and I am in awe of her strength, wit, and wisdom. She's been a vegetarian since the age of seven. She has volunteered with autistic children at the wonderful Brooklyn Autism Center (BAC) each week since she was eight. She's a member of the Humane Society and attends anti-Trump rallies. I honestly don't know where in the hell this kid came from. I have no doubt she'll end up tied to a tree somewhere, protesting something very loudly with an incredible amount of passion.

Whereas my second born, Lourdes, thirteen, well, who the hell knows. When she was ten, she casually asked her father, over breakfast, to define the term "rim job." I was traveling for business that morning, so I (luckily) dodged that conversation, but Markos later found out she had watched the movie *Vacation* without our knowledge. She is an extraordinary child—loving, smart, caring, talented: she wrote, sang, and helped produce a song for me that she and her sisters recorded for my fiftieth birthday gift. I was blown away. She is precocious with a capital P. It should go without saying that I am often told that she is the most like I was as a child—a natural rebel.

Arin, eleven, is most like her father: introspective, shy, a worrier, thoughtful, and with a heart full of love. She is our artist in the making and the one who I think will surprise us the most. She is also the keeper of the driest sense of humor in our family. Her one-liners are comedy gold and she often has all of us doubled over in laughter. And Amelie, eight, runs the house. I think she somehow knew that as the baby of four girls, she'd have to fight for her place in the family. She is hysterically funny, and knows it. She is incredibly bright, determined, and preternaturally comfortable in her own skin.

While I still struggle with mummy guilt and don't like being away from them for any real period of time, they are my guiding stars. I want to show them that if they are fearless and prepared to work hard, anything is possible. My hope is that, fifteen years from now, I'll be sitting in a cocktail bar somewhere sipping a Saint Luna martini with my four girls, aden + anais having become a household name, and I can say to them, "You know what? Your mum did that. I built that at our kitchen table, in the middle of the night, while all of you were sleeping like babies, and if I can do it, you can, too."

I want them to know that whatever their dreams are, they each have what it takes to achieve them; all they need is the courage to leap.

ACKNOWLEDGMENTS

To my family: All of you make my life better and allow me to do what I do. Succeed or fail, I know it's OK when I have you all by my side. You are my net! Markos, you are the most devoted husband a girl could ever ask for. Thank you for your generosity, the love, and the honesty that you give me. And most important, thank you for my babies. Nay Nay, Lulu, Rinny, and Amelish, you are my everything. I am so thankful to have you all in my life; you inspired and saved me. Every day I am proud to be your mum.

Paigey, I literally could not live without you. You make me a better person for having you in my life. You are as necessary to me as air and water and I love you with all that I am.

Rio, my cool nephew, thanks for always talking your old aunty up. I love you.

Suey, it's been forty-five years and we're still going strong. I can't even think of my life without you in it. You have been there for every up and every down; you are my second sister and the true definition of a best friend.

Mum, I know we have not always seen eye to eye, but I also know, when push comes to shove, you would step in front of a truck for me. When I needed it most you were there to support me and for that I am forever grateful.

Dad, they broke the mold when they made you. You made me feel loved and wanted during a time in my life when I was struggling. I am the person I am today in no small part because of how you raised me. I know it was shaky there for a while but I turned out OK in the end, yes?

Granty, my crazy, charming, gorgeous baby brother, thank you for always making me laugh and for having my back. I feel safe knowing I have you in my corner. And thank you to you and Mel for adding your mini-me. Jax, I believe you can fly, too, my darling.

Alicia, you are my second mum and one of the most caring, loving, and kind people I know. I most definitely feel blessed to have you as my mother-in-law. Thank you for being you, and for being the best Abuelita to the girls.

Benny and Mons, my family are everything to me and I am grateful that you guys are part of it. You have always been an incredible uncle and aunt to the girls and I love that we now have Alyssa and Alexander in our lives. I love you all.

Douglas and Juan, my family, thank you for being a constant in my New York life and for being wonderful uncles to my girls. Douglas, your sunburned head was the start of this all. Thank you for being there before aden + anais was anything other than a pipe dream and for always supporting me no matter what. I love you both more than you know.

Kez, Baz, and Scouty, thank you for being my Colorado family. Kez, despite being your second favorite sister, and the fact that you and I hanging together greatly increases our chances of liver failure, I love having you in my life.

Tone and Craig, how could I write a book without a shout-out to you crazy boys? Our friendship shaped me, and forty years on it makes me smile to know that we have another forty years of fun and frivolity to look forward to together. Thank God you both got it right with the lovely Pav and Amanda—bonus.

Mollie Glick, simply the most kick-arse literary agent out there. Thank you for thinking my story worthy of your time and for making this wild ride a little less scary. I have always felt very safe in your hands.

Sara Stibitz, the most patient, collaborative, talented writing partner a girl could ever hope for. You are the OG of ghost writing. This book would literally not exist were it not for you. Thank you for the herculean effort to get this done. You are my hero.

David, my partner, my brother, my pain in the arse. You are one of the smartest, most hardworking people I know, and there is no doubt that aden + anais would not have been the success it is without you. Your loyalty means the world to me and you have always stood steadfastly by my side in both the good times and the bad. You are a true friend and you make me better at what I do.

Alex, what a surprise and incredible support you are. You know me better than I know myself. You are my eyes, my ears and my trusted confidant, and most of all you are a friend whom I love. Thank you for making me laugh, for being skilled in Pokemon, for always being there, and for always having my back.

Samia, my unicorn- and crystal-loving friend. Your positivity, humor, and support mean more to me than you know. Thank you for always being there and for all you did to help me achieve my dream. Your energy and dedication were instrumental in helping to build an incredible business in Europe. You are very much a part of why I am lucky enough to be writing this book. You and your family have become my family—Darren, Yasmin, and Maali, what a bonus you all are. Thank you for all the love and support.

Ciara, you played hard to get but you were worth the effort. Thank you for being so dedicated to both me and aden + anais. You officially win the award for the most sleepovers in the office. Getting to know you the way I did and now being able to count you as one of my closest friends was the real bonus on top of getting a kick-arse CFO like you to join my fledgling business back in the day.

Leslie and Michelle, my NYC sisters, I told you the sun was sure to rise again. Thank you, both, for being there to remind me of the same when I needed it most. Very grateful to have you both in my life.

Sue, how wrong I was about you. The shy newbie in the Santa hat at Locanda Verde who I predicted wouldn't last long in the crazy world of aden + anais could not have proven me more wrong. I will always be grateful for the love and commitment you had for aden + anais. But mostly I am grateful for your unwavering support and friendship. Love you DJ Sab.

My peeps, Ang, Scotty, Beej, Kez, Jason, Sue, Mary Ellen, the heart and soul of the original aden + anais. It's because of you we were able to build such a fabulous company and had so much fucking fun doing it! Thank you for the music, cocktails, Photoshopping, dance moves, videos, inappropriateness, and laughter. Most important, thank you for the hard work, dedication, and passion. You guys are aden + anais! Scotty, Mary Ellen, Jason, Kez, and Sue, an extra-big thank-you for sticking it out till the "end."

Team aden + anais, you know who you are—there are just too many of you to list. Thank you, all, for what you did to help me build the business. I wouldn't be writing this book had each of you not contributed what you did.

Paula and Matt, thank you for the trust and for believing in me and the business. Without you two, aden + anais probably would not have made it. You are true best friends and I love you both very much.

Daniel Hargraves, thank you for going to bat for me when I really needed the help. I owe you. Muchas gracias for all you did for me back in 2008; you helped me save aden + anais. You are the real deal.

Kristina Junger-Godfrey, wow, what a ride, sister, and to think you almost picked the wrong side. You have been instrumental in helping me build the aden + anais brand. The best part of the past ten years, though, is the friendship. Thank you for being my ever-faithful drinking companion and a true confidante. I love you. May your charcoal tablets and green juice keep you up for the challenge for as long as I can still pop a cork.

Samantha Radach, thank you for all the hard work you put into helping me achieve my aden + anais dream. You are absolutely the right person to have in our PR corner. I am beyond appreciative for all you have done to help make this book a success. More important, thank you for not judging every time Kristina and I need to break out the charcoal tablets.

Kelly Reemtsen, I won the lottery when such a talented artist as you agreed to let me use your amazing artwork on the cover of my book. It perfectly represents how I felt building aden + anais. Your work is beautiful, inspirational, thought provoking and just what all girls need to see in 2019. Thank you for agreeing to be part of this project.

Denise Lambertson, my beautiful, talented friend, what a gift it was to meet you in the mountains of Rwanda. Thank you to you and Tim and team LMS for your contribution in getting this book out there.

Elyssa, thank you for taking a chance on a crazy Aussie chick with a muslin blanket way back when. You reinforced my belief in what I was doing long before anyone else even noticed I was there. You rock.

My wonderful friends and test readers, Kez, Baz, Elkie, Doug, Pez, Scotty, M.E., I know it was a big ask and no doubt a laborious undertaking. Only a real friend would agree to a favor like that. Thank you for giving me your time and honest feedback.

Bob, Matt, and Eric, I love you like brothers for all that you have done for me. Thank you for the guidance, the support, the encouragement, and the friendship. You are all men among men and the absolute pinnacle of private equity. If only others could be more like you.

My take-no-prisoners entrepreneurial girlfriends, you are women I admire and you make me want to be better: Chelsea

(FridaBaby), Sarah (S'well), Phyllis (Extreme Solutions), Leslie (Tower Legal Solutions), Julia (Beardwood), Tamsin (Pure Creative Arts), Lisa (Project Gravitas), Fran and Naomi (TomboyX), Rosie (Rosie Pope), Lauren (Park Avenue Skin Solutions), Kari (Earthkind), Joy (Taygan Consulting). I love watching you all kick arse. Thank you for continuing to inspire me.

Stephanie, you are the most encouraging, patient, understanding, and supportive editor out there. I would have told me to shove my head up my arse but you stuck by me and rolled with the punches. I also won the publisher lottery when you decided to get behind my book. Thank you, thank you, thank you.

Rebecca, thank you for jumping in to take the wheel on this book. You are one brave lady. Because of you, it doesn't feel like we skipped a beat! Thank you!

Margo and Lillian, thank you, both, for staying this very long, winding course, and for all you have done to ensure that people actually know that I have written a book.

Adrian, thank you for staying up late to read my proposal. I know that without your support this would not be happening.

Deb and Nick, I am in awe of the amazing work you are both doing with Hopeland. Thank you for allowing me to be a part of it. Your work and my involvement in it fills me up.

Deb, Jen, and Luisa, I meant it when I said that my association with (RED) and the Global Fund—and all that you are achieving—is one of my proudest accomplishments in my entrepreneurial journey. Thank you for inviting me to join the fight. Each of you is a powerhouse woman in your own right and an inspiration to me, and no doubt to countless women everywhere.

Marsha, big shout-out to you for having the vision to start the Women Presidents' Organization back in 1997—we needed it. Anne and Betty, thank you, too, for all that you do through WPO for so many women entrepreneurs out there. Wish I had known about you all when I was starting out and feeling my way around in the dark. You all are very much appreciated.

Lisa, Kerrie, and Katie, you girls are beyond fabulous. Thank you all for championing us and giving us all a platform to shine. I owe you for some of the closest friendships I have and thank you for shining a light on all the amazing female entrepreneurs out there.

Zoe and Pam, I am extremely grateful for the opportunity to work with you and the amazing entrepreneurial women you support as part of the Vital Voices and Bank of America Global Ambassadors Program. What a wonderful thing you are doing for women entrepreneurs all over the world. I couldn't write this book without a shout-out to you dedicated and passionate women. You are making a difference.

Ty Tashiro, a great big thank-you for your time and guidance and an extra-big thank-you for the cheat sheets. I seriously can't believe you have done this three times. You're a machine.

Joey Coleman, many thanks for talking this new author off the ledge. Your words of advice were so very appreciated and recentered me when I was starting to lean.

Marko, thank you for your passion and commitment to aden + anais. We owe Cully, Anais, and Christiane a whole lot for instigating this relationship ten years back. You are a talented artist who helped shape aden + anais. Thank you for all the beautiful images you produced over the years.

ACKNOWLEDGMENTS

Ramona and Giatry, I quite simply would not have been able to build aden + anais if the two of you were not in my life. Knowing that my girls are safe and loved while Markos and I are working is the only reason I am able to concentrate fully on my career. Thank you for being second mums to the girls and for all you do to take care of my family and home when I am not there.

Victoria Young, you are a saint and a healer. Thank you for always making me feel whole again any time I am in your presence. You have a gift.

NOTES

———————

INTRODUCTION

6 **Between 2007 and 2017:** "The 2017 State of Women-Owned Businesses Report," American Express, 2017, 3, http://about.americanexpress.com/news /docs/2017-State-of-Women-Owned-Businesses-Report.pdf, accessed July 13, 2018.

6 **Women make up 40 percent:** Elaine Pofeldt, "Women Are Now Beating Men in This Competitive Field," CNBC, March 6, 2017, https://www.cnbc.com/2017 /02/28/why-women-entrepreneurs-will-be-economic-force-to-reckon-with-in -2017.html, accessed June 13, 2018.

6 **Women of color have:** Pofeldt, "Women Are Now Beating Men."

6 **Still, she was told:** *The Ellen DeGeneres Show*, NBC, season 13, September 10, 2015; see also http://msmagazine.com/blog/2013/05/28/10-things-that -american-women-could-not-do-before-the-1970s; "Forty Years Ago, Women Had a Hard Time Getting Credit Cards," *Smithsonian*, January 8, 2014, https://www.smithsonianmag.com/smart-news/forty-years-ago-women-had-a -hard-time-getting-credit-cards-180949289.

6 **incredible role models:** Alanna Petroff, "The Body Shop Is Getting a New Brazilian Owner," *CNNMoney*, 2018, http://money.cnn.com/2017/06/28/investing /body-shop-natura-loreal/index.html.

6 **Michelle Phan of Ipsy:** Zoë Henry, "How Michelle Phan Cracked the Code for Free Marketing on YouTube," *Inc.*, April 2016, https://www.inc.com /magazine/201604/zoe-henry/ipsy-michelle-phan-youtube-branding.html.

6 **only 2 percent:** Valentina Zarya, "Female Founders Got 2% of Venture Capital Dollars in 2017," *Fortune*, January 31, 2018, http://fortune.com/2018/01/31 /female-founders-venture-capital-2017/, accessed June 13, 2018.

7 **Nearly half won't even:** The 2014 State of Women-Owned Businesses Report, American Express OPEN, March 2014, http://www.womenable.com/content /userfiles/2014_State_of_Women-owned_Businesses_public.pdf.

7 **Those stats, by the way:** U.S. Census Bureau, *Women-owned Businesses: 1997, 1997 Survey of Business Owners,* October 2001, https://www.census.gov/prod/2001pubs/cenbr01–6.pdf.

7 **women may be starting:** Pofeldt, "Women Are Now Beating Men."

7 **women may be starting:** "Launching Women-Owned Businesses Onto a High Growth Trajectory," National Women's Business Council, 2010, https://www.nwbc.gov/2010/10/27/launching-women-owned-businesses-on-to-a-high-growth-trajectory/.

7 **If that's the case, you:** Malin Malmstrom, et al., "VC Stereotypes About Men and Women Aren't Supported by Performance Data," *Harvard Business Review,* March 15, 2018, https://hbr.org/2018/03/vc-stereotypes-about-men-and-women-arent-supported-by-performance-data.

8 **even when, according to:** Sheryl Sandberg and Rachel Thomas, "Sheryl Sandberg on How to Get to Gender Equality," *Wall Street Journal,* October 10, 2017, https://www.wsj.com/articles/sheryl-sandberg-on-how-to-get-to-gender-equality-1507608721, accessed July 13, 2018; Rachel Thomas et al., "Women in the Workplace 2017," accessed July 25, 2018. https://womenintheworkplace.com/.

8 **When women are the direct beneficiaries:** "Scaling up: Why women-owned businesses can recharge the global economy," EY 2009, http://www.ey.com/Publication/vwLUAssets/Scaling_up_-_Why_women-owned_businesses_can_recharge_the_global_economy_new/$FILE/Scaling_up_why_women_owned_businesses_can_recharge_the_global_economy.pdf.

8 **Women-led private tech:** Karen E. Klein, "Women Who Run Tech Startups Are Catching Up," Bloomberg, February 20, 2013, https://www.bloomberg.com/news/articles/2013–02–20/women-who-run-tech-startups-are-catching-up; Adam Quinton, "Start-up Fundraising: The Balance Between Form and Substance in Your Pitch," Women 2.0, November 12, 2015, http://women2.com/stories/2015/11/12/form-versus-substance; Meredith Jones, "Wall Street Has a Problem with Women. Here's Why You Should Worry," World Economic Forum, October 20, 2015, https://www.weforum.org/agenda/2015/10/wall-street-has-a-problem-with-women-heres-why-you-should-worry/.

9 **The McKinsey Global Institute:** "The Power of Parity," McKinsey Global Institute, September 2015, https://www.mckinsey.com/global-themes/employment-and-growth/how-advancing-womens-equality-can-add-12-trillion-to-global-growth.

9 **The US economy:** "The 51%: Driving Growth Through Women's Economic Participation," The Hamilton Project, October 2017, http://www.hamiltonproject.org/papers/the_51_driving_growth_through_womens_economic_participation.

CHAPTER 1: TRUST IN YOUR IDEA

17 **A flood of cheap foreign:** Stephanie Clifford, "U.S. Textile Plants Return, with Floors Largely Empty of People," *New York Times*, September 19, 2013, http://www.nytimes.com/2013/09/20/business/us-textile-factories-return.html ?pagewanted=all.

22 **Women: Stop making:** Jolie O'Dell, "Women: stop making start-ups about fashion, shopping, & babies. At least for the next few years. You're embarrassing me," Twitter, September 13, 2011, https://twitter.com/jolieodell/status /113681946487422976.

22 **we started earning 50 percent:** "Women in the Workforce: United States," Catalyst, 2016, http://www.catalyst.org/knowledge/women-workforce-united-states #footnote16_wsi833g; "Bachelor's, master's, and doctor's degrees conferred by postsecondary institutions, by sex of student and discipline division: 2013–14," NCES, 2015, https://nces.ed.gov/programs/digest/d15/tables/dt15_318.30.asp ?current=yes; "Degrees conferred by degree-granting institutions, by level of degree and sex of student: Selected years, 1869–70 through 2021–22," NCES, 2012, https://nces.ed.gov/programs/digest/d12/tables/dt12_310.asp.

22 **Today, that number:** "Bachelor's, master's, and doctor's degrees conferred by postsecondary institutions, by sex of student and discipline division: 2014–15," NCES, 2017, https://nces.ed.gov/programs/digest/d16/tables/dt16_318.30.asp; see also: "Women in the Workforce: United States," Catalyst, 2016, http:// www.catalyst.org/knowledge/women-workforce-united-states#footnote16 _wsi833g.

22 **As of 1987:** "Degrees conferred by degree-granting institutions, by level of degree and sex of student: Selected years, 1869–70 Through 2021–22," NCES, 2012, https://nces.ed.gov/programs/digest/d12/tables/dt12_310.asp.

23 **And yet, even in:** "The Simple Truth About the Gender Pay Gap," AAUW, September 2017, https://www.aauw.org/research/the-simple-truth-about-the -gender-pay-gap, accessed July 18, 2018.

23 **As one of the study's:** "Simple Truth," AAUW; Claire Miller, "As Women Take Over a Male-Dominated Field, the Pay Drops," *New York Times*, March 20, 2016, https://www.nytimes.com/2016/03/20/upshot/as-women-take-over-a -male-dominated-field-the-pay-drops.html.

24 **However, these service businesses:** "2017 State of Women-Owned Businesses Report," About.Americanexpress.com, 2017, http://about.americanexpress .com/news/docs/2017-State-of-Women-Owned-Businesses-Report.pdf.

25 **The market for female-centric:** Michael J. Silverstein and Kate Sayre, "The Female Economy," *Harvard Business Review,* July 16, 2015, https://hbr.org /2009/09/the-female-economy; Michelle King, "Want a Piece of the 18-Trillion -Dollar Female Economy? Start with Gender Bias" *Forbes,* May 24, 2017,

https://www.forbes.com/sites/michelleking/2017/05/24/want-a-piece-of-the
-18-trillion-dollar-female-economy-start-with-gender-bias/#395f61ef612318
trillionspendingandgrowing; "The Purchasing Power of Women: Statistics," Girlpower Marketing, 2018, https://girlpowermarketing.com/statistics
-purchasing-power-women/; "The case for gender parity," Global Gender Gap
Report 2016, http://reports.weforum.org/global-gender-gap-report-2016/the
-case-for-gender-parity/; "Purchasing Power of Women," *FONA International,*
December 22, 2014, https://www.fona.com/resource-center/blog/purchasing
-power-women.

26 **While a freelancer is looking:** Seth Godin, "The Freelancer and the Entrepreneur," *Medium,* June 5, 2016, https://medium.com/swlh/the-freelancer-and-the
-entrepreneur-c79d2bbb52b2.

CHAPTER 2: HARD WORK BEATS B SCHOOL

43 **Only 3 percent of graduates:** John A. Byrne, "Look Who Harvard and Stanford
B-Schools Just Rejected," *Fortune,* December 18, 2013, http://fortune.com
/2013/12/18/look-who-harvard-and-stanford-b-schools-just-rejected/.

CHAPTER 3: DON'T LET DOUBT STOP YOU

51 **Develop skin as tough:** Maureen Dowd, "E.R.," *New York Times,* July 4, 1999,
http://www.nytimes.com/books/99/07/04/reviews/990704.704dowdt.html;
Patricia Brennan, "PBS's Eleanor Roosevelt," *Washington Post,* January 9, 2000,
http://www.washingtonpost.com/wp-srv/WPcap/2000–01/09/122r-010900
-idx.html.

51 **A recent study evaluated:** Raina Brand and Isabel Fernandez-Mateo, "Women
Are Less Likely to Apply for Executive Roles if They've Been Rejected Before,"
Harvard Business Review, February 7, 2017, https://hbr.org/2017/02/women
-are-less-likely-to-apply-for-executive-roles-if-theyve-been-rejected-before, accessed July 19, 2018.

51 **A study published in:** Tara Mohr, "Opinion: Learning to Love Criticism,"
New York Times, September 27, 2014, https://www.nytimes.com/2014/09/28
/opinion/sunday/learning-to-love-criticism.html; see also Kieran Snyder,
"Women Should Watch Out for This One Word in Their Reviews," *Fortune,*
August 26, 2014, http://fortune.com/2014/08/26/performance-review-gender
-bias, accessed July 19, 2018.

51 **Nearly 76 percent of:** Mohr, "Learning to Love Criticism"; Snyder, "Women
Should Watch Out."

CHAPTER 4: REDEFINE RISK

61 **I mean, the very definition:** Murray Rothbard, "Richard Cantillon: The Founding Father of Modern Economics," Mises Institute, October 26, 2010, https://mises.org/library/richard-cantillon-founding-father-modern-economics.

62 ***Entrepreneur* magazine puts it:** Larry Alton, "5 Things Every Entrepreneur Should Know About Risk-Taking," *Entrepreneur*, February 3, 2016, https://www.entrepreneur.com/article/270320#.

62 **they "lacked the guts":** Adam Grant, *Originals: How Non-Conformists Move the World* (New York: Viking, 2016); "Neil Blumenthal and Dave Gilboa, Co-CEOs and Co-Founders, Warby Parker, to Keynote 2015 Wharton School MBA Graduation," *Wharton UPenn News*, May 18, 2015, https://news.wharton.upenn.edu/press-releases/2015/03/neil-blumenthal-dave-gilboa-co-ceos-co-founders-warby-parker-keynote-2015-wharton-school-mba-graduation/.

62 **The oft-used interpretation:** David J. Hosken and Clarissa M. House, "Sexual Selection Primer," *Current Biology*, January 24, 2011, https://www.sciencedirect.com/science/article%20/pii/S0960982210015198#!; Allen Frances, "The Power of Sexual Selection." *Psychology Today*, February 15, 2013, https://www.psychologytoday.com/blog/dsm5-in-distress/201302/the-power-sexual-selection.

62 **It gets rolled out:** B. Pawlowski, Rajinder Atwal, and R. I. M. Dunbar, "Sex Differences in Everyday Risk-Taking Behavior in Humans," *Evolutionary Psychology* 6, no. 1 (2008): 29–42, doi:10.1177/147470490800600104; Daniel Kruger, "Impact of Social Factors on the Male-to-Female Mortality Ratio," *PsycEXTRA Dataset*, January 1, 2004, doi:10.1037/e351232004–001; Margo Wilson and Martin Daly, "Competitiveness, Risk Taking, and Violence: The Young Male Syndrome," *Ethology and Sociobiology* 6, no. 1 (1985): 59–73, doi:10.1016/0162–3095(85)90041-x; Sebastian Kraemer, "The Fragile Male," *BMJ: British Medical Journal*, December 23, 2000, https://www.ncbi.nlm.nih.gov/pmc/articles/PMC1119278/; "Men overwhelmingly more likely to die of drowning than women, finds Red Cross," Canadian *Red Cross*, June 6, 2016, http://www.redcross.ca/about-us/media—news/news-releases/men-overwhelmingly-more-likely-to-die-of-drowning-than-women,-finds-red-cross.

63 **In the boardroom, too:** Kim Elsesser, "Research Stating 'Women Ask for Pay Raises as Much as Men' Is Misleading," *Forbes*, September 8, 2016, https://www.forbes.com/sites/kimelsesser/2016/09/07/research-stating-women-ask-for-pay-raises-as-much-as-men-is-just-wrong/#40029f503983; Jennifer Ludden, "Ask for a Raise? Most Women Hesitate," NPR, February 8, 2011, http://www.npr.org/2011/02/14/133599768/ask-for-a-raise-most-women-hesitate; Herminia Ibarra, Nancy M. Carter, and Christine Silva, "Why Men Still Get More Promotions Than Women," *Harvard Business Review*, September 7, 2017,

https://hbr.org/2010/09/why-men-still-get-more-promotions-than-women, accessed April 14, 2018; Shana Lebowitz, "A New Study from Lean In and McKinsey Finds Exactly How Much More Likely Men Are to Get Promoted Than Women," *Business Insider*, October 1, 2015, http://www.businessinsider .com/women-are-less-likely-to-get-promoted-2015–10, accessed April 14, 2018; Mary Stergiou-Kita, Elizabeth Mansfield, Randy Bezo, et al., "Danger zone: Men, masculinity, and occupational health and safety in high risk occupations," CIHR/IRSC, December 1, 2015, https://www.ncbi.nlm.nih.gov /pmc/articles/PMC4880472/, accessed April 14, 2018; Business Radio, "Why Are There More Male Entrepreneurs Than Female Ones?," Knowledge@ Wharton, December 14, 2015, http://knowledge.wharton.upenn.edu/article /why-are-there-more-male-entrepreneurs-than-female-ones/, accessed April 14, 2018.

63 **Certain types of risk-taking:** Michael Lawrence Wilson, Carrie M. Miller, and Kristin N. Crouse, *Proceedings of the Royal Society B: Biological Sciences*, November 15, 2017, https://www.ncbi.nlm.nih.gov/pmc/articles/PMC5698637/, accessed April 14, 2018; Chris Von Rueden, Sarah Alami, et al., "Sex Differences in Political Leadership in an Egalitarian Society," *Evolution and Human Behavior*, 2018, doi:10.1016/j.evolhumbehav.2018.03.005; Hannah Devlin, "Early Men and Women Were Equal, Say Scientists," *Guardian*, May 14, 2015, https://www.theguardian.com/science/2015/may/14/early-men-women -equal-scientists, accessed April 14, 2018; Michael Gurven, Kim Hill, and Hillard Kaplan, "From Forest to Reservation: Transitions in Food-Sharing Behavior Among the Ache of Paraguay," *Journal of Anthropological Research* 58, no. 1 (2002): 93–120, doi:10.1086/jar.58.1.3631070.

63 **A 2017 *New York Times* article:** Claire Cain Miller, "Why Women Don't See Themselves as Entrepreneurs," *New York Times*, June 9, 2017, https:// www.nytimes.com/2017/06/09/upshot/why-women-dont-see-themselves-as -entrepreneurs.html, accessed April 14, 2018.

63 **A 2009 EY report:** *Scaling Up: Why Women-Owned Businesses Can Recharge the Global Economy* (New York: Ernst & Young Global Limited, 2009), http:// www.ey.com/Publication/vwLUAssets/Scaling_up_-_Why_women-owned _businesses_can_recharge_the_global_economy_-_new/$FILE/Scaling_up _why_women_owned_businesses_can_recharge_the_global_economy.pdf.

63 **"Until we are willing":** Julie Zeilinger, "7 Reasons Why Women Should Take More Risks," *Huffington Post*, September 25, 2017, http://www.huffingtonpost .com/2013/08/13/seven-reasons-why-risk-taking-leads-to-success_n_3749425 .html, accessed April 14, 2018.

64 **After all, the idea:** Cordelia Fine, *Testosterone Rex: Myths of Sex, Science, and Society* (New York: W. W. Norton, 2017).

64 **Part of what he discovered:** Grant, *Originals*; "Warby Parker Sees the Future of Retail," *Fast Company*, July 8, 2017, https://www.fastcompany.com/3041334 /warby-parker-sees-the-future-of-retail, accessed April 14, 2018.

65 **The study's authors concluded:** Grant, *Originals*; Livia Gershon, "Maybe Entrepreneurs Don't Like Risk Much After All," JSTOR Daily, January 12, 2015, https://daily.jstor.org/maybe-entrepreneurs-dont-like-risk-much; "The Entrepreneur's Motivation," INSEAD Knowledge, November 20, 2017, accessed April 14, 2018, https://knowledge.insead.edu/innovation/entrepreneurship/the -entrepreneurs-motivation-630.

65 **Grant provides plenty more:** Grant, *Originals*.

66 **Compare that to 12.8:** Kathleen Kim, "Risk-Takers? Not Most Entrepreneurs," *Inc.*, November 19, 2012, https://www.inc.com/kathleen-kim/entrepreneurs -more-cautious-not-risk-takers.html, accessed April 14, 2018.

66 **Two years before that:** Malcolm Gladwell, "The Sure Thing," *New Yorker*, June 19, 2017, https://www.newyorker.com/magazine/2010/01/18/the-sure -thing, accessed April 14, 2018.

66 **some of the most famous:** Jessica Livingston, "Steve Wozniak," Founders at Work, http://www.foundersatwork.com/steve-wozniak.html, accessed April 14, 2018; "Pierre Omidyar," *Entrepreneur*, October 9, 2008, https://www.entrepreneur .com/article/197554#l, accessed April 14, 2018; Peter Vanham, "10 Lessons Anyone Can Learn About Success from the Founder of Nike, an $85 Billion Company," *Business Insider*, May 17, 2017, https://www.businessinsider.com /business-lessons-from-nike-phil-knight-2017-5, accessed April 14, 2018.

67 **Pushing women, in:** Julie Zeilinger, "7 Reasons Why Women Should Take More Risks," *Huffington Post*, September 25, 2017, http://www.huffingtonpost .com/2013/08/13/seven-reasons-why-risk-taking-leads-to-success_n_3749425 .html, accessed April 14, 2018.

CHAPTER 5: MUM GUILT

73 **I didn't spend enough:** Lauren Cormier, "Why I'm Embracing the Mommy Guilt," Scary Mommy, September 25, 2017, http://www.scarymommy.com /embracing-the-mommy-guilt/.

78 **Perhaps you've heard:** E. J. Graff, "The Opt-Out Myth," *Columbia Journalism Review*, March/April 2007, http://archives.cjr.org/essay/the_optout_myth.php, accessed April 14, 2018; Kj Dell'Antonia, "After the Opt-Out Revolution, Asking: How's That Working for You?" *New York Times*, August 8, 2013, https:// parenting.blogs.nytimes.com/2013/08/08/after-the-opt-out-revolution-asking -hows-that-working-for-you, accessed April 14, 2018; Sylvia Ann Hewlett and Carolyn Buck Luce, "Off-Ramps and On-Ramps: Keeping Talented Women on

the Road to Success," *Harvard Business Review*, August 1, 2014, https://hbr
.org/2005/03/off-ramps-and-on-ramps-keeping-talented-women-on-the-road
-to-success, accessed April 14, 2018.

78 **So almost everyone thinks this:** Barret Mary Katuna, "Breaking the Glass Ceiling? Gender and Leadership in Higher Education," PhD diss., University of Connecticut, 2014, https://opencommons.uconn.edu/cgi/viewcontent .cgi?article=6581&context-dissertations.

78 **While the opt-out story line:** P. Stone and M. Lovejoy, "Fast-track Women and the 'Choice' to Stay Home," *The Annals of the American Academy of Political and Social Science* 596 (2004): 62–83.

78 **Recent studies have also:** M. McGrath, M. Driscoll, and M. Gross, "Back in the Game: Returning to Business After a Hiatus: Experiences and Recommendations for Women, Employers, and Universities; Executive Summary 2005," Forte Foundation, 2005, 7–9, http://www.fortefoundation.org/site/DocServer /Back_in_the_Game_Executive_Summary—Final.pdf?docID=1261.

78 **It did find, however:** Joan C. Williams, Jessica Manvell, and Stephanie Bornstein, " 'Opt Out' or Pushed Out?: How the Press Covers Work/Family Conflict," *Worklife Law*, January 2006, worklifelaw.org, accessed November 19, 2017.

79 **That number drops to:** Robin J. Ely, Pamela Stone, and Colleen Ammerman, "Rethink What You 'Know' About High-Achieving Women," *Harvard Business Review*, January 16, 2015, https://hbr.org/2014/12/rethink-what-you -know-about-high-achieving-women &cd=1&hl=en&ct=clnk&gl=us&client= safari.

79 **[W]hen high-achieving, highly educated:** Ely, Stone, Ammerman, "Rethink."

80 **Thébaud's study shows:** Sarah Thébaud, "Business Plan B," *Sage Journals*, June 5, 2015, http://journals.sagepub.com/doi/abs/10.1177/00018392155916 27?journalCode=asqa; see also: Andrea Estrada, "Business as Plan B," *UCSB Current*, November 5, 2015, http://www.news.ucsb.edu/2015/016121/business -plan-b; Sarah Thébaud, "What Helps Women Entrepreneurs Flourish?" Council on Contemporary Families, November 4, 2015, https://contemporary families.org/family-friendly-and-women-entrepreneurs-brief.

81 **That is one hell:** Thébaud, "Business Plan B"; Thébaud, "What Helps Women."

81 **Paternity leave is linked:** Bryce Covert, "How Everyone Benefits When New Fathers Take Paid Leave," ThinkProgress, February 13, 2015, https:// thinkprogress.org/how-everyone-benefits-when-new-fathers-take-paid-leave -862836d2f843.

81 **It offers a surprising:** Marcus Noland, Tyler Moran, and Barbara Kotschwar, "Is Gender Diversity Profitable? Evidence from a Global Survey," Peterson Institute for International Economics, February 2016, https://piie.com/publications/wp /wp16-3.pdf; "New Research from the Peterson Institute for International Economics and EY Reveals Significant Correlation between Women in Corporate

Leadership and Profitability," EY, February 8, 2016, https://www.ey.com/us /en/newsroom/news-releases/news-ey-new-research-from-the-peterson -institute-for-international-economics-and-ey-reveals-significant-correlation -between-women-in-corporate-leadership-and-profitability, accessed April 12, 2018.

82 **It's estimated that the:** Brian Neese, "The Hidden Cost of Employee Turnover," Alvernia University Online, March 28, 2018, accessed April 14, 2018, https:// online.alvernia.edu/cost-employee-turnover/; "Calculating the Cost of Employee Turnover," G&A Partners, April 10, 2018, accessed April 14, 2018, https://www.gnapartners.com/blog/how-much-does-employee-turnover-really -cost-your-business/; Suzanne Lucas, "How Much Employee Turnover Really Costs You," *Inc.*, August 30, 2013, https://www.inc.com/suzanne-lucas/why -employee-turnover-is-so-costly.html, accessed April 14, 2018; Beth Greenwood, "The Average Cost to Hire a New Employee," Chron, November 21, 2017, http://work.chron.com/average-cost-hire-new-employee-13262.html, accessed April 14, 2018.

83 **Women whose moms worked:** Carmen Nobel, "Kids Benefit from Having a Working Mom," HBS Working Knowledge, May 15, 2015, https://hbswk.hbs .edu/item/kids-benefit-from-having-a-working-mom, accessed April 12, 2018.

86 **If you've read the:** Klaus Schwab et al., "The Global Gender Gap Report 2015," World Economic Forum, 2015, http://www3.weforum.org/docs/GGGR2015 /cover.pdf, accessed November 19, 2017.

CHAPTER 6: CASH IS QUEEN

91 **While one study found:** Jared Hecht, "State of Small Business Lending: Spotlight on Women Entrepreneurs," *Fundera Ledger*, March 29, 2018, https:// www.fundera.com/blog/the-state-of-online-small-business-lending-q2–2016, accessed July 20, 2018.

91–2 **However, women entrepreneurs are more:** Hecht, "State of Small Business Lending."

92 **Women also tend to:** Hecht, "State of Small Business Lending."

92 **In 2017, female founders:** Valentina Zarya, "Female Founders Got 2% of Venture Capital Dollars in 2017," *Fortune*, January 31, 2018, http://fortune.com /2018/01/31/female-founders-venture-capital-2017, accessed July 20, 2018

92 **When questioning the female:** Sally Herships, "Why Female Entrepreneurs Get Less Funding Than Men," *Marketplace*, October 25, 2017, https://www .marketplace.org/2017/10/25/business/why-female-entrepreneurs-get-less -money-men. accessed April 14, 2018.

92 **Women were asked:** Herships, "Why Female Entrepreneurs Get Less Funding."

92 **In other words:** Herships, "Why Female Entrepreneurs Get Less Funding."

92 **Less than 1 percent:** Daniel Applewhite, "Founders and Venture Capital: Racism Is Costing Us Billions," *Forbes*, February 15, 2018, https://www.forbes .com/sites/forbesnonprofitcouncil/2018/02/15/founders-and-venture-capital -racism-is-costing-us-billions/#baf55e72e4ae, accessed July 20, 2018.

93 **As if to compliment:** Issie Lapowsky, "This Is What Tech's Ugly Gender Problem Really Looks Like," *Wired*, June 3, 2017, https://www.wired.com/2014 /07/gender-gap/, accessed April 14, 2018.

93 **A Women 2.0 conference:** Zoe Barry, "Now Is the Perfect Time to Be a Female Entrepreneur," *TechCrunch*, April 17, 2015, https://techcrunch.com /2015/04/16/now-is-the-perfect-time-to-be-a-female-entrepreneur/, accessed April 14, 2018; Karen E Klein, "Women Who Run Tech Startups Are Catching Up," Bloomberg, February 20, 2013, https://www.bloomberg.com/news /articles/2013-02-20/women-who-run-tech-startups-are-catching-up, accessed April 14, 2018; Peter Cohan, "When It Comes to Tech Start-ups, Do Women Win?" *Forbes*, February 26, 2013, https://www.forbes.com/sites/petercohan /2013/02/25/when-it-comes-to-tech-start-ups-do-women-win/#13f1faf06f3c, accessed April 14, 2018.

93 **When women-led tech companies:** Barry, "Now Is the Perfect Time"; Klein, "Women Who Run Tech Startups"; Cohan, "When It Comes to Tech Start-ups, Do Women Win?"

95 **The Senate Committee on:** Suzanne McGee, "Startup Sexism: Why Won't Investors Give Women Business Loans?" *Guardian*, July 17, 2016, https://www .theguardian.com/business/us-money-blog/2016/jul/17/bank-loan-business -sexism, accessed April 14, 2018; "Happy Birthday to H.R. 5050–Women's Business Ownership Act!" National Women's Business Council, https:// www.nwbc.gov/2016/10/25/happy-birthday-to-h-r-5050-womens-business -ownership-act/, accessed April 14, 2018; Mary Brodie, "Myth: Women Can't Get Investment Dollars," InPower Coaching, July 10, 2017, https:// inpowercoaching.com/myth-2-women-cant-get-investment-dollars-part-1-how -the-investor-side-works/, accessed April 14, 2018; Majority Report of the U.S. Senate Committee on Small Business and Entrepreneurship, 21st Century Barriers to Women's Entrepreneurship, https://www.microbiz.org/wp-content /uploads/2014/07/21st-Century-Barriers-to-Womens-Entrepreneurship.pdf; American Express OPEN, The 2016 State of Women-Owned Businesses Report, http://about.americanexpress.com/news/docs/2016x/2016SWOB.pdf.

96 **What sometimes goes underreported:** "Startup Funding Infographic," Fundable, 2017, accessed September 11, 2018, https://www.fundable.com/learn /resources/infographics/startup-funding-infographic.

96 **In contrast, those who:** Brian Foley, "5 Reasons Bootstrapping Your Business Is the Best Thing You Can Do," *Entrepreneur*, January 18, 2017, https://www .entrepreneur.com/article/276974, accessed April 14, 2018.

96 **Perhaps most important:** Foley, "5 Reasons Bootstrapping Your Business."

96 **Friends and family contribute:** Martin Zwilling, "The Smartest Entrepreneurs Bootstrap Their Startup," The Gust Blog, August 27, 2015, http://blog.gust .com/smartest-entrepreneurs-bootstrap-startup/, accessed April 14, 2018; Ryan Smith, "Why Every Startup Should Bootstrap," *Harvard Business Review*, April 24, 2017, https://hbr.org/2016/03/why-every-startup-should-bootstrap, accessed April 14, 2018; Rajarshi Choudhuri, "The Good, the Bad, and the Ugly of a Bootstrap Startup," Startups.co, May 30, 2017, https://www.startups .co/articles/bootstrap-startup-good-bad-ugly, accessed April 14, 2018; Brian Foley, "5 Reasons Bootstrapping Your Business Is the Best Thing You Can Do," *Entrepreneur*, January 18, 2017, https://www.entrepreneur.com/article /276974, accessed April 14, 2018; Robert J. Lahm Jr. and Harold T. Little Jr., "Bootstrapping Business Start-ups: A Review of Current Business Practices," Address, 2005 Conference on Emerging Issues in Business and Technology, http://citeseerx.ist.psu.edu/viewdoc/download?doi=10.1.1.453.1617&rep= rep1&type=pdf.

97 **The average net worth:** Zwilling, "The Smartest Entrepreneurs Bootstrap"; Smith, "Why Every Startup"; Choudhuri, "The Good, the Bad, and the Ugly"; Foley, "5 Reasons Bootstrapping Your Business."

98 **Susan didn't have a:** Vivienne Decker, "How Susan Petersen of Freshly Picked Created a Multimillion-Dollar Business from Her Kitchen Table," *Forbes*, January 28, 2016, https://www.forbes.com/sites/viviennedecker/2016/01/28/how -susan-petersen-of-freshly-picked-created-a-multi-million-dollar-business-from -her-kitchen-table/#259d133b2b25, accessed July 20, 2018.

CHAPTER 7: EXPECT SURPRISES

116 **In contrast to their greatest:** Press release or publicity materials, the Kauffman Foundation Series on Innovation and Leadership, from Noam Wasserman's *The Founder's Dilemmas: Anticipating and Avoiding the Pitfalls That Can Sink a Start-Up* (Princeton, NJ: Princeton University Press, 2013), http://www .kauffman.org/~/media/kauffman_org/resources/books/founders_dilemmas _surprising_facts.

CHAPTER 9: LEAD YOUR TEAM

144 **EY Winning Women:** "Entrepreneurial Winning Women: Home," Ernst & Young Winning Women, https://www.ey.com/us/en/services/strategic-growth -markets/entrepreneurial-winning-women, accessed July 18, 2018.

151 **Because women are often expected:** "Winning Women"; Menaha Shanmugam, R. D. G. Amaratunga, and R. P. Haigh, "Leadership Styles: Gender Similari-

ties, Differences and Perceptions," PhD diss., University of Salford (Salford, UK: Research Institute for the Built and Human Environment), https://pdfs .semanticscholar.org/b83c/5b565b74ed9169cd56a2a6315056076f3418.pdf.

152 **when we display characteristics:** Alice H. Eagly, Wendy Wood, and Amanda B. Diekman, "Social Role Theory of Sex Differences and Similarities," *The Developmental Social Psychology of Gender* (2000): 123–74, https://www.scholars .northwestern.edu/en/publications/social-role-theory-of-sex-differences-and -similarities-a-current-; Alice H. Eagly and Mary C. Johannesen-Schmidt, "The Leadership Styles of Women and Men," *Journal of Social Issues* 54, no. 4 (2001): 781–97, https://is.muni.cz/el/1421/jaro2009/PSB_516/6390561/the_leadership _styles_of_women_and_men.pdf; Cecilia L. Ridgeway, "Gender, Status, and Leadership," *Journal of Social Issues: A Journal of the Society for the Psychological Study of Social Issues*, Winter 2001, 637–55, http://onlinelibrary.wiley .com/doi/10.1111/0022–4537.00233/full; Cecilia L. Ridgeway and Shelley J. Correll, "Unpacking the Gender System," *Gender & Society* 18, no. 4 (2004): 510–31, doi:10.1177/0891243204265269; Alice H. Eagly and Blair T. Johnson, "Gender and Leadership Style: A Meta-analysis," *Psychological Bulletin* 108, no. 2 (1990): 233–56, doi:10.1037//0033–2909.108.2.233.

153 **Learning to be transparent:** Ray Dalio, *Principles* (New York: Simon & Schuster, 2017), 137.

CHAPTER 10: THINK BIGGER

165 **We're about being in business:** David Zax, "37signals Earns Millions Each Year. Its CEO's Model? His Cleaning Lady," *Fast Company*, October 25, 2016, https://www.fastcompany.com/3000852/37signals-earns-millions-each-year-its -ceos-model-his-cleaning-lady, accessed April 26, 2018; see also: Jessica Stillman, "Slow Business: The Case Against Fast Growth," *Inc.*, September 18, 2012, https://www.inc.com/jessica-stillman/slow-business-fast-growth-is-not -good-for-the-company.html, accessed April 26, 2018.

CHAPTER 11: KNOW WHEN TO SELL

179 **However, they weren't:** Anna Klaile, "Why Are So Few Women Promoted into Top Management Positions?" October 6, 2013, https://kauppakamari.fi/wp -content/uploads/2014/10/annaklaile-why-are-so-few-women.pdf, accessed July 18, 2018.

CHAPTER 12: TRUST YOUR INTUITION

214 **There is plenty of:** Rebecca Harrington, "When Companies Are in Crisis, Female CEOs Are More Likely to Be Blamed Than Male CEOs," *Business Insider*, November 1, 2016, https://www.businessinsider.com/female-ceos-blamed-company-scandals-2016-11.

CONCLUSION

223 **Contributions from the aden + anais:** "(RED) Impact," (RED), https://www.red.org/impact, accessed July 21, 2018.

224 **Around the world:** *World Development Report 2011* (Washington, DC: The International Bank for Reconstruction and Development/The World Bank, 2011), https://siteresources.worldbank.org/INTWDRS/Resources/WDR2011_Full_Text.pdf.